# BRIDGES 3

**S.D. Robinson**
Series Editor

# ·BRIDGES·

## 3

S. D. Robinson · S. Bailey · C. Bartel · M. Beattie · D. Townsend

Prentice-Hall Canada Inc., Scarborough, Ontario

**Canadian Cataloguing in Publication Data**

Main entry under title:

Bridges 3

For use in schools.
ISBN 0-13-082074-1

1. Exposition (Rhetoric) — Juvenile literature.
2. English language — Composition and exercises —
Juvenile literature. I. Robinson, Sam, 1937–

P91.2.R64 1986   808′.042   C85-099551-5

**Accompanying Material**

Bridges 1,2,3,4 student texts and Teacher's Guides

© 1986 by Prentice-Hall Canada Inc., Scarborough,
Ontario

Prentice-Hall, Inc., Englewood Cliffs, New Jersey
Prentice-Hall International, Inc., London
Prentice-Hall of Australia, Pty., Ltd., Sydney
Prentice-Hall of India Pvt. Ltd., New Delhi
Prentice-Hall of Japan, Inc., Tokyo
Prentice-Hall of Southeast Asia (PTE) Ltd., Singapore
Editora Prentice-Hall do Brasil Ltda., Rio de Janeiro
Prentice-Hall Hispanoamericana, S.A., Mexico

**Credits**

Project Editors: Rebecca Vogan and Paula Pettitt
Production Editor: Miriam London
Production: Joanne Matthews
Design: Michael van Elsen
Illustrators: Loris Lesynski and Christina Munck
Composition: Attic Typesetting Inc.

ISBN 0-13-082074-1

7 8 9 0   BP   00 99 98 97

**Policy Statement**

Prentice-Hall Canada Inc., Secondary School
Division, and the authors of *Bridges* are commit-
ted to the publication of instructional materials
that are as bias-free as possible. The student text
was evaluated for bias prior to publication.

The authors and publisher also recognize the
importance of appropriate reading levels and
have therefore made every effort to ensure the
highest degree of readability in the student text.
The content has been selected, organized, and
written at a level suitable to the intended audience. Standard readability tests have been applied
at several stages in the text's preparation to
ensure an appropriate reading level.

Research indicates, however, that readability is
affected by much more than word or sentence
length; factors such as presentation, format and
design, none of which are considered in the usual
readability tests, also greatly influence the ease
with which students read a book. These and many
additional features have been carefully prepared
to ensure maximum student comprehension.

# TABLE OF CONTENTS

# PREFACE

*Bridges 3* is about communication: writing, listening, speaking and viewing. It also deals with language and the value of language for today's students. *Bridges 3* is not a replacement for literature books or a reading series. Rather it is a **companion programme** designed to extend students' experiences with communication.

*Bridges 3* is the third book in a four-text series designed for Canadian students in grades 7–10. *Bridges 3* is complete in itself and students need not have studied *Bridges 1* or *Bridges 2* in order to use this book.

There are fourteen communication chapters in *Bridges 3*. The **writing process** is an integral part of these chapters and the stages of this process— prewriting, writing, revising, editing and publishing—form the base of the text. Other communication skills such as speaking, listening and viewing are layered on top of this theoretical foundation.

The six resource chapters focus on the concepts of language usage, grammar, sentence combining and the skills of listening and viewing. These chapters are a repository of information, activities and exercises and can be used in an incremental way when required by work in other chapters or according to the needs of specific students or classes.

*Bridges 3* is essentially a book of activities. Many of these activities encourage students to work in pairs or small groups, an important component of the writing process. Students are carefully directed to help each other as they learn to evaluate each other's writing and provide objective feedback. However, most of these group activities can be adapted and used as independent or whole class work. This adaptability is part of the flexible nature of the text, allowing for as much teacher control over the programme as possible. For example, it is possible to follow the sequence of *Bridges 3* and achieve a good programme. If this is not appropriate, the chapters and activities can be easily reorganized to achieve a suitable order of presentation.

*Bridges 3*, then, is our commitment to helping students become more effective communicators not only in the classroom but in every aspect of their lives. We hope that this text will play a part in achieving this common goal.

# ACKNOWLEDGEMENTS

The *Bridges* Series grew over a period of four years. It is not the product of any one person or of a group of people. Rather, it is the result of the hard work of many people, each of whom has left a special mark on the series.

As a result, we the authors of *Bridges* have many people to thank for their help and encouragement and downright hard work. We sincerely acknowledge these contributions.

Several teachers field-tested early drafts of chapters for *Bridges 3*, pointing out the good and clearly telling us what would and would not work in classrooms. Our appreciation, then, to these teachers: Gordon Bland, Neville Hosking, Gloria Lennox, and Margaret Mayotte.

We also owe a special thank you to those at Prentice-Hall who guided this series from its first stumbling steps to this finished product. Joe Chin and Joanne Matthews are to be commended for their untiring efforts in coordinating art and manufacturing. To project editors Rebecca Vogan and Paula Pettitt and production editor Mia London—thank you for the care and attention, and even love, that you have given to *Bridges*. Your cooperation and helpfulness got us over many a rough spot, and your professionalism has made *Bridges* a better series.

To Dorothy Greenaway, who worked with *Bridges* from its first stages, thank you for being a first-rate editor. Without your cheerfulness, your optimism, and your drive, we would still be mired in the jungle of first drafts.

The authors,
S.R., S.B., C.B., M.B., D.T.

# Credits

Every reasonable effort has been made to find copyright holders of the following material. The publishers would be pleased to have any errors or omissions brought to their attention.

# Sources

p.6: "Axiom", Stephen Scriver. Reprinted from *Between the Lines* by Stephen Scriver (Thistledown Press, 1977) with permission.

p.36: "My Skates", Aina Arro. Used by permission.

p.42: "People and Places" reprinted with permission of *Road and Track*.

p.49: "The Road to Nijmegan", Earle Birney. Reprinted by permission of McClelland and Stewart, The Canadian Publishers.

p.62: "Comic Book Language", © 1978 by Stan Lee and John Buscema. Reprinted by permission of Simon and Schuster Ltd.

pp.89–90: Reprinted from *2500 Anecdotes for All Occasions*, ed. Edmund Fuller © MCMXLII, MCMLXX by Crown Publishers, Inc. Used by permission of Crown Publishers, Inc.

p.93: *The Castaway*, Roland Topor found in D. Booth and S. Skinner, *ABC's of Creative Writing*, Globe/MCP, 1981.

p.94: Excerpt from "All the Years of Her Life" from *Morley Callaghan's Stories* by Morley Callaghan. Reprinted by permission of MacMillan of Canada, A Division of Canada Publishing Corporation.

p.95: Excerpt from "Voodoo", Fredric Brown. Used by permission.

p.101: "Cars", David Mosley. Used by permission.

p.102: "Pizza", Yasmin Dossabhoy. Used by permission.

p.107: "Getting It On", Robert Currie. Reprinted from *Diving Into Fire* by permission of Oberon Press.

"My Old Cat", Hal Summers, *The Book of Cats*

pp.108–109: "Something I Don't Understand", Erfa Alani. Used by permission.

pp.109–110: Courtesy Canada Wide/Lois Maxwell

p.115: "To Hold A Poem", A.J.M. Smith from *Poems Collected and New* by A.J.M. Smith, © Oxford University Press, 1967. Reprinted by permission of W.E. Toye for the Estate of A.J.M. Smith.

p.116: Excerpts from *The Canadian Inventions Book: Innovations, discoveries and firsts* by Janis Nostbakken and Jack Humphrey, published by Grecy de Pencier Publications, Toronto, © 1976, pp.46–47.

pp.117–125: Courtesy of Dr. Edward de Bono, *Cort Thinking Program*, Pergamon Press. All copyright stays with Direct Education Services Limited.*

p.119: Excerpts about accessories and safety paint adapted from *The Canadian Inventions Book* by Janis Nostbakken and Jack Humphrey, published by Grecy de Pencier Publications, Toronto © 1976, pp.48–49.

p.121: Excerpts adapted from *The Canadian Inventions Book* by Janis Nostbakken and Jack Humphrey, published by Grecy de Pencier Publications, Toronto © 1976, pp.46 and 48.

p.123: "All-terrain vehicles..." adapted from *The Canadian Inventions Book* by Janis Nostbakken and Jack Humphrey, published by Grecy de Pencier Publications, Toronto, © 1976, p.50.

p.134: Excerpt from *In Search/En Quête* courtesy Department of Communications and *Macleans*.

p.135: Excerpts from *The Plug-In Drug* by Marie Winn. © 1977 by Marie Winn Miller. Reprinted by permission of Viking Penguin Inc. Excerpts from The Royal Commission on Violence in the Communications Industry, 1976, Learning and Media, Volume 5, p.194. Reprinted by permission of the Queen's Printer for Ontario.

p.166: "The Seeds of Brotherhood", Buffy Sainte-Marie. © 1967 Gypsy Boy Music, Inc. Used by permission.

pp.168–169: "Our School System Fosters Inequality." Used by permission of Doris Anderson, columnist, *The Toronto Star*.

p.171: Excerpt adapted from *Something Beau-*

# Photos

*The thinking skills on pages 117 to 129 are three selected from the sixty lessons of the Cort Thinking Program. Norah Maier, Director, Thinking Program, University of Toronto Schools, is responsible for full program information and the perceptual approach to improve thinking.

*Will She Round the Point?*, painted by Ancher, engraved by Terick

# BEGINNINGS

People like to connect with each other—to communicate. You do this naturally, without much thought. No one has to tell you how to talk with your friends.

But communication can be much more than friendly talk. It can be big business, such as telephone companies or the CBC and CTV television networks. Because communication plays such a large role in our lives, it is the subject of this textbook.

Reading, writing, speaking, listening and viewing are the skills of communication. *Bridges 3* has been designed to help you with four of these communication skills—writing, speaking, listening and viewing. Developing reading skills is left to other textbooks.

## Communication

The two pictures in **Beginnings** are about communication. *Will She Round the Point?* tells about Newfoundland during the nineteenth century. *Wind Song* shows the Canadian prairies in the twentieth century.

*Wind Song*, Neil Wagner

## *Activity 1    Two Paintings*

1. In your notebook, write your response to *Will She Round the Point?*

   *Note*: A response is one kind of word or idea association about some object. You should write down what this painting makes you think about rather than what it is.

2. Next, write a description of *Will She Round the Point?* in your notebook.

   *Note*: To write a description, look carefully at the painting and write down what you see rather than what it makes you think about.

3. Repeat questions 1 and 2 for *Wind Song*.

4. As a class, share your responses to these paintings. Then share your descriptions.
   a. What thoughts did the paintings make you consider?
   b. From your descriptive statements, what can you say about life in Newfoundland in the nineteenth century? the prairies in the twentieth century?
   c. How are these paintings alike? How are they different?

5. As a class, talk about the way these paintings communicated with you.

The discussion in Activity 1 introduces you to the topic of **communication**. It prompts you to search your own mind to discover again what you already know. The other activities in *Bridges 3* will extend your thoughts and your awareness about communication. They will provide some answers, and they will also leave some questions because the topic of communication is such a complex one.

What exactly is *Bridges 3* about? First, it introduces you to the **writing process**, a system that will help you with all of your writing tasks. It will also give you practice with **speaking**, from talking in dyads, to working in groups, to making formal presentations. You will also learn the skills needed for effective **listening**. And you will begin to think about the skill of **viewing**, learning about your visual community.

## *Activity 2    The Art of Communication*

1. Study the *B.C.* cartoon on page 3.

2. In your notebook jot down notes for yourself about the meaning of this cartoon. On what grounds does *the prosecution rest*?

3. Discuss this cartoon as a class. What does it say about the subject of this textbook—communication?

*Activity 3   The Beginning of the Year*

1. On a new page in your notebook, write a paragraph or two as quickly as you can to summarize for yourself what the word communication means.

2. Using another new page, list several goals in the area of communication that you plan to achieve this year.

3. Leave plenty of extra space around your writings in questions 1 and 2. From time to time during the year, review your definition of communication and your goal statement. You may change them as you learn more about communication.

# A Writing Folder

One way to note your progress during the year is to use a **writing folder**. You can keep samples of your writings in such a folder. Some schools pass students' folders on as students move from one level to the next, making it easier for both students and teachers to see the growth in writing ability.

Here are some hints to help you set up a writing folder.

- Use a plain, manila file folder. Loose leaf notebooks and accopress binders work well, too.

- Create a table of contents for your folder, and keep it up to date as you add new work.

- Plan to use the **checkpoint system** below to assess the types of work you are doing:

## Checkpoint

Every two months, take time to review the writing you have done, and write a page or so of notes for yourself about your progress. Here are some ideas to guide your thinking.

+ Summarize the kind of writing that you have been doing—descriptions, reports, and so forth.

+ Write a paragraph or two to yourself to outline what you have achieved with your writings and what you have done particularly well.

+ Note, too, what you might do to improve your work. Don't be too hard on yourself; give yourself a limited number of objectives, no more than five.

+ Write a kind of contract for yourself in which you definitely state what you plan to do with your writing for the next two months or until you come to the next checkpoint.

# Journals

Many students find that **journal writing** is both pleasant and useful. It is pleasant because journals can be fun to write—and fun to read years later. It is useful because journals often help students improve their writing.

The rules for journal writing are simple.

• Plan to write in your journal at a specific time each day. Once you have started writing regularly, you might reduce the number to two or three times a week. Or you could write consistently for a short time, stop writing for a while, and then start again.

• Ideas are important. Don't worry about the mechanics of writing and don't be concerned to correct your writing.

• Journals are personal writings. But they are not diaries. You can expect to share your journal writing with others. If you want to write entirely for yourself, start a diary and keep it at home.

• Find a special notebook for journal writing or set aside a special section of your language arts notebook.

## Activity 4    Angel Nose

1. Read the *Peanuts* cartoon above from the point of view of Peppermint Patty.

2. In your journal, invent the entry that Peppermint Patty might write after making this phone call.

3. Work in pairs and share your responses with each other. Talk about the following items:
   a. the interest of your journal entries
   b. the freedom and lack of concern with the mechanics of writing
   c. the personal nature of the journal entry

4. Write your own personal journal entry about a miracle you have experienced.

## Activity 5  *Journals—Getting Started*

1. Take five minutes of each English class for one week to write your personal journal entry.

2. During the second week, reduce the number of times you write in your journal to two or three.

3. Once you have started keeping a journal, keep up the practice.

## Activity 6  *Thinking About It*

1. Read the following poem about hockey.

**Axiom**

If a team knows its basics
but isn't in shape
it can't execute

If a team is in shape
but doesn't know its basics
it executes chaos

If a team knows its basics
and is in shape
it will win...

unless the refs are crooked
   or the ice is poor
   or the puck doesn't bounce right
   or the goalie is cold
   or...

Therefore: HOCKEY IS LIFE
   Stephen Scriver

2. What does this poem make you think about? Write a note to yourself to suggest your thoughts.

3. In your experience, do you agree with the poet's thoughts about life?
   a. If you agree write notes for yourself to give an example of the way life is.
   b. If you disagree, write notes to yourself to tell what you think life is like.

4. This poem compares life to the game of hockey.
   a. Suggest some other comparison that could be used to tell what life is like.
   b. Construct a collage that will explain your comparison.

   *Note:* You construct a collage by cutting out pictures or words from magazines or newspapers and gluing them on a piece of paper or poster to give a visual image of your comparison.

   c. Share your collage with a classmate. Ask him or her to tell you what the collage is about and compare your interpretations.

# CHAPTER 1

## SHADOWS

# IMPRESSIONS

A shadow is mysterious. It can change size and shape. It can be black and solid, or grey and faint. At times, it seems to be something alive and then, suddenly, it disappears.

The words you write or speak are not like shadows. They leave a more lasting record, an impression of thoughts and feelings. This chapter is about those lasting impressions and the writing process, a system that will help you with your writing tasks.

To learn this system, you are invited to explore the mysterious world of shadows.

## You're Invited

*To What?* *A secret meeting with your shadow.*

*Where?* *In the halls, at noon, after school, wherever it makes an appearance.*

*When?* *As soon as possible.*

*Why?* *To make some observations that will help you capture your shadow in words.*

# THE WRITING PROCESS

The way you use words is as personal as your fingerprints or your shadow, yet all of you go through more-or-less the same stages when you write. The diagram on the side shows these stages and the way they fit together to form the **writing process.**

**The Writing Process**

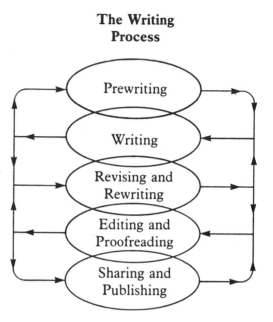

When you write you probably don't follow these stages exactly as if they were a series of steps. You have a highly personal pattern for recording your thoughts, and this pattern will no doubt change for different writing tasks or assignments.

For instance, if you know a great deal about your writing task, you will probably skip most of stage 1, prewriting. (You completed it before you began the writing task.) You will enter the writing process at stage 2, writing, and record your ideas as rapidly as you can. You will probably be revising, a stage 3 process, as you are writing the first draft, a stage 2 task.

If your subject is new to you, you may change your pattern of writing. You would most likely spend a lot of time at the prewriting stage, stage 1, gathering ideas. You can and perhaps should engage in several prewriting activities, exploring your subject from different perspectives, before beginning to write your draft.

Your writing style will change depending on your writing task. But much of the time you will follow the stages of the writing process, particularly as you are learning the craft of writing. This chapter will help you understand these stages by looking at them one at a time.

As you go through each stage, you will explore the world of shadows. Using the power of your imagination, you will be bringing your own shadow to life.

Before you begin to explore this subject, you need to know what you will eventually be asked to write.

**Your Writing Task**

After you use your imagination to bring your shadow to life, your task is to express ideas and feelings about your *live* shadow. This writing will be shared with your classmates. Your purpose is to entertain them.

# STAGE 1:  PREWRITING

During stage 1, you prepare for the task of writing by gathering information and thinking about your subject. You search for ideas by writing, talking, listening, viewing, and reading. You also make some decisions about how to present these ideas. It might help to answer certain questions:

- What is my purpose?
- Who is my audience?
- What details will I include?
- What impressions do I want to create?
- What form will I use?

For the writing task in this chapter, the first three decisions have been made for you. Your **purpose** is to write a unique statement that will entertain your **audience**, your classmates. The **details** you include will be largely determined by the length of your statement. The **impression** you create and the **form** you use to create it are sometimes assigned in the writing task. In this writing exercise, these decisions are left to you.

The prewriting activities in this chapter will help you with these decisions. First, you will observe your reaction to your own shadow and compare it to some information about shadows in folklore and shadows in photographs. These activities will help you decide on what impression to communicate about your shadow. Then you will have to choose a form for your writing. There are three forms from which you may choose—a paragraph, a letter, or a script for a play.

## Shadows in Folklore

Folklore tells us that people throughout the ages have interpreted their shadows in many ways.

1. **In folklore shadows are the soul, life, essence, or strength of the individual person.**
   - The people of the Amboyna Island in the Sea of China feared to go out of their houses at midday. In that equatorial latitude their shadows at noon were tiny, and they were afraid they might lose their souls.

- The strength of the Mangaian warrior hero from the Cook Islands in the southern Pacific was believed to vary with his shadow. His strength was greatest in the morning and least at noon.
- In parts of Transylvania, Romania, people believed that the shadow of a living person could be built into a house. Passers-by were warned not to come near a house while it was being built lest their shadows were caught and they died.
- In ancient Arabia people believed they would be paralyzed if a hyena stepped on their shadows.

2. **Some cultures teach that shadows have independent lives of their own.**
   - In some English folktales it was believed that people could not escape their shadows because the shadows were a witness to their actions. When people died their shadows became their accusers.
   - Some West African cultures believed that a person had four souls, one of which was the shadow-soul. It was important to keep in the shade at noon in case the shadow-soul was lost. The shadow-soul rested after sunset and arose with renewed power in the morning.

## Activity 1A    Exploring Shadows in Folklore

1. In pairs, discuss which explanation for the existence of shadows you could believe in:
   - Shadows are the soul, life, essence, or strength of an individual.
   - Shadows have independent lives of their own.

2. On your own, write a short explanation for your choice in question 1.

3. If you know any myths or have more information about shadows, write them in your notebook.

4. Be prepared to talk about your ideas in class.

## Activity 1B    Comparing Ideas in Folklore to Photographs

1. On your own, examine each of the shadows in the following photographs. Decide whether you see each shadow as separate within the photograph, or whether you see it as part of whatever is casting it.

2. In pairs, discuss your findings. What shadows do each of you see? How do you each perceive them?

3. As a class, talk about your answers. Why might there be differences in the way individuals in your class view these photographs?

## *Activity 1C    Deciding on Your Impression*

1. The following boxes contain questions about the two reactions to shadows. Choose one box to write about. Jot down your response to these questions in your notebook.

2. Be prepared to share your ideas as a whole class.

**Reaction 1    Your shadow is your life, essence and strength. It is part of you.**

1. How does your shadow change?

2. How are you and your shadow alike?

3. Do you have power over it?

4. Do you think of your shadow as an annoying copycat?

5. Are you flattered that it follows you?

6. Is it a silent eyewitness? If so, what has it seen?

7. Is your shadow a friend or an enemy?

8. Would anyone like to capture it because it contains your strength? Who? Why?

9. Do you enjoy its presence? When? Why?

**Reaction 2    Your shadow has an independent life of its own. It is not part of you.**

1. How is your shadow different from you?

2. How does it change?

3. When is it invisible? What happens to it?

4. Could your shadow develop ideas of its own? What ideas? Why would it want to?

5. Is it friendly? When? Why?

6. When it witnesses your actions, does it want to be a tattletale, a gossip, a fan? Why?

7. Does your shadow like to follow you or is it your prisoner? Does it resent you or want to haunt you?

You have explored ideas about your shadow in these prewriting activities to help prepare for the major writing task in this chapter. You have also given some thought to the impression this writing will make. There is one decision left to make at the prewriting stage: the form of your writing.

## Activity 1D    Deciding on Form

1. Read the following list of forms and choose the one you would like to use.

| a paragraph | a letter | a short play |
|---|---|---|
| • a narrative or story in which your shadow tells of an experience<br><br>• a pen portrait in which you describe observations about your shadow | • to your shadow in which you tell how you feel about it<br><br>• in which you assume your shadow's voice:<br>  * telling something about you to someone else<br>  * plotting against you<br>  * praising you | • a dialogue in which someone cross-examines your shadow about a back-biting story it tells<br><br>• a memoir during which your shadow confesses, complains, and tells of its misery |

# STAGE 2:  WRITING

In this stage you work entirely alone. You will usually want to write as quickly as you can, concentrating on getting your ideas down on the page. Write fast and write as much as possible. You can always make changes later.

The next activity will help you begin the writing task.

## *Activity 1E    Writing about Shadows*

Answer only one of the following three questions. Write on every second line so you will have room for changes at the next stage of the writing process.

1. A paragraph. Write down one sentence that says something about your topic. Use that sentence to start writing as fast as you can and as much as you can about the shadow's experience or about the pen portrait.

2. A letter. Place the address of the writer (you or your shadow) in the upper right-hand corner of the page. Date your letter. On the left side of the page, write the imaginary address of the person to whom the letter is sent. You could address your letter to a specific person or *To Whom It May Concern*.

3. A script. If you are writing a script for a short play, a dialogue, or a memoir, decide on an appropriate time and place for the action to take place. In two or three sentences, write a description of the

setting for your script. Then decide on the people involved and begin to write the dialogue.

Once you have started to write using your chosen form, work alone to finish your first draft.

# STAGE 3: REVISING AND REWRITING

Once you have finished your draft, the next stage of the writing process is to revise and rewrite. At this stage, much of the real work of writing occurs because you rethink what you have written.

Writing that is specific in details, is logically connected, and uses emphasis carefully will be more entertaining to your audience. Revision activities will help you create several choices. From these choices, you can decide what is the best way to express your ideas for your audience—your classmates.

## *Activity 1F    Rethinking Your First Draft*

1. Read your first draft quickly. Then add at least one additional idea to your writing.

2. Decide what mood, or general feeling, your writing has. Underline the words that produce this mood. Can you change any other words in your writing to help add to this mood?

3. Write an alternative opening or *topic sentence* for your writing. Try taking the best idea from your draft and using it in a new opening sentence. Try to capture your reader's attention as quickly as possible.

4. Look at the length of your sentences.
   a. Choose two of the shorter sentences and rewrite them, adding more details by answering these questions: When? Where? Why?
      *Note:* You can write your revised sentences above the original sentences in your draft, or place them on a separate page.
   b. Choose two of your shorter sentences and combine them using any of the following words: because, as, since, while, if, before, after.
   c. Choose a series of thoughts in your writing that you want to emphasize. Rewrite two of your longer sentences by breaking

them into two or more shorter sentences. This will create a more dramatic effect because it quickens the pace of the sentence.

5. Examine the beginnings of your sentences.
   a. Rewrite two of your sentences by adding an opening word or phrase that answers one of these questions: Where? When?
   b. Rewrite three or four sentences that go together. Try to repeat words or ideas as often as possible.
      • If the repetition in these sentences sounds all right when you read them aloud, then keep these sentences.
      • If this repetition sounds awkward, discard these sentences and think of them as a good try.

## *Activity 1G    Rewriting Your First Draft*

Now that you have experimented with some revisions, it is time to rework your thoughts and compose a second draft.

1. Study the changes that you made in Activity 1F. Keep the ones you believe improve your writing and ignore the rest. Remember, you make the final decisions about your work.

2. Write a second draft of your personal statement about your shadow.

# STAGE 4:   EDITING AND PROOFREADING

When you reread your second draft, you may want to make some final changes to the words in your work. These changes are usually smaller than those you made at the revision stage. This process is called **editing**.

## *Activity 1H    Editing Your Writing*

1. Reread your second draft, concentrating on the verbs and the phrases that show time.
   a. What time, or *tense*, do you use to talk about your shadow in the first sentence—the present or past tense?
   b. Does the time or tense shift from past to present or present to past in any of the sentences that follow? Does this shift in tense confuse the reader?

2. Can you substitute stronger verbs for the ones you used in this draft?

3. If necessary, make a clean copy of your writing.

**Proofreading** is a process during which you check the mechanics of writing. Mechanical problems include errors in spelling, punctuation, capitalization, or paragraphing.

### *Activity 1I   Proofreading Your Second Draft*

1. Reread your draft version one more time. This time, pay less attention to your ideas as you reread. Read word by word, slowly looking for problems with the mechanics of writing.

2. Pay particular attention to the following concerns:
   - misspelled words
   - sentences that do not start with capital letters
   - words that should be capitalized but are not
   - words that should not be capitalized but are
   - errors in showing possession with an apostrophe
   - any misuses of such homophones as:
     their, there, they're     its, it's     to, too, two

### *Activity 1J   Preparing the Final Copy*

After you finish editing and proofreading, you may have a messy copy. If you are going to have others read your writing, you may want to make a completely polished copy of your work. Here are some suggestions to make it easy for your audience to read and enjoy your writing.
- Write your work on a separate page.
- Leave margins around both sides of your work and at the top and bottom of the page.
- Use ink for your final copy and try for a good clear handwriting.

# STAGE 5:   PUBLISHING AND SHARING

The final stage of the writing process is the publishing and sharing of your work. You have captured a mysterious thing, your shadow, with words and others will be interested in your work.

## *Activity 1K    Publishing and Sharing*

You can share what you have written in many ways. Here are some ideas to help you.

1. Your class can have a sharing day when everybody exchanges writings.

2. You could dramatize the shadow's voice and use a projector to cast your own shadow.

3. Your class could publish a booklet on shadows and find a way to make it available for others to read.

You have now completed your first piece of writing in *Bridges 3*. By writing, you have become acquainted with the writing process—a system that helps you write more easily.

After you have shared your work with others, don't forget to store it in your writing folder. You may want to look back at your first piece of writing in the future.

# Final Impressions—Looking Back

Beyond a shadow of a doubt, the writing process helped you with your work. Remember what you have learned and the stages of the writing process: prewriting, writing, revising and rewriting, editing and proofreading, publishing and sharing.

## *Activity 1L    Shadowplay*

1. Look carefully at the images on the opening page of this chapter on page 8.

2. Create the same animals (a dog, swan, horse, puma, rhinoceros and eagle) by manipulating your hands and fingers.

3. Move your fingers to create action and bring your characters to life.

4. Work with a partner to create a shadow drama. Create two images and have them interact to tell a story.

*Settler Shooting Ducks—Immigrant Train Crossing the Prairies*, W.G.R. Hinds

# WILD GOOSE CHASE

To go on a *wild goose chase* means to spend valuable time on something that is not worthwhile. You chase something that is not worth having once you have caught it. This phrase, which is called an **idiom**, can also mean to hunt something that cannot be caught.

Perhaps you feel that writing is a wild goose chase. You may feel that what you have written is not valuable or that the words you use don't capture what you want to say. Don't worry. Such reactions are quite normal when you hunt ideas.

In this chapter, you will examine some techniques for a successful hunt. You will flush out your ideas and learn how to use and control them as you write. But, as a hunter, you must appreciate the most important quality you can bring to a hunt: persistence.

# PERSISTENCE

The phrase *a wild goose chase* did not discourage many of the early European settlers who depended on the Canada Goose for food and feathers. Here are some ways they chased and caught wild geese.

- Grain soaked in cheap whiskey and scattered on feeding grounds would make the geese so tipsy that hunters could walk in and pick them up or shoot them at close range.
- Along the New England coast, hunters disguised their boats and themselves as small icebergs. They placed chunks of ice around the bow and

along the sides and wore white clothing. They would scull their craft to within gun range of a flock.

- Hunters used live decoys by separating mated pairs from their young. The birds would call to each other and attract young birds to within shooting range.
- More recently hunters have even used portable tape recorders to play actual goose calls to lure other geese within range.

Such techniques have now been declared illegal, but many hunters still lie behind blinds, in pits, or in snow-covered fields with a white sheet for cover, waiting for geese. They go to all this trouble because they appreciate the meal the birds make. Unsuccessful hunters always admire the ability of the Canada Goose to outwit them.

Perhaps the same thing is true when you write. You develop persistence because you do not want to be outwitted. You want to explore your ideas by reading, writing, listening, viewing, and discussing. You want to compare your ideas and pursue the best ones. You do this at the **prewriting stage** in the **writing process**.

# THE PREWRITING STAGE

In the first stage of the writing process, the prewriting stage, you gather ideas. There are many sources from which you can gather information.

- **printed material**—by reading and looking at pictures, maps, newspapers, or diagrams
- **electronic media** such as television and radio—by watching television or films, or listening to radio
- **other people**—by discussing ideas and asking questions

*Activity 2A    Test Yourself*

1. Look at this question and write your response immediately in your notebook:
   *Question:* How did early hunters of the Canada Goose demonstrate that they were persistent?

2. Compare what you wrote with the information given about the question on pages 23 and 24 and the picture on page 22.

From this activity, you can probably see that something has to happen in your head for information to become an idea that you can express. Printed material, electronic media, and discussions with others provide you with information. To find ideas in this information, to trap them on paper, you must be constantly hunting—reading, looking, observing, watching, listening, discussing, and asking. And to improve your ideas, you have to relate the new information to what you already know.

In this chapter you will learn some prewriting techniques that will help you capture your new ideas and relate them to what you already know. Here is a list of these techniques:

- recalling past experiences
- creating thought webs
- making associations
- finding possibilities
- questioning

## The Writing Task—A Fowl Problem

The subject of your writing will be a *fowl problem*. You will be on an idea hunt. Exactly what happened in the picture on page 26 is your quarry. Your task is to capture this event in words by creating an imaginary story about it.

You will share your writing—the message you find at the end of your idea hunt—with your classmates. Your message should help them realize that in any communication situation, there are a variety of possible communicators, purposes, audiences, messages, and forms of communication.

To help you with the idea hunt in this chapter, you will be using prewriting techniques in a carefully planned order, but remember that each idea hunt is different. When you hunt down ideas on other topics you may have to use the techniques you learned in this chapter in a different way or in a different order.

The prewriting activities will help you to understand one system for hunting ideas. The activities will also lead you to the prewriting decisions you need to make to complete your writing task on the *Fowl Problem*.

You will probably not complete all of the activities in this chapter at one time. It would be helpful to summarize the hunting techniques as you learn them and to record your prewriting decisions.

### *Activity 2B    Record Your Hunt*

1. Prepare a chart to record your prewriting decisions entitled *My Prewriting Decisions*.

You will find directions to complete this chart as you go through the prewriting techniques and activities outlined in this chapter.

**Fowl problem**   A Canada Goose with an arrow through its neck was found waddling around the Packanack Lake golf course in Wayne, N.J. Humane Society workers say the goose is difficult to catch since it can still fly away from pursuers.

# Technique 1: Recalling Past Experiences

You probably have had many experiences hunting for lost things. The following activity will help you remember the approach you used to find them.

## *Activity 2C   Helping a Hunter*

1. Pretend you are in the situation below:
   Your school is hosting a volleyball tournament. A visiting team member has lost a jacket in the locker room. Your coach has asked someone to help this player find the jacket. The locker room is strewn with clothing and equipment from all four teams.

2. Working in pairs, write a dialogue between the person asked to help and the player who has lost the jacket. Record this conversation in your notebook.

To write about the imaginary hunters in the last activity, you probably recall past experiences when you hunted for something. By using the prewriting technique of *recalling a past experience* you have prepared yourself for an idea hunt. You have remembered a method you used in the past and tried to relate it to the new situation presented in Activity 2C.

# Technique 2: A Thought Web

Does the conversation below sound familiar?

> "Yes. I lost my jacket."      "What does it look like? Maybe I've seen it."

The next activity, **a thought web**, will help you focus the *Fowl Problem* in your mind. A thought web helps you record characteristics and associations about a subject and fix them in your head. It also requires you to begin to organize your ideas, to arrange them so that a pattern emerges.

## *Activity 2D   A Thought Web*

1. In your notebook, draw a circle and write the subject in it like this:

{ *fowl problem* }

2. Examine the picture on page 26 and read the information under the picture. Record the ideas you think of by copying the example below and adding at least five more circles to the web:

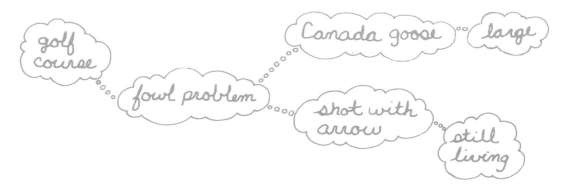

3. Save this record of your observations of the facts. The ideas in your thought web will help you clearly identify the subject of your message when you start to write.

# Technique 3:   Associations

Does this conversation sound familiar?

| | |
|---|---|
| "I've lost my jacket."<br>"If I knew that, it wouldn't be lost!" | "Well, where did you put it?"<br>"Well, what I mean is, where were you when you last remember seeing it or having it? Trace your steps. Fix the scene in your mind." |

The next prewriting technique, **making associations**, will help you imagine the circumstances of the *Fowl Problem*.

## *Activity 2E   Making Associations*

1. Keep your thought web from Activity 2D in mind and try to imagine how the event happened and where on the golf course it happened.

2. Travel to this place in your imagination.
   a. List any six people you would associate with this place.
   b. List any five objects you would associate with this place.

# Technique 4:   Providing Possibilities

"…and that's the last time I remember having it."
"That gives me an idea. It was there when I……"

"Maybe it's mixed in with some other teams' clothes. Check the empty lockers."

When you hunt, you need to explore **all kinds of possibilities**. You can work with many people to stimulate your ideas or you can think alone. Your purpose is to produce as many ideas or solutions to a problem as possible within a short period of time. Once you have some ideas you can make your first prewriting decision: **choosing a point of view**.

## Activity 2F    Possibilities and Finding a Point of View

1. Form groups of about three students and appoint a *recorder* who will keep track of the ideas generated by the group.

2. In four minutes, make a list of all the possible people who could be connected with the *Fowl Problem*. They could be eyewitnesses to the event, or perhaps they learned of it from others since the event has become a national news story.

3. As the recorder slowly reads out the group's list, copy all the suggestions into your notebook.

4. From this list, choose one character that interests you. You will be reacting to the *Fowl Problem* from the point of view of this person.

5. Record your first decision—the point of view for your writing—in your Prewriting Decision Chart.

# Technique 5:   Questioning

"I'm going to be in trouble if I can't find it."

"Could any of your teammates have taken it by mistake?"

The prewriting technique of **questioning** can help you decide on the message of the character you created in Activity 2F. To help think of the emotional reaction your character might have to the *Fowl Problem*, imagine that you can interview this imaginary person.

## *Activity 2G   Interview Your Character*

1. Write a series of at least eight questions that you could ask about the event behind the *Fowl Problem*.

2. These following words will help you think of possible questions: Who? What? Where? When? How? What if? Should? Could? Would? Are? Is? Can? Will?

3. Answer your questions as you imagine your character would answer them.

4. In two or three sentences, summarize your character's emotional response to the problem in your Prewriting Decision Chart.

## *Activity 2H   The Purpose of Your Character's Message*

1. Keep in mind the reactions you imagined in the last activity. Which of the purposes below might your character have?

| | | |
|---|---|---|
| to brag | to threaten | to thank |
| to inform | to suggest | to gossip |
| to shock | to confess | to complain |
| to narrate | to explain | to apologize |
| to protest | to persuade | to assess |

2. Choose one or two of these purposes for your character's message and record your decision in your Prewriting Decision Chart.

You have completed some decisions about your writing task. You have established the point of view of your character, you have decided how your character will react, and you have determined your character's purpose. The next decision is to determine the audience.

## *Activity 2I   The Audience*

1. Decide to whom your character would most likely send a message.

2. Record your decision in your Prewriting Decision Chart.

## *Activity 2J    The Form*

1. Your last decision—the form—depends on your previous decisions. After examining your decisions, choose a form that seems appropriate to your character, the message, the purpose, and the audience. Here is a list of forms you might use.

| | | |
|---|---|---|
| a personal letter | a memo or note | a poem |
| a business letter | an editorial | a dialogue |
| a diary entry | a report | |
| a journal | a news article | |

2. Record your final decision in your Prewriting Decision Chart.

# CONTINUING WITH THE WRITING PROCESS

You have spent considerable time exploring the nature of your writing task. Now it is time to go on with the other stages of the writing process.

## *Activity 2K    The First Draft*

1. Review the prewriting decisions you recorded in your Chart. Reread your imaginary interview with your character from Activity 2G.

2. Write a first draft of your ideas, a statement, using your chosen form. And just as a reminder, your writing task is to write about the *Fowl Problem* in order to interest your classmates.

## *Activity 2L    Revising*

1. In groups of three or four, share your work. Each group member should read his or her statement to the rest of the group.

2. Each student should write down two positive comments about this statement.
   a. Share these comments among the group.
   b. As a group, talk about the main achievement of each piece of writing.

The writer should then decide whether or not the group members understood the statement in the way he or she wanted them to.

3. Repeat this procedure for each writer in the small group.

4. Working in pairs, exchange papers. Read your partner's paper a second time.
   a. Look specifically at the verbs used. For each verb, suggest two other verbs that could have been used.
   b. For each verb, suggest an adverb that could be used to describe the verb.

5. Return the paper to your partner.

## Activity 2M   The Final Draft

1. Study the suggestions and responses made by the group and by your writing partner.

2. Use the suggestions you like and ignore the others.

3. Decide what you want to say in your final draft.

4. Write your paper and get ready to share with your audience—your classmates.

## Activity 2N   Editing and Proofreading

1. Read your paper one more time, looking for errors in
   - spelling
   - capitalization
   - shifts in verb tense, from past to present or present to past. (It is usually wise to use one tense throughout a piece of writing.)

2. Form *special editing groups* to catch any problems with the mechanics of writing.
   a. Choose one student to look at all the pieces of writing for problems with spelling.
   b. Choose another student to check the capitalization in all the pieces of writing.
   c. Have another student look carefully at the use of verbs.
      - Is the use of tense consistent? Do all verbs suggest the same time—present or past?
      - Do the verb forms *agree with the subject* in number?

## Agreement of Verbs

All verbs must agree with their subjects.
When the subject is singular, regular verbs add an *s*.

Subject            Predicate or Verb

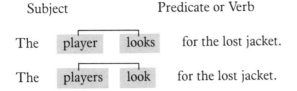

The player looks    for the lost jacket.

The players look    for the lost jacket.

Some verbs are irregular. They have their own way of changing from singular form to plural form.

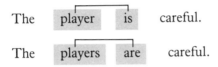

The player is    careful.

The players are    careful.

## *Activity 20    Publishing and Sharing*

1. Share your writing.
   a. Form groups of four or five students.
   b. As each person prepares to share his or her statement, he or she should
      • read out the prewriting decision chart that introduces the imaginary response
      • share the response with the group

2. As a group, decide on how to present your group writings orally to the whole class.

3. Be sure to save your final draft in your *writing folder*.

# The Final Shot

In this chapter you have stalked ideas by using some prewriting techniques—recalling past experiences, creating thought webs, making associations, providing possibilities, and questioning. These techniques have led you to prewriting decisions. Once these decisions were made you were better able to capture your ideas and create an imaginary story.

The Aurora is one of the world's exotic sports cars. It takes its name from the place where it is built—Aurora, Ontario. When you look at this car, you see a unity containing all parts: the chassis, the transmission, the body, and the engine. These components unite to give the magnificent car you see before you.

A paragraph is like the Aurora. Both are made of components that combine to give a unity. This chapter will explain the components of a paragraph.

# AURORA

All writers need to know how to write a paragraph. A **paragraph** is a collection of sentences grouped together because they deal with one central idea. These sentences form a unity of meaning. They may begin with an overview kind of sentence, called a **topic sentence**. And they may end with a sentence that summarizes the main idea of the paragraph: the **concluding sentence**.

Effective writing and car-building have one thing in common—they need careful planning. Just imagine what would happen if the makers of the Aurora did not have an organized plan for assembling the components of this car! Once you know how to write a well-organized paragraph, you can communicate your ideas more effectively. Future writing assignments will be less complicated and more successful.

This chapter will introduce you to the components of the paragraph and teach you how to assemble them to produce a well-organized unity of meaning. You will practise writing three different types of paragraphs:

- descriptive paragraphs
- narrative paragraphs
- expository paragraphs

| A descriptive paragraph provides a picture of an incident, a person, or a thing. | A narrative paragraph tells a story. | An expository paragraph explains something. |
|---|---|---|

Not many writers produce *pure* paragraphs. That is, there are very few paragraphs that do nothing but describe something, or tell a story, or explain. But it is probably a good idea for you to look at the different kinds of paragraphs in isolation, as presented in this chapter, to better understand the structure of more complex paragraphs.

# DESCRIBE IT AS IT IS...
## Descriptive Paragraphs

**My Skates**

1. My skates are my most treasured possession and they are worth more than a king's ransom to me.

2. With white leather boots from Austria, smooth as silk, yet thick and padded, I can soar like an eagle.

3. With my Coronation Ace blades from the United Kingdom, I can trace the most definite circles.

4. These ultrasharp blades, shining like silver, allow me to execute jumps and spins to perfection.

5. My skates are everything to me—they are my pride and joy!

Aina Arro, grade-nine student

As all well-written paragraphs should, this one has a beginning, a middle, and an end. It has a topic sentence that captures your attention immediately, a middle section with supporting details, and a satisfactory end.

## *Activity 3A    What's in a Paragraph?*

1. Working alone, once again read the paragraph *My Skates*.

2. Copy the chart below in your notebook and answer the following questions to complete it.
   a. Choose the *one* sentence from this paragraph that states the main idea—the topic sentence.
   b. Choose the sentences that support the main idea and add details—the body of the paragraph.
   c. Choose the *one* sentence that ends the paragraph and sums up the main idea—the concluding sentence.

**The Components of a Paragraph**

| Components | Sentence Number(s) |
| --- | --- |
| The Topic Sentence | |
| The Body of the Paragraph (details) | |
| Concluding Sentence | |

# Describe It in a Paragraph

Just as an artist uses forms and colour to describe something, a writer uses words for the same purpose. Good writers pay careful attention to the descriptive detail in their writing.

## *Activity 3B    My Greatest Treasure*

1. Look at these two pictures. Each represents someone's greatest treasure.

2. Use a thought web, like the one in the example below, to explore your ideas.

3. Working alone, use the ideas you generated in your thought web to write continuously for five minutes on the topic of *My Greatest Treasure*. Keep your ideas flowing and your pen moving on the page for the entire five minutes. If you can't think of anything to write, write the word *treasure* over and over again.

4. Share your paragraph with a writing partner.
   a. Read your writing aloud while your partner listens. Then, listen while your partner reads.
   b. Ask your partner questions about his or her greatest treasure. Encourage your partner to think more about the value of this treasure, why it's important, some adventures he or she has had with it, when it was acquired and so on.

5. Working alone, plan an interesting paragraph about your treasure that you can share with an adult.
   a. Write a topic sentence stating the main idea of your paragraph. For example, "My cat Bushy is my greatest treasure."
   b. Write three or four sentences to support your main idea. You might explain why you hold this treasure in such high esteem, how you acquired it, or its physical characteristics.
   c. Write one sentence that summarizes your thinking and provides a good conclusion to your paragraph.

6. Read over what you have written. If you are happy with it, store it in your writing folder. If you are not, go back to question 5 and go through each step again with either your original topic or a new one.

**Contest Rules: Describe It!!**

In one paragraph, describe the unique experience of driving a Lamborghini. Most people will have to imagine this one!

The winning paragraph will evoke the sense of beauty, speed, and power associated with being behind the wheel of one of the world's finest cars.

Can you be a winner?

## *Activity 3C    You Can Be the Winner!*

1. Work in groups of about three students. Brainstorm to come up with as many descriptive words as possible to respond to the above contest.
   - Nominate one group member to record the work of the group. The recorder will have to listen carefully to everything said and write down all the ideas suggested by the group members. (If you are the recorder, make certain that you add your own ideas to the list.)

2. When you are finished, listen as the recorder reads the group's words, suggestions, and phrases aloud.

3. Working by yourself, choose from the group list the words and phrases that you like best and write them in your notebook.

4. Write continuously on the topic *Driving My Lamborghini* for five minutes.
   - Keep your pen going steadily for the full five minutes, without stopping. If you can't think of anything to say, keep writing

*Lamborghini* until something pops into your mind and you get started again.

• Remember to describe the total experience. Appeal to all the senses as you record the sights, the sounds, the smells, the textures, the feelings, and the sensations.

5. Choose a writing partner to help you think more about your entry in the *Describe-the-Lamborghini* contest.
   a. Student A reads aloud while Student B listens. Student B's job will be to listen carefully for those words, phrases, and sentences that most accurately and vividly describe the experience. She or he should make notes on these to give Student A feedback at the end of the reading.
   b. Then Student B reads while Student A does the listening.

6. Help each other write the next drafts of your *Lamborghini* paragraphs by providing some alternatives.
   a. Write another topic sentence for your partner's paragraph.
   b. Write three sentences to support the new topic sentence.
   c. Write another concluding sentence for your partner's paragraph.
   d. Talk with your partner about the effectiveness of your original sentences and the new alternative sentences.

7. Look once again at your original paragraph. Make your own decision about what you want to keep and use in your next draft and what should be thrown away.

8. Write your descriptive paragraph in response to the contest rules for *Driving My Lamborghini*.

9. Share your finished paragraph with your partner by reading it aloud. Listen while your partner reads his or hers to you. Store your paragraph in your writing folder.

# TELL IT AS IT HAPPENED...
## Narrative Paragraphs

You are a sports writer attending a car race where this incident happened. It is your job to narrate the details for your readers. You were there. Tell what happened.

## *Activity 3D   Action...Camera...Roll...*

1. Look at the picture of the racing car. Study the position of the car. Look at the skid marks on the track and the smoke coming from the overturned car. Where is the driver? Is he or she safe?

2. Working alone, imagine this scene five seconds before the picture was taken. Now go forward, one step at a time, and imagine the sequence of events that lead to the scene in the picture. Make some quick notes about the details in your notebook.

3. Choose a writing partner with whom to work.
   a. Using your notes to help, tell your partner your version of the incident.
   b. Listen and look at the picture while your partner in turn recounts his or her version.

4. Talk with each other about your work. Are you satisfied with the story each paragraph narrates? Why or why not?

5. Use the results of this discussion to write the next draft of your paragraph. Be sure that you don't just recopy your first draft. Think about your paragraph and the best possible way to narrate the story involved with the car accident.

6. Store your writing in your folder.

In the next activity you will combine narration and description. You will have to use both action and descriptive words.

## Activity 3E  Tell It and Describe It

1. Read *People and Places* silently. As you read, imagine the scene.

### PEOPLE AND PLACES

A 2½-year-old Massachusetts toddler wearing a red sweatshirt inscribed with the words "Destruction Is My Business" climbed behind the wheel of his grandmother's car and proceeded to wreak HAVOC in the parking lot of an ice cream store. Police said the youngster climbed out of his car seat and got behind the wheel when his grandmother stopped to get something out of the rear of the car. He then put the car in reverse and ran over his grandmother's foot, before backing onto the street and back into the parking lot. He went around the parking lot and out onto the road in reverse four times. Somehow he managed to put the car in drive, ran over a concrete embankment and pushed a dumpster into a parked 1973 Chevrolet. Although the child was unhurt, the grandmother was treated and released for scrapes and bruises on her left ankle.

*Road and Track*, May, 1984

2. Rewrite the paragraph. Bring it to life by adding more descriptive details and more effective action words. Try to let your reader really see the characters and the objects and to feel and hear what is happening.

3. Form groups of three or four students.

   a. Take turns reading your paragraphs aloud while the other group members listen. Make notes of the most effective words, phrases, and sentences.

   b. Take turns giving each group member oral feedback on the paragraph he or she has written. Tell the writer what is good about his or her writing—what works.

4. Working on your own, use this feedback to revise your paragraph.

---

- *Add:*       Add any details necessary to make the paragraph more lively, colourful, and entertaining.

- *Remove:*    Take out anything that does not have a specific purpose, is unclear, or is dull.

- *Replace:*    Substitute any words, phrases, or sentences that are unclear with ones that convey your meaning more exactly.

- *Rearrange:*   Make any necessary adjustments to the order of the words or phrases in the paragraph.

---

5. Write a good copy of your paragraph and share the final draft with your group.

6. Keep your paragraph in your writing folder.

# EXPLAIN IT TO ME...
## Expository Paragraphs

Quite frequently you need to explain something to others—to clarify how to do something, to give directions, to make something, or to give some information. You will have to use this skill quite often in a type of writing called **exposition**.

When you write a how-to... paragraph, you must provide the necessary details for the reader. You have to be careful to present details in the order the reader needs them.

## Activity 3F   Make It Perfectly Clear....

1. Working with a partner, take turns choosing a topic from the box of *How-to...* topics below. Give an oral explanation of *How-to....*

2. Using one of the topics given in the box, or one of your own choice, write a *How-to...* paragraph. Be as specific as you can and provide all the details that your reader will need.

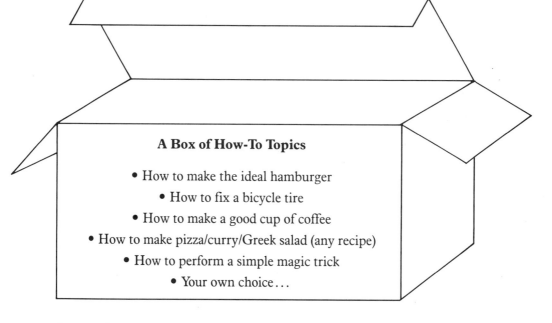

**A Box of How-To Topics**

- How to make the ideal hamburger
- How to fix a bicycle tire
- How to make a good cup of coffee
- How to make pizza/curry/Greek salad (any recipe)
- How to perform a simple magic trick
- Your own choice...

3. Working with a different partner, take turns reading your explanations aloud. Your partner should listen and prepare a response to each of the following questions. Write your responses at the bottom of your partner's work.
   a. What is the best thing about your partner's instructions? Explain your answer.
   b. What is the effect of the topic sentence?
   c. What is the effect of the concluding sentence?

4. You are now ready to revise your paragraph, using the outline given in the box in Activity 3E on page 43.

Explanations are part of everyday life. The more you explain things the better you get at explaining, and the easier it becomes.

## *Activity 3G   How to...*

The following activity gives you the opportunity to do some humourous writing about a how-to topic.

1. Working with a partner, take turns choosing a topic from the list below and explain *how-to*... orally.

   - How to tidy my bedroom in five seconds flat.
   - How to irritate a friend/teacher/parent.
   - How to demolish a pizza in six easy steps.
   - How to dodge...
       washing the dishes.
       mowing the lawn/shovelling snow.
       running an errand.
   - How to outwit my sister/brother/cat/dog/self.

   Each partner should get two or three chances to select a topic and explain it orally.

2. Choose one of the topics listed or a humourous topic of your own choice. Write a *How-to*... paragraph.

3. Working with your partner, take turns reading your paragraphs aloud.

4. After your partner has finished, comment on each of the following questions orally.

   a. Were all necessary details given?
   b. Were they given in the proper order?
   c. Was the explanation clear and easy to follow?
   Listen while your partner responds to each question about your paragraph. Make any necessary adjustments to your work.

5. Revise your paragraph using the outline given in Activity 3E on page 43 as a guide.

6. Write a good copy of your paragraph after you have proofread it carefully.

7. Get together with a group of four or five students and have some fun listening to each other's humourous paragraphs. Nominate one student to organize the order of speakers and to chair the gathering. Choose one paragraph to be read for the whole class.

8. Keep the paragraph in your writing folder.

## *Activity 3H    Some Real Life Situations*

In this activity you will use your skills at writing paragraphs to communicate effectively in real-life situations.

Working alone, read over the following list of situations. Choose the three you like best and complete them by writing a paragraph of 8 to 10 sentences on each one.

1. You are a fashion designer/car designer/architect and you have completed one of your best designs ever. Describe it.

2. You are a police officer/traffic warden and you have just been involved in one of the funniest incidents of your career. Narrate it to a co-worker.

3. Your younger brother or sister has asked you to explain how to play football/basketball/hockey. Explain it.

4. You were a witness at a traffic accident involving a pedestrian and a cyclist. You will need a record of the details of the accident for future reference. Describe it as you saw it.

5. You are a newspaper columnist and you recently met a famous person whom you admire greatly. Describe the meeting for your readers.

6. You are a retired airline pilot/lawyer/farmer/ship's cook (any career you like) and you are writing your memoirs. You are now at the point where you are describing the most exciting event of your career. Describe it.

7. You are a teacher (any subject area you choose) whose class will be covered by a supply teacher. You have an acceptable code of behaviour for your students. Explain it.

8. Your own choice.

# Paragraph Building

The activities you have done throughout this chapter will help you when you do any of the following writing tasks:

- write or tell stories
- give or write directions
- write reports or letters
- give or write instructions

As you worked through the chapter, you listened, you talked, you read, and you wrote.

The next time a teacher asks you to

- write a paragraph about Samuel de Champlain,

  or

- write a paragraph explaining how the Canadian National Railway was built,

  or

- write a description of Canada's most exciting sports car,

you will be able to do this easily and successfully. Good describing, telling, and explaining!

*Infantry Near Nijmegen, Holland,* Alex Colville.
   Alex Colville was one of the Canadian artists commissioned under the Canadian War Art Programme to record the war in painting.

# CHAPTER 4

## ON THE ROAD TO...

So peering through sleet as we neared Nijmegen
I glimpsed the rainbow arch of your eyes
Over the clank of the jeep
your quick grave laughter
outrising at last the rockets
brought me what spells I repeat
as I travel this road
that arrives at no future

Earle Birney, "The Road to Nijmegen"

On November 11 each year, Canadians celebrate Remembrance Day. We remember the more than 100 000 men and women who died during World Wars I and II. Many people have thought about these wars and about their horrors and glories. Alex Colville remembered the wars in *Infantry Near Nijmegen, Holland* (pronounced Nye-may-gan), painted in 1946. Earle Birney, a Canadian poet, put his thoughts into the poem, "The Road to Nijmegen". They were expressing their opinion about a specific topic.

# WHAT CAN YOU SEE AND FEEL?

## *Activity 4A    Nijmegen*

1. Study Alex Colville's painting on page 48 and then write your response in your notebook to the following questions.

   a. What expressions do you see on the faces of the soldiers? Describe them as fully as you can.

   b. What ideas about war does Colville express in the painting? List them in your notebook.

   c. What are your feelings about war? Do you agree with the feelings expressed in Colville's painting? Why or why not?

2. Read the excerpt from Earle Birney's poem, "The Road to Nijmegen", and as a class talk about the opinion Birney presents.

3. Write your response to Birney's poem. Include the ideas and feelings this poem stirs within you.

   *Remember*: If you write a *description*, you provide a factual account of a scene. A *response* asks you to express what the poem makes you think about and how it makes you feel—no matter how unrelated your ideas might be to Birney's poem.

4. Using Colville's painting and Birney's poem, write a description of the road to Nijmegen. You can add a few details to this scene from your own imagination.

5. Store your work in your writing folder.

6. Use this writing to stimulate further writing in your journal.

# EXPRESSING OPINIONS

People express opinions all the time. It's human to want to communicate with others and to find a way to connect your mind with theirs. Some opinions are sound; others are questionable. Some have reasons and facts to support them while others are vague generalizations without value. It is necessary for you to learn to express your own opinions and to judge the value of the opinions of others.

## *Activity 4B    Youth Today*

You have been invited by your local radio station to present an opinion on a topic of importance to young people. Your interview will be broadcast on the programme, *Speak Out*.

1. Working with a group of four or five students, list at least five issues you believe are really important to today's youth.
   - Appoint one member to be the group leader.
   - Appoint another to record the ideas of the group.

2. Find out how important each issue is in the opinion of the members of your group.
   a. Use a ranking system from 1 to 5.
   b. Each member assigns a number value to each item. 1 is the least important and 5, the most important.
   c. Add the group ratings for each item. The most important issue is the one that gets the highest total score.

3. Discuss the issue your group has rated as most important.
   *Note*: The recorder should not participate in this discussion. He or she should only make notes on the various opinions expressed.

a. Go around the group once, allowing each member to make one statement about the issue. Do not discuss anyone's statement further at this time.

b. Go around the group again allowing any member to contribute a second or third statement on the issue.

*Note*: Each member of the group should be encouraged to express at least one thought or opinion on the subject. Indeed, it is the group's responsibility to create a group feeling in which all members feel comfortable expressing opinions and thoughts. Each member of the group should try to support and encourage others to express themselves.

4. Once you have gone around the group twice, open the topic for discussion.
   * Back up your opinion with reasons and examples, and ask others to do the same.
   * See if you can challenge any of the opinions expressed in your group, even your own. Remember, it takes a great deal of skill and tact to challenge an opinion without attacking the person who stated it.

5. As a group, listen while your recorder presents a summary of the discussion. The recorder should note all of the opinions expressed, telling which ones were rejected, which ones were supported, and why.

6. Working together as a group, compose an essay of two or three paragraphs. Appoint one group member, not the recorder, to do the actual writing while the other members suggest ways to express the ideas. The essay you finish with should present your stand on the issue. In some groups, the essay may have to consider opposing points of view and show that there are several different opinions about the topic.

7. Work together as a group to make an audio-tape of your essay to be read on the radio programme *Speak Out*. The announcer should introduce the reading as a topic of importance to young people and read by one of the teenagers in the community. You might choose some music to be played as an introduction to your piece so that your audience is prepared for the reading.

8. Exchange tapes among small groups or play them for the whole class. (You might even ask your principal to play some of your class's more successful tapes over the school's public address system.)

# DISCUSSION IS IMPORTANT

During a discussion, you have the opportunity to explore ideas from many different viewpoints. In other words, the collective thinking of a group can be more powerful than the independent thinking of an individual. Each member of a group should be encouraged to express opinions. The end product will depend on both the thinking of group members and the interaction among them.

When you discuss something, you don't have to challenge the ideas or change the minds of the people in your group. Instead, a discussion allows group members to explore different ideas, and to have many people offer thoughts and viewpoints. As you listen to the discussion, the ideas of the other group members may help you clarify or expand your own thoughts or opinions. You don't have to agree with everything you hear. You don't even have to agree with yourself. However, you do have the responsibility to really listen to what others are saying.

## *Activity 4C    Beauty Pageants*

1. Form small groups of four or five members.

   - Select a recorder to take notes of the group's discussion.
   - Select a chairperson to be responsible for conducting the discussion. The duties of the chair are these:
     - Keep the members of the group on topic, occasionally reminding them of it if necessary.
     - Make sure that each group member has a chance to speak.
     - Encourage and thank members for their contribution, and, where possible, eliminate comments and remarks that tend to discourage thought and free expression of opinion.
     - Report the results to the class.

2. As a group, make a list of questions you could ask about the topic: *Beauty Pageants*.

   Example:
     Who enters beauty pageants?
     What are the advantages of entering beauty pageants?
     Who might object to beauty pageants and what are some of their objections?

3. As a group, categorize your questions. One list will contain support questions; the other, critical questions.

4. Discuss your questions to discover the group's *pro* and *con* opinions about beauty contests.

5. The chair for each small group should then present the opinions of the group to the whole class.

6. As a class, talk about the reports. Discuss your findings.
   a. What was the general attitude towards beauty pageants in your class?
   b. What are the advantages and disadvantages of beauty pageants to
      • the people who enter them
      • society as a whole

*Extension*: If your class feels strongly about beauty pageants, form a special small group to write a letter to the editor of your local newspaper. Give your class's opinion about beauty pageants such as The Miss Teen Canada Pageant, The Mr. Universe Contest, or the Miss World Contest.

# DISCUSSION SUPPORTS WRITING

Group discussion is an excellent prewriting activity. It helps you clarify ideas and collect information on a topic such as the information you need for a class speech.

## A Communication Task: A Three-Minute Talk

Prepare a three-minute talk for your class. This talk should give your opinion about a topic of interest to you and to the students in your class. Your talk should

- state your opinion clearly
- support your opinion with reasons, examples, and explanations
- consider the opposite point(s) of view and refute opposing ideas
- draw a conclusion

### Activity 4D    Discussion as Prethinking

**Opinion Topics**
1. School attendance should be voluntary.
2. "No More Wars"
3. Lotteries should be banned.
4. The rich have all the advantages.
5. Censorship should be abolished.
6. Canada needs a dictator.

1. Choose a topic that interests you. Several topics have been listed in the box above. Choose one of them or find one of your own.

2. Form a group of about four people. Each student should lead the group in a discussion of his or her topic.
   a. Listen carefully to the ideas expressed by the group as they discuss your topic. As they speak, make notes of any points you can use in your upcoming talk.
   b. When it is time to discuss another group member's topic, do your best to contribute to the discussion and to provide lots of material and ideas for her or his talk.

Writing can be used for two purposes—to communicate ideas to others and to explore ideas for yourself. When you write an exploratory draft, your intent is to think and discover ideas and ways to arrange them. This is called a **thought draft**. You write thought drafts quickly, with the main purpose of getting ideas out of your mind and onto your page.

## Activity 4E    Writing Your Thought Draft

1. Collect notes from your group discussions in Activity 4D and classify them into support and criticism statements.

2. Decide on which side you want to be. Use the ideas from the group discussions to build up your opinion. Always have examples and facts ready to back up your argument.

3. Write a *thought draft* based on your discussion in Activity 4D. Write your ideas quickly. You simply want an overview of your opinion at this stage.

    *Remember*: Nothing is ever black or white. You may have a strong opinion about something but you may also have reservations about the issue—this is natural! There are always grey areas to deal with.

4. Keep opposing ideas in mind and, if necessary, consider them in your thought draft. Acknowledge the grey areas as well as those areas you completely reject. You should at least be prepared to consider opposing opinions in case there is a discussion after your talk.

## Activity 4F    Revising and Rethinking Your Opinion

1. Exchange papers with a writing partner and help each other think some more about your topics. Use the following questions as a guideline to review your partner's thought draft.
    a. What is the main opinion expressed in your partner's thought draft? Underline it.
    b. Write out at least two one-sentence opinion statements for your partner that could be used at the beginning of his or her talk.
    c. Number the examples or reasons your writing partner presents in his or her paper. If possible, suggest two or three additional reasons that could be used. Write them down for your writing partner.

d. Look for the conclusion at the end of the paper and underline it. Write out at least two other concluding statements that could be used.

e. Try to find a quotation for your partner to use as a way of supporting an idea or finishing up the paper. Write it out and give it to your partner.

f. Suggest three possible titles that are appropriate for this paper and write them down for your partner.

g. An appropriate joke or anecdote can give a nice finishing touch to a talk. Try to find one to give your partner to use in his or her talk.

2. Exchange papers again so that each partner has his or her own.

3. Write the first draft of your opinion speech.
   a. Read over the ideas you got from your writing partner.

   *Remember*: This is your writing. You have the responsibility of choosing only those ideas and suggestions you want to use.

   b. Use any of your partner's suggestions you think will improve the quality of your writing and any new ideas that you have to write your second draft.

# STAND UP…AND TALK

In everyday life, you often give your opinions freely without advance preparation. You sum up your facts, organize your ideas, and then speak— perhaps all of this in under ten seconds. Sometimes you must give your opinions more formally. You know you will be expected to discuss your opinion and you have some time to consider your ideas.

## *Activity 4G    Before You Speak*

1. Read over the written talk you prepared and wrote in Activities 4D, 4E, and 4F.

2. On an index card approximately 8 cm by 12 cm, write the title of your speech on the top line.

3. Write one or two words that will help you remember the first line of your talk, just enough to get started.

4. Use point-form notes to list the main points of your talk. Use large print and write headings or main ideas only.

5. Write down notes to help you remember your final sentence.

6. Go off by yourself and practise your talk. It should be about three minutes. Don't memorize it; instead, know the content so well that you can talk about it easily and naturally.

## *Activity 4H   As You Speak*

Here is some advice to help you deliver your three-minute speech.

1. Just before going to the front of the room, take six deep breaths. Deep breathing will help you relax and keep your throat loose.

2. When it is your turn, take your index card(s) with you and walk to the front of the classroom.

3. Greet your audience with "good morning" or "good afternoon," followed by

   • Madam /Mr. Chairperson (the student nominated by your teacher)

   • _____ (your teacher's name)

   • Fellow students

4. Establish eye contact with individual members of your audience. Select friendly faces in different parts of the room. Take turns looking at them as you speak.
   • Always talk to the friendly faces in your audience.
   • Try to find a friendly face at the back of the room and project your voice so that he or she can hear everything you say.

5. Relax. Smile. Glance at your notes to remember how to start. Look at your audience, particularly the people at the back of the room...and begin.

6. Talk to your audience as if you were taking part in a discussion. Be as natural as you can. Tell your audience why you hold your opinions. If you begin to see puzzled looks, you may have to explain things in greater detail than you had planned.

7. Speak slowly and confidently as you deliver your speech. Look at your index cards only as a reminder of the next major point in your speech or to check that you have covered all of your points.

8. Finish your speech by thanking your audience before returning to your place.

# Down The Road

This chapter has helped you think about your opinions and the reasons you hold them. You have learned how to express your ideas in a group discussion and how to support them with reasons. You also learned how to gather and organize your ideas. Finally you took the plunge—you presented your ideas in a formal speech.

Take every opportunity you can to speak before a group. The more you do it the easier it gets and the more your confidence grows. Think about your audience and its unique needs as you prepare your speech. You will have interesting decisions to make just as Sally does in the cartoon below.

# THE GREAT CANADIAN COMICS CAPER

During the early 1940s American comic books were refused entry into Canada, and such comics as *Superman, Batman and Robin*, and *Captain Marvel* were no longer available. The ban had nothing to do with the comic books themselves. It was caused by World War II. The War Exchange Conservation Act, 1940, imposed restrictions on importing certain non-essential items from other countries. American comic books were just one item no longer allowed into Canada.

To compensate, Canadian writers and illustrators for the first time turned their attention and talents to creating all-Canadian comic books. The characters you'll meet in this chapter are from that period in Canadian history. Through them you will learn to recognize some techniques that writers and illustrators use to produce their characters and you'll have a chance to use these techniques to create your own characters. The final product for the chapter will be your own **splash page**, the first page of a comic book story.

The splash page to the left mentions Cy Bell. Cyril Vaughn Bell is credited with publishing—inventing?—the first Canadian comic book. As you can see, Canadian comic book artists and writers were not above poking some fun at themselves and their main characters.

## The Talk of the Trade

Like most businesses, the comic book industry has its own language with which to talk about the various elements that make up a typical comic book page. The splash page on the next page points to some of the elements that make up comic book language.

A: The first page of a story, with a large introductory illustration, is called the **splash page**.

B: Letters drawn in outline, with space for colour to be added, are called **open letters**.

C: Copy that relates to a title is a **blurb**.

D: The name of the story is, of course, the **title**.

E: A jagged outline around the lettering is called a **splash balloon**.

F: One of the illustrations on a page is a **panel**.

G: The space between panels is the **gutter**.

H: *Krrak*, *Pow*, and *Zat* are **sound effects**.

I: Copy that represents what a character is thinking is a **thought balloon**.

J: The little connecting circles on thought balloons are **bubbles**.

K: Copy that represents what a character is saying is a **dialogue balloon**.

L: The connecting "arrows" on dialogue balloons that show who is speaking are **pointers**.

M: The words in balloons that are more heavily lettered than the other words are **bold words**, or **bold lettering**.

N: The **credits** give the names of the writer(s) and illustrator(s).

O: The technical information showing who publishes the magazine, when and where, is the **indicia** (pronounced in-dee-shah) and is usually found on the bottom of the first page.

P: Copy in which someone is talking to the reader, but which is not in a dialogue balloon, is a **caption**.

## *Activity 5A    Looking for Lingo*

1. Take another look at the opening page of this chapter on page 60, *Some Panthers Don't Wear Skates*.

2. Identify as many of the typical elements from a comic book, A-P, as you think apply to this splash page.

3. In your notebook, write the letters that correspond to the elements you think are illustrated in *Some Panthers Don't Wear Skates*.

4. For each element not illustrated on this splash page, suggest how it could be included. For example, where could the illustrator have used open letters?

# REVEALING CHARACTER

Comics, by definition, are a number of pictures in a sequence that tells a story. The proportion of words and pictures varies but the pictures in comic books are always at least as important as the words. Nevertheless, it's rare to find comics without words.

In this section you'll look at the combination of words and pictures in comic books to see how writers and illustrators have created **main characters**. You'll see that characters are revealed through **how they look, how they act, what they say, what they think**, and **what others say about them**.

## What Characters Look Like

The first thing you notice about people is **physical appearance**—what they look like. Often, physical appearances provide clues to personality traits. The following questions will guide your thinking about characters and their personality traits:

- What do they look like?
- What aspect of their physical appearances suggests something about their personalities?
- What are their names?
- What do names suggest about characters?

Authors often make use of the idea of a relationship between physical appearance and personal characteristics when they write short stories and novels. Heroes or heroines are usually associated with good characteristics, and villains, with less than attractive characteristics.

In real life, however, you have to make certain that you don't stereotype people on the basis of how they look—their physical appearance. There really is, for example, no strong relationship between beauty and goodness, even though many advertisements try to convince you that there is. In other words, you will have to remember that physical appearance is not really tied to personality.

### *Activity 5B    Hey, Look Me Over!*

1. **Study the following splash page on page 65 for** *Nelvana of the Northern Lights and the Ether People.* **Focus your attention on the physical appearances of both Nelvana, whose name as an ordinary citizen is Alana, and the Ether People.**

2. In your notebook, make two headings:

| ALANA | ETHER PEOPLE |
|---|---|

Under each heading, write as many words and phrases as you can think of to describe the physical appearances of Alana and the Ether People. No detail is too small to mention. Your descriptions might begin like this:

| ALANA | ETHER PEOPLE |
|---|---|
| tall | short |
| neatly dressed | chubby |
| one fist clenched | pointed ears |

Try to list eight to ten descriptive words for each character.

3. Read over your physical descriptions. On the basis of the characters' appearances decide what you believe they are like. Try to find at least three words for each physical description that suggests something about the character's personality.

4. Answer the following question in your notebook: Why have you linked certain physical appearances to the character traits you've identified?

5. As a whole class share your views on what you believe Alana and the Ether People are like. Explain what aspect of their physical appearance is linked to each character trait.

   a. Do class members have similar ideas about the character traits of Alana and the Ether People?

   b. Has the class linked certain character traits with a particular physical appearance?

## What's in a Name?

With comic strip characters, names are very important. It should come as no surprise to you that in *Nelvana of the Northern Lights*, Alana is the heroine, the good character, and the Ether People are the villains, the evil characters. Do their names add to what physical appearance tells you about the personalities of the characters?

## *Activity 5C    A Rose By Any Other Name*

Look at these following comic book characters and their names.

1. Write the name of each character in your notebook. Add two or three words describing what you think the personality of each character is.

   *Remember*: Base your description on the picture of the character and the character's name only.

Mister Kolak

Nitro

Wing

Polka Dot Pirate

2. Share your thoughts about each character with a partner. How similar are your opinions?

3. Talk about the names of each character. Do you think the names are good choices? Why or why not?

## Activity 5D    Characters of My Own

In the following activity, you will start to create your own comic book character.

1. From the list to the side, choose two characters for your own comic book splash page. Then choose the main personality trait you'd like each one to have. Write the characters and the traits in your notebook.

   Your characters could be opposing characters, one good and one evil as in the *Nelvana...and the Ether People* splash page, or they could be both good or both evil.

2. Think of a name or nickname for your characters to fit the traits you've given them. Remember, names help capture the character's personality. Write each character's name in your notebook beside the characters and the traits you've chosen for them.

| Character | Trait |
|-----------|-------|
| detective | kind |
| child | generous |
| television star | cowardly |
| nurse | brave |
| criminal | sneaky |
| father | thoughtful |
| mother | humourous |
| singer | suspicious |
| ballet dancer | dishonest |
| teacher | mean |
| wrestler | friendly |
| lawyer | shy |
| mechanic | polite |
| secretary | rude |
| police officer | lonely |
| space creature | joyous |
| your own choice | your own choice |

## Activity 5E    Here's Lookin' At You

1. In your notebook or on a separate piece of paper that can be attached to your notebook, draw pictures of your characters. Don't be too concerned about the beauty of your drawings. Use stick figures if necessary.

2. Add something to each character's appearance that clearly indicates the personality trait you've given him or her.

3. Write the characters' names beside the pictures.
   *Note*: Be sure to leave room around your drawing for a partner to write comments and thoughts about your work.

## *Activity 5F    It Looks Like This...*

Work with a partner for this activity.

1. Exchange pictures of your comic strip characters with your partner.

2. At the bottom of each picture, write one word that identifies one personality trait of the character.

3. Write one or two sentences describing each character.

4. Exchange pictures again. You should now have your own pictures with the word and sentence descriptions that explain what your partner thinks your characters are like.

5. Together, talk about how closely your partner's description matches your intention.
   a. What in the physical appearance of each character suggests the trait and the description your partner gave?
   b. How does the name of your character suit the kind of personality you want him or her to have?

6. Based on the discussion with your partner, you may want to add or alter the physical appearance or the name of your characters.

# What Characters Act Like

Just as physical appearance and name can suggest something about characters, **characters' actions** help reveal their personalities. And what characters do depends on where they are and what is happening to them—the **setting** and **plot**. In comic books these elements of the story must be established quickly,' often on the splash page. These stories are short and there is little opportunity or time to spend giving details about the plot and the setting.

## *Activity 5G    The Where and the What*

Look back at the splash page for *Nelvana... and the Ether People* on page 65.

1. Read the splash page. Note the setting, the time and place of the story, and the plot or story idea. The captions provide much useful information.

2. Write the setting and the plot information in your notebook. Your chart might look something like this:

| Setting | | Plot |
|---|---|---|
| *Time* | *Place* | *Story idea* |
| past—radio transmitters still used | Canadian Arctic far north | science fiction space invasion takeover of Earth |

## Activity 5H   The Where and the What

1. Read the splash page on page 63.

2. In your notebook write the setting and plot information for this splash page as you did for *Nelvana...and the Ether People* in Activity 5G.

3. Compare your ideas for the setting and plot with those of a classmate.
   a. How similar are the settings you have suggested for this story?
   b. How similar are the plots?

## Activity 5I   Your Own Where and What

1. From the suggestions listed below, choose a setting and plot for the comic book characters you created in Activity 5D. Write your choices beside the pictures of your characters.

| Setting | | Plot |
|---|---|---|
| *Time* | *Place* | *Story idea* |
| scary night | a ship | science fiction |
| 1800s | a castle | a chase |
| today | a city | getting caught for doing something |
| the future | a foreign country | |
| Prehistoric Era | the Rockies | getting away |
| last summer | at the lake | winning fame |
| 2250 AD | in the forest | losing a fortune |
| once upon a time | in a bank | learning a secret |
| your own choice | Utopia | an explosion |
| | your own choice | a birth |
| | | your own choice |

Now that you have two characters, a main personality trait for each, a name for each, and a setting and plot for the story's action, let's look at comic book characters in action.

## *Activity 5J   See What I Do*

Look at the actions of Rex Baxter and Gail Abbot in the following two panels from *Dime Comics*.

1. In your notebook answer the following questions about these characters.
    a. What is each one doing? State two or three specific actions for each character.
    b. What is each one like?
    c. How do their actions reveal what they are like?

2. As a whole class, share your responses to these questions. You'll come back to these panels in a later activity.

Illustrators use various techniques to show action in comic books. Their techniques help readers understand the action and movement in a comic book story.

## Activity 5K    The Lines Have It

*Study the panels below from Nelvana... and the Ether People.*

1. As a whole class, identify any drawing techniques that show action. Determine how each drawing demonstrates a specific action. For example, do circular lines always suggest a specific kind of movement?

## Activity 5L    Adding Lines of Your Own

1. Review the physical appearances, personality traits, names, setting, and plot situation for the characters you created in Activities 5D, 5E, and 5I.

2. Decide on a sequence of actions for your characters.

3. Sketch one large panel or one main panel plus one or two smaller panels to show your characters in action. Omit the dialogue and the captions; you will add them later. Don't worry about your drawings for these panels. Stick figures are fine.

4. Keep your panel(s) in your notebook to use in a later activity.

# What Characters Say

So far you have been creating your characters from the outside. That is, you've tried to tell what your characters are like by showing what they look like and how they act.

The way characters speak—the words they choose, the way they use them, their tone of voice—can reveal a lot about their personalities. A well-written conversation can do a tremendous amount to suggest what characters are like. But that conversation must be **in character**. That is, it must be appropriate to the character who is speaking.

## *Activity 5M    Who Said That?*

1. Listen carefully as someone reads the words spoken by the following comic book people. The words are in a box on page 87.

a.

b.

c.

d.

© 1971 Nelvana Limited

2. In your notebook write the letter that belongs with the picture of each character. As you hear the words, pick out one main word or phrase and write it beside the letter that belongs to the character you think said it.

3. After you have heard all the dialogue and matched it with one of the characters, write a sentence to explain why you matched certain words with a certain character.

4. As a class, share your matchings and the reasons for them.

   *Note*: The answers appear in a box on page 87.

## Activity 5N  Who Said What?

Work in pairs for this activity.

1. Study the pictures of the characters below along with the excerpts from their dialogue that appear in the box on page 75.

2. With a partner, match the words with the characters. You and your partner must agree on the matchings.

3. For each matched character and dialogue, decide why you matched that character with that dialogue.

a. Okay TX-5 message received...I'll try and guide you down...you're over the field now...bank to the right!

b. Sure an' it's car number thirrrty thrrree I'm afterr callin'! Will ye be kind enough t'turn off Dick Tracy and listen to orrrders?

c. Listen, youse guys! When de Penguin pays a visit it means trouble, so do what you want with the mug—*but get rid of him*!

d. The strip is supposed to be true to life...and yet, if I draw the truth...all of young Canada will denounce me as a liar!

e. They're in here, Boss. Just wait'll I get me mitts on them... UGH!!

4. As a class, share each pair's matchings and discuss the reasons for the matchings.

a. What can you tell about the characters and their situations from each of the dialogue excerpts?

The answers appear in a box on page 87.

4

5

© 1971 Nelvana Limited

## Activity 5O  Once Again, With Words

Do the panels below look familiar? Here are the Rex Baxter/Gail Abbot panels you studied in Activity 5J, this time complete with words.

1. Read the characters' words in the dialogue balloons. What do the words reveal about each character?

© 1971 Nelvana Limited

2. In your notebook write the words and phrases that you think reveal each character's personality. What is it about the character that these words reveal?
   *e.g.* Rex Baxter: *Nonsense*—shows determination, fearlessness

3. Read the responses you made to the questions in Activity 5J. How does your estimate of the characters' personalities, based on their actions, compare with what you think the characters are like, based on their words?

## *Activity 5P    Once Again, With Words and New Roles*

Below are some panels showing Wing, a comic book heroine, in various situations.

1. Read the words given in dialogue balloons. What do they reveal about Wing's character?

© 1971 Nelvana Limited

2. As a class, discuss the words and phrases that you think reveal Wing's character. What is it about her character that the words reveal?

3. Compare Wing's character with that of Gail Abbot shown in Activity 5O.

Once again it's time to turn your attention to your own comic book characters. You have created two characters and placed them in an action sequence in previous activities.

## Activity 5Q   Speak Up for Yourself

1. Look at the action panel(s) involving the characters that you created in Activity 5L.
2. On the panel(s) you've drawn, add dialogue suitable to each character and the situation. Place the dialogue in *dialogue balloons* and use *pointers* to show who is speaking. Punctuation marks, capital letters, bold lettering, and lines can all help convey the tone of the character's voice.

# What Characters Think

Thoughts can also reveal character. In fact, thoughts can be more revealing of character than words. Thoughts show the true inner self of the character. Most writers use this technique sparingly.

## Activity 5R   Hmm

© 1971 Nelvana Limited

1. Read the above panel from *Nelvana ... and the Ether People.*

2. In your notebook list at least three things Keene's thought tells the reader about him.
   *e.g.* Corporal Keene is suspicious.

The thoughts of Betty Burd in the splash page for *Perils of the Jungle* shown on page 63 give the reader background information to the story as well as a first indication of what Betty Burd is like.

In the following panels from *The Brain and the Mummy Man* note that in the left thought balloon the vision that the Brain sees inside his mind is revealed. In the right thought balloon, this vision disappears.

© 1971 Nelvana Limited

## *Activity 5S    A Second Thought*

1. Take one piece of dialogue from the panels that you drew for your own splash page and change it to thought in a thought balloon. Or add a panel that includes a thought balloon for one of your characters.

# What Others Reveal About Character

Up to now, it is the character alone who has revealed his or her personality through looks, actions, words, and thoughts. But other characters, too, play a part in revealing the personality of the major character through what they say or think or how they react in situations involving the main character. Some examples follow.

## *Activity 5T   Others' Opinions*

1. For each panel below, describe what the looks, actions, and words of one character tell you about the other character(s) in the panel. Write your responses in your notebook.

© 1971 Nelvana Limited

2. As a class share your responses to question 1. What are the clues in other characters' looks, actions, and words that help reveal the main character in each panel?

# WRITING AND ILLUSTRATING

In the first part of this chapter you've learned the techniques writers and illustrators of comic books use to reveal the personalities of their characters. Along the way you've created your own characters and actions for them. In the following section you'll do more on your comic book splash page.

---

**Revealing Character**

Here is a summary of the techniques that writers use to create characters:

- They describe characters' appearances.
- They give characters appropriate names.
- They have characters act in appropriate ways.
- They make characters talk in certain ways.
- They tell what characters are thinking.
- They show what other characters say and think about them.

---

## Activity 5U   Earning the Credits

1. Look again at the panel(s) you've drawn for your splash page.

2. Put the panels together. You may want to add, remove, rearrange, or replace one or more of the panels. You should have one large panel or one main panel with one or two smaller ones that highlight your characters.

3. The characters, together, should be portrayed in at least four of the five ways shown in this chapter. These ways are listed in the box above.

4. Make sure you have a title for your comic book story. It should be placed prominently somewhere on your splash page. You might write the title in all capital letters, open lettering, bold lettering, or in any combination of eye-catching devices.

5. The captions on the splash page are your way of telling readers the setting and plot for your story. Reread your captions to make sure the audience has the information it needs to understand the story line.

6. Sign the credits on the splash page.

# GETTING REACTION

So, what does an audience think of the characters on your splash page? Let's find out.

## *Activity 5V    Comic Critics*

1. Work in pairs for this activity. Exchange splash pages with your partner.

2. Read your partner's comic book splash page.

3. On a separate piece of paper do the following after studying your partner's splash page.
   a. Write the names of the main characters.
   b. Beneath each name write one word that gives the main personality trait of that character.
   c. Write one sentence about how the physical appearance of each character reveals his or her personality.
   d. Identify one action that reveals each character's personality. Write that action beneath the character's name.
   e. Copy the words or phrases from the speech balloons that reveal each character's personality. Write these words or phrases underneath his or her name.
   f. Write one sentence describing how the actions, words, or thoughts of one character reveal the personality of another character.

4. Exchange splash pages and comment sheets so that you and your partner each have your own.

5. Read your partner's comments about your splash page. Was your partner's description of what your characters are like and how they are revealed similar to your intentions? The following chart may help you organize this information.

| | Your intentions | Partner's identification |
|---|---|---|
| character's main traits<br>character looks like<br>character acts like<br>character says<br>character thinks<br>other characters | | |

Discuss with your partner any point in your comparison where you differ substantially.

6. Using your partner's 'comic' comments, revise your splash page as much or as little as you decide is necessary.

# CHECKING THE ARTWORK

Here is a guide to some of the more commonly used techniques in comic book art.

## SYMBOLS USED IN COMIC STRIP ART

**Word Encasing (Bubbles)**

indicates the person to whom the 𝒥 is pointing is speaking.

indicates thoughts from the person to whom the little circles lead.

usually indicates voices from a television, radio, or telephone. Sometimes it just indicates loudness.

is used for "meanwhile..." etc., and longer narration.

indicates that the person to whom the 𝒥 is pointing is whispering.

**Lettering**

EXAMPLE is used in regular speech.

EXAMPLE indicates LOUD tone of voice.

EXAMPLE indicates louder tones of voice, or can be used in sound effects such as:

Usually coloured in yellow or red.

 There are also many different lettering styles used in titles, or "logos," such as **PHOENIX**

## The Words Themselves

**?** usually comes at the end of a sentence, indicating a question, but sometimes put in a bubble alone, meaning astonishment.

**!** also indicates astonishment, and can be put at the end of a sentence.

@✻!#% is used to censor such words as

✻#%✻ and !✻%@#

⋝ ⋜ around a word indicates it is not actually being said, such as ⋝AHEM⋜

## Art Symbols

 around someone's head means unconsciousness.

 used the same way as except it means dizziness.

 sometimes means movement, or hesitation when used around someone's head.

 put in back of an object means fast movement from one place to another.

💡 is usually put in a "bubble" and indicates an idea. Sometimes labeled "IDEA".

around someone's face indicates either physical perspiration or nervousness.

 An object drawn in dotted lines indicates that it cannot be seen by characters in the comic book. It is invisible—except to you!!

is usually put in a "bubble" to indicate sleep. Zs alone can be used.

## *Activity 5W    The Art's in the Right Place*

1. Using the guide given above, check the artwork on your splash page. Checking one item at a time will help you focus on each art technique.

2. Make any changes on your splash page you think necessary.

# INDICIA

Indicia, you might remember, means *publishing* in comic book language, and publishing is the last step for your splash page. Who knows? Perhaps it is the first step in your career as a comic book writer and illustrator.

## *Activity 5X    Out on the Stands*

You can share your comic book splash page in one of the following ways.

1. Your class can publish the splash pages as a collection. Give the collection a title, such as *New Canadian Comic Classics* or *Great Beginnings* or ....

2. Display the splash pages in your classroom, hallway, or school entrance.

3. Publish some or all of the splash pages in your school newspaper. Stagger their publication over a number of weeks or months.

4. Select a few splash pages to submit to a local newspaper for publication.

5. Share your splash pages with younger students, such as those in grades 4 to 8.

# In Our Next Episode

You've worked hard at creating and portraying characters in a variety of ways. It almost seems a shame to leave your creative efforts at the first page stage. Well, maybe you don't have to...

## *Activity 5Y    Completing the Comic*

1. As a class study the splash pages you have created.

2. Choose five or six of the splash pages to complete in groups. Then decide on the groups that will work on them. Each group should complete the comic book story it thinks might follow from the splash page.

3. Share, display, and publish the completed comic books.

So what do characters in comic books have in common with characters in literature? Lots of things. Although comic book characters are revealed quickly and as much through illustrations as through words, the techniques that writers of comic books and writers of literature use are similar. Both kinds of writers reveal their characters through descriptions of how the characters look, what they do, what they say, what they think, and how other characters react to them. Comic book writers are able to use visual aids to reveal their characters that are not available to writers of literature.

## *Activity 5Z    From Visuals to Words—A Character Sketch*

1. Put your splash page in front of you. Look at it carefully.

2. Write a description of one of the characters on your splash page. You cannot use any visuals. You must reveal the character to the reader through written description only. Again, describe the character by using the character's looks, actions, words, and thoughts. You can include another character in your description so that the second character's looks, actions, words, or thoughts reveal something else about the first character's personality. What you've written is called a *character sketch*.

This chapter introduced you to the main techniques of revealing character. Whether you sketch your character through drawing or through writing, the methods for revealing character to an audience are the same. Characters are revealed through **how they look, how they act, what they say, what they think,** and **how other characters react to them.**

**Dialogues to Use with Activity 5M**

Here are the dialogue pieces to read with Activity 5M. As someone reads them, students try to match the dialogue with the characters pictured in Activity 5M.

1. We must crush this evil at its roots!—I have a plan...which may achieve this purpose—our lives will be in constant danger! We may even be forced to live the rest of our days in another world! It's our lives or those of countless millions on this Earth! What is your answer...?

2. Hi, Sugar...Lookin' fer someone?

3. ...Thank heavens...I've invented a new drug that will help our boys at the war... these men were trying to force the formula from me!!

4. I call on my brother Tanero, to come to my side and help rid our country of this evil thing.

**Answers**: a – 4; b – 3; c – 1; d – 2.

**Answers for Activity 5N**

1 – c; 2 – d; 3 – e; 4 – b; 5 – a.

*Merrymaking*, Cornelius Krieghoff

Cornelius Krieghoff's painting now hangs in the Beaverbrook Art Gallery in Fredericton, New Brunswick. Dancing, singing, card-playing, and storytelling were essential ingredients of the sort of evening of merrymaking shown in the painting. In the following chapter you will find out more about the art of storytelling and by the end of the chapter you will be a practised storyteller, ready to join in the merrymaking.

## ONCE UPON A TIME...

Storytelling makes events come alive.

In the days before radio and television, people used storytelling to entertain and instruct one another, and to pass down literature and folk tales from one generation to another.

The art of storytelling was dying out in North America until groups of people across the country decided to form **storytelling groups**. Such groups meet regularly and members have the chance to tell old stories and to listen to new ones.

# STORYTELLING

Storytelling takes practice. Professional storytellers say it takes time and effort to learn to tell stories well. One of the most basic forms of the oral story is the anecdote.

## Telling an Anecdote

A simple story about a single event is called an **anecdote**. Here is an example.

> An astrologer foretold the death of a lady whom Louis XI [of France] passionately loved. She did, in fact, die; and the King imagined that the prediction of the astrologer was the cause of it. He sent for the man,
>
> ➡

intending to have him thrown through the window as punishment. "Tell me, thou pretendest to be so clever and learned a man, what thy fate will be?" The astrologer, who suspected the intrigues of the King, and knew his foibles, replied: "Sire, I foresee that I shall die three days before your Majesty." The King believed him, and was careful of the astrologer's life.

Edmund Fuller, ed. *2500 Anecdotes for All Occasions*

## Activity 6A   Car Wash

**Work in pairs to complete the following activity. Decide who will be Student A and who will be Student B.**

1. **On your own, think about what just happened at the car wash in the cartoon on the side. Picture it in your mind.**

2. **Form pairs to complete the next step in which you tell each other an anecdote based on the cartoon.**

   a. **Student A tells an anecdote, playing the role of the mother. What might she tell a friend as they prepare to play tennis?**

   b. **Student B tells an anecdote about the same incident playing the role of the father, about one month later. What would he say to a friend as they prepare to go for a jog?**

**HERMAN®**

"This idiot opened all the windows halfway through the car wash."

## Activity 6B   He was a Real Beauty...

Again, work with a partner to do this activity.

1. On your own, read and look at the cartoon on the side.
   a. Who are these people?
   b. What took place before the incident pictured in the cartoon?
   c. What do you think will be the outcome of this scene?

2. Student A tells the story of the cartoon as an anecdote to Student B as if she or he were the son, telling the story to a friend over the phone later on that evening.

3. Student B tells the story to Student A as if he or she were the father or the mother, telling the story to a relative a week later.

HERMAN®

© Universal Press Syndicate

"You wouldn't let me have a dog. You wouldn't let me have a cat!"

## Activity 6C   About Anecdotes

1. With your partner, talk about the telling of anecdotes. What was successful about the stories you told for Activities 6A and 6B? What worked? What didn't work?

2. Help each other compose a list of the factors involved in telling an anecdote successfully. Then both partners should write this list in their notebooks.

3. As a class, compare lists and prepare a master list describing the characteristics of a good anecdote.

## Activity 6D   It Happened to Me

1. On your own, think about something silly that happened to you. It's probably easier to think of something that happened in your dim, distant childhood.

2. Sit at your desk and, for four minutes, write about your anecdote. Keep your pen moving, always adding details about the situation you are remembering. It won't bother anyone if you decide to stretch the truth just a little—for emphasis and humour.

3. Meet in groups of four or five and tell your anecdotes to each other.
   a. Be sure to listen carefully to all the anecdotes told in your group because you may be the *storyteller* chosen to tell one of your group's anecdotes to the whole class.
   b. Close your notebook so that you are not tempted to read your anecdote. Instead, tell it from memory—just as if it were a story.

4. Decide which member will be the group storyteller.
   a. Draw lots among the members of the group to see who gets the chance to be the *chief storyteller* for the group.
   b. The chief storyteller chooses an anecdote to tell to the whole class, on behalf of the small group.
      • He or she cannot tell his or her own anecdote but must choose the anecdote of another member of the group. It is permissible for the storyteller to add details to the anecdote, and even to borrow ideas from the other anecdotes told in the small group.

# Stories Everywhere

The best stories are told simply but dramatically, and the speaker's voice has a very important role to play. You can use your voice to add atmosphere, drama, suspense, or surprise to a story.

You can achieve many different effects just by altering your voice. Experiment with different tones of voice and different volumes as you work on the next activity.

## *Activity 6E    Your Voice—An Instrument*

1. Read this anecdote silently. Think of the details of the story and form mental images of them.

2. Memorize as much of the story as you can so that you are able to tell it without looking at the text.

3. Reread the story and decide how you will use your voice to tell it dramatically.
   a. How will you use your voice to convey the desolation of the opening?
   b. How will you describe the arrival of the helicopter?
   c. What tone of voice will you use to express the hopelessness of the ending? How can you use pauses for dramatic effect?

4. Using a variety of tones, volumes, and the dramatic qualities of your voice, tell the story of *The Castaway* to your partner. Listen while your partner tells you the story.

---

**The Castaway**

The man on the raft had only hope to keep him alive now. The bones showed through his thin face. An endless moan escaped his trembling mouth. His eyes were bright with fever. He had been clinging to life for more than a month now on this wretched collection of planks.

All at once a new sound reached his enfeebled brain: a buzzing noise imagined in his delirium no doubt. But it wasn't—it really was a helicopter approaching slowly, flying over the raft. Saved! He was saved! The castaway danced about clumsily.

In the meantime a rope-ladder had been lowered from the helicopter. A man dressed in rags, his emaciated face overgrown with a coarse beard, was pushed brutally on to the top rungs.

The helicopter turned away and disappeared.

Now there were two castaways on the raft.

Roland Topor

---

## Activity 6F    You'll Never Believe This One...

1. Think of a good story to tell. It will probably be about something funny or a strange, unusual experience.

2. Decide how you are going to tell your story.
   • What details will you dramatize?
   • What details will you leave out?
   • How will you use your voice?

3. In groups of four or five students, take turns telling your stories. Listen carefully while the other members of the group tell their stories.

4. Working with a partner, take turns giving each other constructive feedback. You can do this orally. Use the following questions to help you structure your comments.
   • Did the story begin close to the main idea and move along, maintaining interest throughout? Comment on the flow of the story.
   • Was the storyteller's voice used effectively to add interest and excitement to the story? Pick out one way your partner did this and comment on the method's effectiveness.
   • Was listening to the story a pleasant, entertaining experience? Comment on something that made it enjoyable.

# WRITING SHORT STORIES

The best stories come from your own experience, what you know about, the situations you've been involved in, and the people you know.

The key to good story writing—as it is to good story telling—is the ability to create **believable situations** and **believable characters**.

## How to Begin...

Short stories often begin with "What if..."

> What if a young boy is caught shoplifting by the owner of the store he works in?

The outcome of this particular *What if...* was the short story "All the Years of Her Life" by Morley Callaghan.

> They were closing the drugstore, and Alfred Higgins, who had just taken off his white jacket, was putting on his coat and getting ready to go home. The little gray-haired man, Sam Carr, who owned the drugstore, was bending down behind the cash register, and when Alfred Higgins passed him, he looked up and said softly, "Just a minute, Alfred. One moment before you go."
>
> Morley Callaghan, "All the Years of Her Life"

What if a wife who is considering divorcing her husband goes to Haiti for a holiday and learns voodoo while she is there?

The result of this *What If...* is a story by Fredric Brown.

Mr. Dicken's wife had just returned from a trip to Haiti—a trip she had taken alone—to give them a cooling off period before they discussed a divorce.

  Fredric Brown, "Voodoo"

## Activity 6G   What If...

1. Read the following suggestions for a *What if...* story.

- What if a young boy or girl meets the person of his or her dreams?

- What if a young person dares to do what he or she fears most?

- What if you and a group of friends run out of gas on a dark lonely road, twenty kilometres from the nearest gas station, on a stormy night?

- What if a historical figure is reincarnated in the form of a cat?

- What if...your own choice.

2. Choose the *What if...* situation that most appeals to you.

3. Explore your *What if...* situation by writing continuously about it for five minutes. Add as much detail as possible to your writing.

   *Note*: Keep your pen working for the entire five minutes. If you can't think of anything to write, just keep writing the last word on your page over and over again until something new comes to mind.

4. Exchange work with a writing partner. Take your partner's *What if...* and write continuously for five minutes on her or his topic. Give both pieces of writing on your partner's topic back to her or him.

## Activity 6H    Story Time

You have two prewriting starters before you, the one you wrote and the one your writing partner wrote for you.

1. If you believe you need more ideas to write your short story, ask someone else to do some fast writing for you, or talk about your *What if . . .* situation in a small group.

2. When you are ready, begin the first draft of your short story. Plan to make it about three pages long.

> • Your opening paragraph(s) should hint at the main plot of your story but not give the ending away.
>
> • Think of something very specific and real for your opening. **Show** the readers what is happening; don't **tell** them.
>
> • Use dialogue if it is appropriate to the kind of short story you are telling.
>
> • Keep your reader in suspense until the very last sentence if you possibly can.

## Activity 6I    Read It Over—Revising

1. Read your story aloud to a writing partner. As you read, make quick notes of any changes you need to make.

2. Listen while your partner reads his or her story to you. Look for possible changes.

3. Return to your own story and make any alterations you think necessary.

4. Exchange papers with the same partner or perhaps a different writing partner. Help each other revise your writing by commenting on each of the following issues. Write your responses to your partner's story on a separate sheet of paper.

    a. Is the story believable? Comment on two details that add to its credibility.

    b. Are the characters real? Comment on something the writer has done to make the character(s) seem real.

    c. Is all the information given relevant to the story? If the answer is *no*, put a bracket around any sentence(s) you feel is unnecessary.

d. Does the story need any additional details or information? If the answer is *yes*, make suggestions about additional material to improve the story.

5. Read over your partner's comments. You may not agree with all of them. Incorporate only those suggestions you think will improve the quality of your short story. It is, after all, your writing, and you decide what it should contain.

6. Now, write a second draft of your story. You might plan a cover page and some illustrations.

## *Activity 6J Look Carefully—Proofreading*

1. Use the checklist below to help proofread your writing.

a. Start at the end of your story and read it backwards to yourself, one sentence at a time.

- Each sentence should form a complete thought, expressed simply and clearly.

- In a story such as this one, you might be using **sentence fragments** for special effect. Make certain that the fragments are working as you intended. If you are using dialogue, you will probably find sentence fragments here because people often use them when they talk.

b. Make certain that you have capitalized your title correctly as well as all proper nouns—place names and people's names.

c. All paragraphs should be indented. If you are using dialogue, make certain that you begin a new paragraph when each new speaker begins to talk.

d. Look for spelling errors, particularly with the following troublesome homonyms.

- their—belonging to them as in *Their dog.*
  there—suggesting a direction, as in *The house is over there.*
  they're—contraction for they are, as in *They're going to be there.*

- two—a number, as in *Two books.*
  to—suggesting a direction from one place to another, as in *I am going from Montreal to Corner Brook, Newfoundland.*
  too—means also, as in *Can we go too?*

2. Work with a writing partner. Read your partner's work aloud to him or her, watching for any writing problems such as spelling mistakes. Help make your partner's work as correct as possible. Your partner will then do the same for you.

3. Talk with your partner about illustrations that might enhance your stories.

## *Activity 6K   The Final Draft*

1. Choose a clean, fresh page for the final draft of your story.

2. Centre your title on the page and leave one line between the title and the beginning of the story.

3. Write your short story, making a special effort to write as neatly and legibly as possible. Your story should be about three pages long.

4. Remember to indent paragraphs. Pay particular attention to paragraphing if you are using dialogue.

5. If appropriate, add illustrations and a cover page.

## *Activity 6L   The Delivery*

You wrote your short story for an *audience* of your classmates but you can also share your story with others. Here are some possible ways.

1. Form groups of five or six students, students with whom you have not been working as writing partners. Take turns reading your stories aloud to each other.

2. Share your work with all your classmates by arranging a classwide story-reading session. Appoint a chairperson to introduce each participant and to set up a schedule for story reading.

3. Share your work with people outside the classroom:
   a. Make a copy of your story, dedicate it to a special person such as a parent, and give it as a gift on a special occasion.
   b. Make a class anthology of short stories and display it in your school library.
   c. Give your class anthology to your local library so that it can be circulated there.
   d. Send a copy of your story to a story-writing contest. Watch for advertisements for such contests.

e. Take your class anthology to a Senior Citizens' Home and leave it for the residents to read. Better still, go and talk with these residents about your work or invite them to visit your classroom and respond to your writing.

# Merrymaking

This chapter focussed on storytelling and story writing. You learned to tell and write short stories as well as practising your skills in speaking, listening, writing, and reading. Best of all, you are now an experienced storyteller. Like the people in Krieghoff's painting on page 88, you have found another way to make people happy.

Tyger, Tyger

Tyger, Tyger, burning bright
In the forests of the night
What Immortal hand or eye
Dare frame thy fearful symmetry?

William Blake

# TYGER, TYGER

Look at the picture of the tiger on the opposite page. Notice its powerful body, the strong legs, the huge paws, the set of the shoulders, the squareness of the head, and the menacing teeth and claws. Imagine the movement of its lithe body as the tiger stalks its prey.

To describe such a powerful, beautiful beast, you must choose your words very carefully—both for their visual effect and for their sound appeal. In this chapter you will learn how to work with words. You will write poems.

Some of your poems will be personal; you write them for yourself. Others will be shared with your classmates and friends and perhaps presented in a poetry reading.

# CINQUAINS

A **cinquain** (pronounced sang-kane) is a short poem of **five lines**. Cinquains are written to a pattern. The writer's aim is to capture the essence or the heart of a subject in only five lines.

The following cinquains were written by grade-nine students.

**Cars**

Cars
Sleek, aerodynamic,
Bright, shiny, blue
Even better in orange.
Mine.

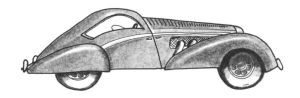

David Mosley

### Pattern For Writing Cinquains

- The first line contains one word, although not necessarily the subject of the poem.
- The second line contains two words.
- The third line contains three words.
- The fourth line contains four words.
- The last line contains one word that may be repeated from the first line.

**Pizza**

Pizza.
Hot, mouthwatering
Cut into slices
Pepperoni, cheese, tomatoes, peppers
Gone.

Yasmin Dossabhoy

# Write Your Own Cinquain

Chinese poets claim that the best writing is that which is trimmed to the bone—bare-bones writing. All unnecessary words are taken away; only the essential ones remain.

## Activity 7A   The Best Things in Life

1. In your notebook, make a list of *My Favourite Things*.

2. Working with a partner, take turns reading your lists aloud to each other. As you read, place an asterisk (*) beside any items you would like to explore further.

3. Choose one topic and explore it further by writing down everything connected with it in your notebook.

4. Use the ideas you generated in question 3 to write a first draft of a cinquain in your notebook.

5. Read your poem aloud to yourself.
   - Substitute any words that are not precise enough.
   - Rearrange the order of words or phrases if you think it is necessary.

6. Reread your poem to make certain it says exactly what you want it to say.

In the following activity you will turn a visual image into a word picture.

## Activity 7B    A Word Picture

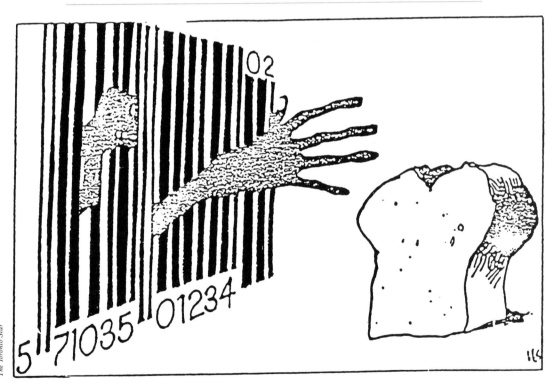

1. Working with a partner, take turns describing the above cartoon. Talk about what this cartoon is trying to communicate. It is not an easy cartoon to understand.

2. Working by yourself, write continuously for four minutes in your notebook about the cartoon. This fast-writing activity may help you discover what you think about the cartoon.

3. Read over what you have written. Underline any words and phrases that are particularly effective in describing this cartoon.

4. Experiment with arranging some of your words and phrases into patterns similar to the pattern of a cinquain.

5. Arrange and rearrange your words and phrases until you are satisfied that you have created a word picture of the cartoon.

6. Share your poem with a partner and listen to a reading of your partner's poem.

## *Activity 7C    Tyger, Tyger*

Work as a class to compose a cinquain.

1. Look once again at the statue of the tiger on page 100.

2. List at least twelve adjectives to describe it.

3. List at least twelve *-ing words*, such as *snarling* and *stretching*, to describe it. *-ing words* are called *participles*.

4. List at least six adverbs to describe its movements.

5. Use this *word cache* to create your group cinquain about the tiger.

To write a cinquain, you have to follow a set form—a five-line poem with a specific number of words. In the next section, you will concentrate on choosing words for your poem without the guidance of a specific form.

# Sound Is All Around

Poetry and music have a lot in common. Poets, advertisers, and writers of song lyrics all know the value of choosing words for their sound appeal. Sounds are all around you—the roar of city traffic, the chirruping of birds in the early morning, the lapping of waves on a beach.

## *Activity 7D    Sounds of School*

1. Listen to the *school sounds* around you, and make a list of them in your notebook.

2. Go over your list with a group of four or five students, and listen while the other group members read their lists.

3. Work together to compose a group poem entitled "Sounds of School."
   - Nominate one group member to do the recording of ideas while the others make suggestions.
   - Don't stifle any ideas or reject any as "bad"; record all of them.
   - As a group, select the ideas you like best and put them together into the form of a poem.

4. Each group should read its poem to the whole class.

5. Working on your own, use the words from your lists, change them into phrases, or make your words into sentences. Arrange these words, phrases, and short sentences to make a poem.

## Activity 7E  Sights and Sounds

1. Working by yourself, imagine what it would be like to be one of the following. Choose the one you find the most interesting.

a. the wind

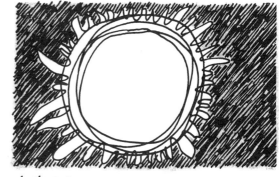

b. the sun

c. a bird

d. a storm

2. Write continuously in your notebook for four minutes on your chosen topic. Keep your pen moving and the image of what you are describing firmly in your mind. Describe yourself as the image as fully as possible.

3. Examine your *fast writing*. Select the important words and phrases and short sentences from this writing and arrange them on your page to shape a poem.

4. Work with a partner. Help each other by suggesting new words and details to improve each other's descriptions.

> Try for a *bare-bones* description of your subject. Include only words and phrases that are absolutely essential to communicate your ideas and feelings.

5. Recopy your poem, arranging the words so that the shape of your poem also helps communicate your meaning.

6. Read your poem to a partner.
   a. Ask your partner to respond to your poem by completing the following phrase in writing.

> What I like best about your poem is...

   b. Listen to your partner's poem and respond in the same way.

# LYRIC POETRY

A **lyric poem** expresses emotion or feeling. It can be about joyful feelings such as friendship, love, and excitement, or about sad feelings such as loneliness, sorrow, and even death.

The first example below of a lyric poem is an **ironic poem,** in which the poet expresses his feelings about a flood that hit Moose Jaw, Saskatchewan, during the 1950s. The poem, in a very gentle way, tells us that people can say and do very odd things. The second poem presents the strong feelings of the poet.

**Getting It On**

This is Sam the Man Spenser again
back for another 55 fantastic minutes
While the news was on ladies and laddies
I had one sick fella on the phone
Wanted me to play that John R. Cash song
How high's the water Momma?
Five feet high and risin ·
With the crest still to hit River Park
we'll have none of that      No siree
It's golden oldies all weekend
the best of early fifties rock
taking you back to where it all began
But first a public-service message
on behalf of the guys at EMO
Puh-lease stay off the telephones
at least whenever possible
Our man at Sask. Tel.
reports lines burning up
They can hardly handle the load
Guess everybody's phoning
to see how high the water is
So you take it to heart
out there in radio land
Now let's get it on again
with the hot songs from the cool fifties
If you've got a favourite
give us a call right here
at the key to the world's breadbasket
CKCB in Moose Jaw

   Robert Currie

The second example was written on a sad occasion, the death of a well-loved pet.

**My Old Cat**

My old cat is dead,
Who would butt me with his head.
He had the sleekest fur.
He had the blackest purr.
Always gentle with us
Was this black puss,
But when I found him today
Stiff and cold where he lay
His look was a lion's,
Full of rage, defiance:
Oh he would not pretend
That what came was a friend
But met it in pure hate.
Well died, my old cat.

   Hal Summers

# How Do You Feel?

Lyric poems explore feelings and emotions that need to be explored. Talking or writing about feelings is not easy but it can help you understand those feelings more fully.

---

## Activity 7F   Your Journal—for Ideas

---

1. Use your journal to express your feelings. Write about feelings and emotions that confuse you or ones you would like to understand better.

2. Sit down and write. Let your mind wander over things that have puzzled you. Try to find words that will express your ideas on paper.

3. After you have read Erfa's journal entry below, use your own journal to write on *Something I Don't Understand*.

   *Remember*: Your journal is a good place to try out ideas and topics that could provide the raw material for future poems.

---

Erfa used her journal to explore feelings of frustration. In the following entry, she expresses her inability to deal with all the demands being made on her and all the changes taking place in her life.

## Something I Don't Understand

Right now there are quite a few things I don't understand. (In fact I'm not all that sure I understand anything), but the one thing that confuses me the most is the change in myself.

I'm not the same person I was yesterday. The things which once occupied my every spare moment (skipping ropes, picture books, puzzles) now sit in a forgotten corner collecting dust. I no longer think about the things I once thought about. My mind is cluttered with thoughts of unimportant, trivial things (like if my hair is neat and what I'll wear tomorrow). I also think about things that once seemed too far away to worry about, things like where I'm going and what the future holds for me. I ask new questions all the time: questions which seem to be answerless.

I'm not quite sure where I am now. I'm distant from my yesterdays. I'm no longer the carefree person I used to be. I don't even know what my future paths are.

Irfa Alani

## Writing Your Own Lyric Poem

### *Activity 7G    A True Story*

Last week a young woman rode her bicycle in the streets of Toronto. Beside her ran her unleashed husky dog.

From around a corner appeared a blind man, walking carefully, his hand firmly clenched on the harness of his guide dog. The patient black Labrador is his master's eyes, constantly watching for obstacles or vehicles which could create a danger for the sightless man. The guide dog has been trained to ignore other dogs, so it was unprepared for the vicious attack.

The husky smashed into it with brutal force, its fangs searching for the throat. As the man cried aloud, blood spurted from the Labrador. The woman yelled at the husky, who paid no heed. In desperation she

→

jumped off her bicycle and flung it at the husky, who broke off the attack.

The woman didn't leave her name with any bystander. She just rode away down the street followed by her unleashed dog. One hundred stitches were required to close the dreadful wound sustained by the Labrador, and the blind man has lost his "eyes."

Lois Maxwell, *The Toronto Sun*

1. Read the newspaper excerpt above to yourself.

2. Working with a partner, take turns giving your *personal reaction* to the story. Describe your feelings and emotions about it.

3. Listen as your partner describes the emotions and feelings that he or she experienced.

## Activity 7H    A Web of Ideas

1. Make a thought web in your notebook of topics about which you have strong feelings. Think about issues that always get an emotional response from you.

Example:

2. Think about a time when someone made you red with anger, or a time when you were so happy you thought you were walking on air. Add these experiences to your thought web.

3. Read over the following questions. They may help you remember a time when you were emotionally involved in a situation. If

you answer *yes* to any of the questions, stop and add the episode to your thought web.

---

- Have you ever lost a friend or a pet?

- Have you ever been saddened by an experience, a story, or a scene?

- Have you ever been moved by the beauty of an act, an experience, or a sight?

- Have you ever been frightened by an event, an experience, or some news?

- Have you ever been overjoyed by some news, an experience, or an event?

- Have you ever had a strong friendship with another person?

---

4. Pick one of the ideas from your list. Think about it by writing continuously on the topic for five minutes. Time yourself. Within the five minutes, do not pause or allow the flow of your ideas to be interrupted. Dig deep into your memories to find the details that describe your thoughts, feelings, and emotions.

5. Read your writing to yourself.
   a. Which lines express your ideas and your feelings effectively? Underline them.
   b. Which words are particularly effective at describing a feeling or an emotion? Use a different-coloured pen to underline them.

6. Write a rough draft of a poem that expresses the idea you have been exploring in writing. Arrange the words, phrases, or complete lines that you created in question 5 in the form of a poem. Experiment with your arrangement. Look for the poem-shape that communicates your thoughts most effectively.

## Activity 7I    Read It Aloud ... Revision

1. Read the poem you wrote in Activity 7H aloud to a writing partner. Then listen while your partner reads to you.

2. Help each other revise, or rethink, your poems.
   a. Writing on a separate page, suggest three possible titles for your partner's poem.

b. Complete this statement in response to your partner's poem.

> The most important words in this poem are . . . . . . . . . . . . . . . . . . .
>
> . . . . . . . . . . . . . . . . . . . . . . . . . . . . . . . . . . . . . . . . . . . . . . . . . .
>
> because . . . . . . . . . . . . . . . . . . . . . . . . . . . . . . . . . . . . . . . . . . .
>
> . . . . . . . . . . . . . . . . . . . . . . . . . . . . . . . . . . . . . . . . . . . . . . . . . .

c. Choose the one line in your partner's poem you like best. Write it on your page and tell your partner why you like this particular line.

3. Exchange your poems and comments so each has his or her own.

4. On your own, read the comments your partner made about your poem. Use these comments as well as your own second thoughts to revise your poem.

5. Write a second draft of your poem.

## *Activity 7J  Another Look: Editing*

1. Plan to complete yet another draft of your poem. Use the following questions to guide this second look at your poem. This time you will look at the specific words you have included in your poem.
   a. Read each line of your poem separately and take out any word that is not absolutely essential to the meaning of the poem. (Remember *bare-bones writing.*)
   b. Ask this question about each line of your poem:

   > Can I replace any word in this line with a stronger word?

   If the answer is yes, try to do so.
   c. Look closely at the order of the lines in your poem.

   > What would happen if you arranged your lines in a different order?

   If you find a new arrangement that you like, make the change.

2. Write out a third version of your poem.
   a. Choose a clean page for your final draft of the poem.
   b. Centre the title on the page.
   c. Leave at least one line between the title and the beginning of your poem.
   d. Leave margins around your poem on the top, bottom, and both sides.

## Activity 7K    A Final Look: Proofreading

1. Proofread your poem for mechanical errors. Use the checklist below to help you with your proofreading.

- Are there mistakes in spelling?
- Does each line of your poem start with a capital letter—unless you specifically chose not to?
- Have you used punctuation marks to help the reader understand your meaning?

Correct any mistakes you find.

2. Store your work in your writing folder.

# A POETRY READING

A **poetry reading** is a time for sharing. Poets take part in readings to give their readers a chance to hear poems read by their authors. **Poetry is meant to be heard as well as read**.

## Activity 7L    Poets All

1. Select some of the poems you wrote as you worked your way through this chapter.

2. Think about your poems and, on your own, practise reading them aloud.

3. As a class, choose a student to draw up a programme for a poetry reading session. This student will introduce each reader.

4. Consider using appropriate background music as you read your poems. You might also consider showing slides or pictures.

5. When it is your turn, read slowly and clearly. Enjoy reading your poems. After all, you made them.

## Activity 7M    Publish and Share

1. Working with a group of four or five students, choose your best poems to include in a class anthology. Nominate a group member to arrange your work. Each member of the group should contribute at least three poems.

2. Make copies of your favourite poems, dedicate them to a friend or relative, and give them as gifts on a special occasion.

3. Make a *Poetry Display* in your classroom.

## Activity 7N    William Blake

1. Reread the poem by William Blake on page 100.

2. Think about these questions:
   a. Why does Blake say that the tyger is "burning bright"?
   b. What is the tyger's "fearful symmetry"?
   c. What is the answer to the question raised in the poem?

3. What is your reaction to this poem? What does it make you think and feel?

4. Is this an effective lyric poem? Why or why not?

5. Rewrite this poem in your own words. How does your version compare with that of William Blake?

6. Use the thoughts that the poem stirs within your head and heart to write your own poem.

# A Fearful Symmetry

You have written many different types of poetry during this chapter. You have thought about words—their meanings and their sounds. You have talked about poetry, you've listened, and you've written your own poems.

### To Hold A Poem

I would take words
As crisp and white
As our snow; as our birds
Swift and sure in their flight;
As clear and as cold
As our ice; as strong as a jack pine;
As young as a trillium, and old
As Laurentia's long undulant line;

Sweet-smelling and bright
As new rain; as hard
And as smooth and as white
As a brook pebble cold and unmarred;

To hold in a poem of words
Like water in colourless glass
The spirit of mountains like birds,
Of forests as pointed as grass;

To hold in a verse as austere
As the spirit of prairie and river,
Lonely, unbuyable, dear,
The North, as a deed, and forever.

A.J.M. Smith

Henry Seth Taylor of Stanstead, Quebec built Canada's first steam carriage in 1867. The Stanstead Journal wrote: "This mechanical curiosity is the neatest thing of the kind yet invented." It was the first self-propelled vehicle made in Canada and is also one of the oldest in the world.

William Still and Frederick Featherstonhaugh of Ontario were responsible for building Canada's first electric car in 1893 which was in good use for fifteen years.

Canada's first gasoline driven carriage was constructed in 1897 by George Foote Foss in Sherbrooke, Quebec. His car was more practical than most other automobiles of the day and travelled for 80 km on 4.5 L of gas. Foss drove his wonderful new vehicle for five years through winter and summer alike.

# WHEELS

The vehicles shown on the opposite page represent some of the bright ideas in early Canadian motoring.

Inventions, innovations, discoveries, "firsts" often begin with wondering, with asking questions such as "What if...?" or "How could I...?" When ideas are made concrete, they become inventions—solid, touchable, usable ideas.

Ideas can lead to inventions; inventions can raise issues and issues can invite opinions. This chapter is about different ways to consider an idea. Few ideas are as straightforward as they might seem at first. Before you discuss an issue or develop an opinion, you should first examine the idea behind it. This chapter will help you with strategies for doing just that— considering an idea.

You will practise using three strategies designed to sharpen your thinking skills. The strategies were developed by Dr. Edward de Bono and are part of the *Cort Thinking Program* published by Pergamon Press.

- **Plus/Minus/Interesting (pmi)** is a strategy that encourages you to consider all the aspects of an idea, not just the most obvious one.
- **Examine Both Sides** is a strategy that helps you think of arguments opposed, or contrary, to the ones you hold initially.
- **Considering Consequences** is a strategy that helps you think about the consequences of an idea—what might happen in the future as a result of a present decision.

## What If...?

In 1897 a Quebec dentist, Dr. H. Casgrain, adapted his car by replacing the front wheels with skis and fitting the back tire with a studded wooden rim.

His innovation to the car was uniquely his own, and was a first for Canadian vehicles.

## Activity 8A    What if . . . ?

Study the picture above of the Casgrain vehicle. Think about why he adapted his car the way he did.

1. In your notebook write out the bright idea that Casgrain had.
   a. What question or problem led him to make the innovations he did?
   b. Why did he use skis instead of wheels? Why did he use a studded rim?

2. As a class discuss your thoughts about Casgrain's idea.
   a. How many of the students came up with similar explanations for his innovations?
   b. Who came up with a unique possibility?
   c. How many different ideas did the class generate?

# PLUS/MINUS/INTERESTING (PMI)

Some ideas are instantly great, some immediately awful or...just a minute now.... There's an angle you may not have thought of before.

Sometimes an idea is more, or different, than it first appears. To avoid making hasty decisions about the value of an idea, it might be worthwhile to explore the **pluses**, the **minuses**, and the **interesting aspects** of an idea.

## Accessories Anyone?

In the early days of Canadian motoring the array of auto accessories available was amazing.

The **Motormeter**, a small thermometer for the radiator cap, would tell the engine temperature.

Flower vases were designed for the doorposts of closed cars. Fancy lights and anti-rattling accessories were also sold.

A **"Fat-Man" steering wheel** was made to fold or slide up for easy access to the driver's seat.

You could even buy an inflatable figure of a person to set behind the wheel of your car to ward off auto thieves.

Spark plugs had brass umbrellas to keep out the dampness.

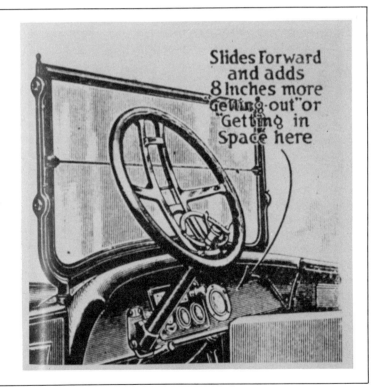

Slides forward and adds 8 inches more "Getting-out" or "Getting in" Space here

A more recent idea is a **safety paint** for automobiles, invented in 1974 by Neil Harpham of Prince Edward Island. His paint contains glass beads that allow for the maximum amount of reflection and the minimum amount of glare. Cars become visible at night for up to one kilometre under another car's high beams.

## *Activity 8B    Looking Around an Idea*

For the following activity, you will think about Harpham's idea by doing a *pmi* on it.

1. Reread the paragraph about Harpham's idea for safety paint and make three headings in your notebook: plus, minus, and interesting. Form groups of three or four students to think about Harpham's idea.

2. Under the *plus heading* write down all the positive reasons your group can collectively think of in favour of Harpham's idea. Under the *minus heading* write down all the negative aspects of Harpham's idea. Under the *interesting heading* write down just that—all the interesting or intriguing things about Harpham's idea that, together, you can think of. Don't be concerned if some of your *pmi's* are slightly far-fetched. Take a chance. Aim for ten reasons in each category.

3. Answer the following questions by yourself in your notebook.
   a. Did you see advantages to the safety paint idea after doing the pmi that you had not seen before? What were they?
   b. What disadvantages to the idea did you see after doing the pmi that you hadn't seen before?
   c. What aspects of the idea listed under the interesting heading were new or unexpected to you?

You've considered the idea of safety automobile paint in two ways: through a group pmi and through your own thinking about the pmi. Now you'll take your thinking one step further.

## *Activity 8C    Your Own Stand*

1. Based on your exploration of the idea of safety automobile paint, write your own paragraph about its desirability, its lack of desirability, or both.

2. Reform the group of three who did the pmi in Activity 8B. Take turns reading your individual opinions to each other. As you hear the views of the other group members, listen for the similarities and differences among the opinions.

3. You all began with the same information because the pmi was

done together. Compare your final views by discussing the
following questions orally.

a. In what ways are your opinions similar?

b. In what ways are they different?

c. What accounts for the similarities and differences?

# EXAMINE BOTH SIDES

Some ideas seem to have obvious positive and negative aspects to them from
the moment they are presented. People are either heartily in favour of or
bitterly opposed to a new bright idea. Take the automobile for instance. The
following items from the early 1900s show how people saw some of the
positive and negative aspects of the automobile when it was first introduced
into Canadian life.

In 1903, Ontario speed limits
were set at 11 km/h within
91.5 m of a horse-drawn vehicle.
If motorists drove *in a manner
likely to frighten a horse* there
was a penalty of $25 or 30 days
in jail for first offenders.

This Russell car ad in 1906
shows another side to the introduction of the automobile in
Canada. It stresses:

- reliability—they keep running
- popularity—get in line with
  the others
- healthiness—enjoy our glorious
  open air and sunshine

Around 1900, Maher's Horse
Exchange near Yonge and Bloor
Streets in Toronto sold between
600 and 700 horses a week at
regular auctions. There were
millions of horses in Canada, on
farms as well as in cities.

The Car You See Running

# THE RUSSELL

You see more RUSSELLS on the streets than any other car

**Because:**

1. People recognize that they represent the best value in motoring this
   year and purchase them.
2. After purchase, the owner finds they keep running and is out
   enjoying every available minute.

Get in line with the others—get a RUSSELL
and enjoy our glorious open air and sunshine.

Model A—12 H.P. Touring Car - - - $1,300
Model B—16 H.P. Touring Car - - $1,500
Model C—24 H.P. Touring Car (de luxe) - $2,500

WRITE FOR CATALOGUE

Canada Cycle & Motor Co., Limited
General Offices and Works:—TORONTO JUNCTION

## *Activity 8D    On the Other Hand*

1. Your class will divide into teams of equal number. Half of you, Side A, will support this new invention, the automobile. You think it should become the major form of transportation in Canada. The other half, Side B, will be opposed to it. You favour retaining the horse.

2. By yourself in your notebook list all the arguments you can think of for your side of the issue. Side A will list arguments in favour of the automobile and against the horse as the major form of transportation. Side B will list arguments supporting the horse and opposing the automobile.

3. Meet with one or two other people who have also considered arguments for your side. Share your lists. Together you may think of more arguments than you did individually.

4. Together decide which are the strongest arguments. Mark them with a checkmark or asterisk. These points will form the basis for the argument you present in the panel discussion.

# Holding a Panel Discussion

Here are some guidelines for holding a panel discussion.

---

### A Panel Discussion
A panel discussion is an informal group discussion before an audience. In a panel discussion,

- There are usually three to seven panel members who sit in front of an audience.

- The chairperson or moderator introduces the topic and the speakers.

- The moderator usually opens the discussion with an appropriate question and calls on one of the panel members to begin. There is no set order for the speakers.

- The panel members talk over the topic informally in voices loud enough for the audience to hear easily.

- After a certain fixed time the moderator invites the audience to participate, either by asking questions or contributing ideas and information.

---

*Activity 8E    A Panel Discussion*

1. Following the guidelines for holding a panel discussion given in the box above, your class will be organized into one large or two smaller panel discussions. Both sides of the automobile versus horse issue should be represented on the panel(s).

2. To panel members: present your views on the issue from the points you listed in Activity 8D.
   To the audience: Be prepared to ask questions or make comments during the question period that follows the discussion.

You prepared arguments for one side of the automobile versus horse issue, but now, as a member of the panel or as part of the audience, you've heard viewpoints from both sides of the issue. If asked, you should be able to present the other side's viewpoint as well as your own.

# CONSEQUENCES

Some ideas change over time in ways that the originators may or may not have anticipated.

The invention of the gasoline engine made possible automobiles, airplanes, the oil industry, and a great deal of pollution. If all the consequences had been foreseen at the time of its invention, perhaps the inventors of the gasoline engine might have decided that electric or steam engines would be a better invention. A new invention or idea may have consequences that go on for a long time. In thinking about an idea, you should always consider the consequences. And remember, consequences can be immediate (now), short-term (1-5 years), medium-term (5-25 years), or long-term (over 25 years).

In 1937 while living in Manitoba, John Gower came up with the idea for the **Jiger**, the first truly successful off-road vehicle. All-terrain vehicles (ATVs) are easily recognized by their balloon-type, low pressure tires called fat cats. They can manoeuvre freely on all types of terrain, adapting with speed and ease from water to desert to rocky bluffs to ice and snow. Some even float on a cushion of air! They are of special interest to farmers, hydro workers, miners, lumber workers, fishers and hunters—in fact, anyone who needs to get from one area to another quickly and safely no matter what the conditions.

*Activity 8F    Consider the Consequences*

1. As a class think about the consequences of all-terrain vehicles. List the immediate, short-, medium-, and long-term effects.

2. As consequences are offered by class members, write them down in your notebook. Your consequences list might include the following:

**ATV Consequences**

1) Immediate —people with ATVs are not restricted to travelling on roads
—ATVs open up the countryside more than before

2) Short term —decline in sales of conventional automobiles as sales of ATVs increase

3) Medium term —environmental damage related to the use of ATVs

4) Long term —road construction and maintenance becomes obsolete as ATVs become the main form of transportation

3. In groups of three, study your lists of consequences. Compare the immediate, short-, medium-, and long-term consequences of increased ATV use by answering the questions below.
a. How do the consequences change over time?
b. At what point or points are the consequences reversible?
c. How do the consequences—immediate, short-, medium- or long-term—affect you?
d. How do all the consequences affect others?
e. Which of the four types of consequences do you think is most important? Or are they all equally important?

# YESTERDAY AND TOMORROW

The bright ideas in this chapter have revolved around wheels, specifically when they are adapted to vehicles. We take the automobile in its present state for granted. Hasn't it always had four wheels and a gasoline engine? Not quite. The initial designs of automobiles were as varied as the model types of today are. Look again at the vehicles shown on page 116: one is three-wheeled, one is steam-powered, one is electric. They are ideas that never quite got rolling, but perhaps the time has come to reconsider these options to the gasoline-powered automobile of today.

As a driver in 2023, you need to be concerned about the kinds of vehicles that will be available to you. So concerned, in fact, that perhaps you should check out some vehicle options for the twenty-first century. Once you've decided on a workable bright idea for an automobile of the future, write your ideas down in an **editorial**. Your views might be used in the final panel discussion of the chapter.

Here are three ideas for considering vehicles in the twenty-first century:

• Look at the energy sources of vehicles of the future. Perhaps vehicles will be
    steam-driven
    electric
    solar-powered
    nuclear-powered
    powered by some other energy source you can think of

• Look into possible accessories for vehicles of the future. Reread the early accessory options listed on page 119. Decide on one accessory that you think no vehicle in the year 2023 should be without.

• Look into design features for vehicles in the twenty-first century. What might the dream vehicle of the future look like? Decide on one design idea that you think will add to the aesthetic appeal of vehicles in 2023.

## *Activity 8G    What Will You Be Driving?—*
### *Prewriting*

1. Choose one of the options listed above for a futuristic vehicle.

2. Decide on one strategy for thinking about your idea. You might do a *pmi* on it, *examine both sides* (the new idea versus present cars), or list *consequences*.

3. In your notebook, write out the idea you are considering and the strategy you've chosen to help consider it.

4. Using your chosen strategy, list all the reasons or arguments or consequences you can think of concerning your bright idea for a vehicle of the future.

5. Meet in groups of two or three and share your ideas about a futuristic vehicle. Together you may be able to make additional suggestions about each other's ideas.

## *Activity 8H    My Choice Is . . . —Writing*

1. Reread your strategy notes, all the points you listed in Activity 8G.

2. Write your views on a futuristic vehicle in the form of an editorial. Your audience will be your classmates. See the advice given in the box to write your editorial.

### The Editorial

- An editorial is a short article that expresses the views of one person on important topics of the day.

- The purpose of an editorial is to discuss a topic in the news or to comment on a topic of general interest.

- An editorial is written in essay form with clear, well-organized paragraphs.

- Language in an editorial is simple and direct. Specific, commonly understood words and phrases are used; "flowery" language is avoided.

- The views in an editorial are based on knowledge or experience and are presented in a fair and reasonable manner.

## *Activity 8I    Under Review—Revising*

Work with a partner for this activity.

1. Exchange writings.

2. Read your partner's editorial about a vehicle for the future.

3. Use the following points to help you comment on your partner's writing.

   a. Underline the writer's beginning sentence about his or her idea for a vehicle of the future.

   b. On the back of your partner's writing, write two other sentences that might be used to begin this editorial.

   *Note*: A beginning sentence, or *topic sentence*, does two things:
   - It grabs the reader's attention.
   - It sets the stage for the ideas presented later.

   c. Number the arguments that support the writer's view about a futuristic vehicle.

   d. On the back of the writing, ask two questions about the vehicle that you think the writer hasn't answered in the editorial.

   e. Look at each paragraph separately. Paragraphs in an editorial should be short and to the point so that the reader can easily follow what the writer is saying. Circle the key words and phrases in each paragraph that you think express the writer's main point.

   f. Language should be clear and suitable for the audience reading the editorial. Put a question mark above any words that you think are not appropriate to the audience.

   g. Underline the writer's ending sentence that restates or summarizes his or her views about a vehicle for the future. On the back of the editorial, write your own statement, summarizing the main ideas in the editorial.

4. Exchange writings again so that each of you has your own.

5. Read your partner's comments and suggestions about your writing. Discuss anything with your partner that you don't understand about the comments.

6. Rewrite your editorial using only those comments and suggestions from your writing partner that you think will clarify your editorial.

## Activity 8J  Finishing Touches—Editing and Proofreading

1. Read your writing slowly, one sentence at a time, beginning at the end of your writing and working backwards. Reading your writing from the bottom to the top will help you focus on one thing at a time as you check for mechanical errors.

   a. On the first reading, look for errors in punctuation.

   b. On the second reading, look for errors in capitalization.

   c. Next, look for errors in spelling.

   d. Last, look for errors in complete sentences. Read one sentence at a time and make certain that each sentence forms a complete thought.

2. Make the necessary changes to the writing.

## Activity 8K  Into the Twenty-First Century— Publishing and Sharing

1. Organize a panel discussion among the people who chose the same writing option in Activity 8G. Refer to the guidelines in the box on page 122 for holding a panel discussion.

2. Brainstorm to gather a list of audiences who might be interested in reading your views, perhaps a government agency, an automobile manufacturer, or a patent office. As a class select two or three editorials to send to one or more of the possible audiences you listed.

3. Have someone older than you—a grandparent, an older neighbour, a senior citizen in your area, or anyone who remembers what automobiles were like thirty years ago—read your writing and respond to it. Older people are in a position to compare automobiles of thirty years ago with your ideas for automobiles in the future.

# Wheels for the Future

In this chapter you've examined some *wheel* bright ideas by applying three specific strategies to them. You've used one of these strategies to help explore an idea of the future. Most ideas have implications that aren't immediately obvious. **Pmi's, examining both sides** and **considering consequences** are techniques to help you organize your thoughts when considering an idea.

(April 15, 1969)

"Your set is safe radiation-wise . . . have you checked the programs they've been exposed to?"

# HERE COMES THE JUDGE

*Television* comes from the Greek word *tele* meaning *far* and the Latin word *videre* meaning *to see*.

Television is one of the biggest single influences on your life. It influences your language, your clothes, and your beliefs about the world around you. Since television invades your daily life, you need to be aware of its effects on you.

So, where television is concerned, you are the judge. You have to be, if you're going to be in control of the one-eyed monster or the plug-in-drug— two terms that critics of television have used. In this chapter, you will examine some opinions—including your own—about television. You will learn how to look at television programmes closely by writing a **Critical Review** of a specific programme.

## *Activity 9A    An Opinion About Television*

1. Look at the cartoon about the family and the T.V. repairperson on the opposite page.

2. Working with a partner, decide what this cartoon is saying about children and television. Do you agree with the cartoon's message?

3. Present your ideas on question 2 in a class discussion to see how many different opinions about the cartoon exist in your class. Can the class come to a *consensus* or agreement about the view or opinion the cartoon puts forth?

# TALKING ABOUT TELEVISION

## Here to Serve You

Like all the mass media, television exists to communicate. It is here to serve you.

### Activity 9B    The Purposes of Television

1. In your notebook, complete the following chart using your own ideas.

2. Compare and contrast your chart with those of two or three of your classmates.

**Purposes of Television in Your World**

| Purpose | Programme Examples | Age Groups Most Affected |
|---|---|---|
| 1. to entertain | Saturday night videos | 12–30 |
| 2. to provide information | *The Journal* | 12–80 |
| 3. | | |
| 4. | | |
| 5. | | |

## *Activity 9C    A Discussion: Television's Purpose*

1. Working with two or three classmates, read each other's charts and draw at least three conclusions about the purpose of television.

2. Have one group member record your conclusions and present them to the class.

3. Create a master list of suggestions, using ideas from each group.

4. Write the class's conclusions in your notebook and keep them in mind as you continue through the chapter.

# Products of the T.V. Generation

Television has been a subject of much thought and discussion. According to some observers, it has had a number of negative effects on people who have grown up watching it. Some critics say that children who watch a lot of television do not develop their minds because they do not play and use their imaginations. Others claim that children and adults read less now than they did thirty or forty years ago—because of television. Some doctors talk about television diseases like T.V. spine, T.V. trance, and T.V. eyes. You should think about and evaluate these facts.

Think of your own experience as a T.V. watcher. You fit into the statistics somewhere. Perhaps you watch an *average* amount of T.V. Perhaps you are *above average* or *below average*. Take a look at the chart below.

| Age Group | Average Amount of T.V. Watched Per Week |
|-----------|------------------------------------------|
| 2 a (years) to 5 a<br>7 a to 11 a<br>Teenagers<br>Average Viewing Time Per Canadian Home | 23 h<br>22.5 h<br>23.3 h<br>42 h |

Exactly what these statistics mean is surprising. By the time you entered kindergarten you probably spent more hours in front of the T.V. than you spend in your first four years at school. No wonder some people are concerned about the influence of television on children.

# Some Pros and Cons of Television

Comments and statistics related to television viewing give you some food for thought. But television has been praised as an excellent communicator of entertainment and information as well as condemned as a plug-in-drug that can hinder your creativity and thinking.

## *Activity 9D    A Panel Discussion About Television*

1. In small groups, read over and discuss the information and questions presented in the chart *T.V. and Your Mind* on page 135.

2. As you discuss the material, think of arguments both for and against the charge that each statement brings against television. Record your ideas in your notebook for easy reference.

3. One person from each group will serve on a panel to present your group's opinions to the whole class. Remember the guidelines for panel discussions.

- **Panel members** should sit at the front of the classroom.

- A **moderator** or **chairperson** should present questions from *T.V. and Your Mind* to the panel members, allowing each one to comment.

- **Members of the audience** should raise their hands if they wish to make a comment or ask a question of a panel member. Wait until the moderator acknowledges you before you begin to speak.

## T.V. and Your Mind

1. "Not unlike drugs or alcohol, the television experience allows the participant to blot out the real world and enter into a pleasurable and passive mental state." *The Plug-In Drug*.

   - Do many people use television to escape reality because they find it dull?
   - Do people really **switch off** their minds while they watch television?

2. "For the television generation, the separation between the real and the unreal becomes blurred; all of life becomes dreamlike..." *The Plug-In Drug*.

   - Have you ever heard people say after they attended a live event, "We should have stayed home and watched it on T.V."?
   - Why do people sometimes find T.V. more exciting than real life?

3. "Cartoon characters who fly through the air or get crushed to death and revive again instantly can warp a child's sense of what is real and not real." *The Plug-In Drug*.

   - To what extent might this charge be true?
   - Do children really confuse entertainment with real life?

4. Television seriously distorts both teenagers' and adults' sense of reality. A recent Ontario Royal Commission gives the following information:

   "Almost half of the teenagers in a recent report indicated that crime programmes 'tell about life the way it really is'. Homicide is the most frequent television crime, but in real life homicide accounts for only a fraction of one per cent of actual crime."

   - Why do people want violent scenes on television?
   - Does television violence distort teenagers' view of the real world?

5. "In the first five years of the T.V. medical drama *Marcus Welby, M.D.*, the fictitious Dr. Welby received over a quarter of a million letters from American and Canadian viewers, most of them asking for medical advice."
   T. Goranson, "T.V. Violence Effects: Issues and Evidence."

   - Why would people write to a fictitious television doctor?

4. As you listen, make notes related to the panel and audience discussion of each of the points in *T.V. and Your Mind*.

5. After the discussion, work as a class to draw conclusions—both pro and con—about the possible influence television has on people's thoughts and actions. Keep your conclusions in your notebook.

# RESPONDING TO TELEVISION: A CRITICAL REVIEW

## Standards for Judging Television Programmes

What makes a television show good? What makes one bad? The answers to these questions are matters of personal opinion once again, but you should establish some standards for evaluating T.V. shows. If you do, you can exercise choice as a viewer.

## *Activity 9E    T.V.: The Good, the Bad*

1. Working with three or four other students, list some standards by which you can judge television shows.

2. As you talk, each person should write down the group's suggested standards for analyzing T.V. programmes.

3. Use some or all of the following sentence stems to guide your talk:

---

*What makes a good...*                    *What makes a bad...*

---

comedy show?

adventure/action show?

soap opera?

children's show?

science fiction show?

---

Add other choices to the list if you can.

---

# The Language of Criticism

Now that you've set some standards, you need a vocabulary that will help you express yourself clearly in an actual review of a T.V. programme.

## *Activity 9F    A Critical Review: Getting Started*

1. Set up the *word cache chart* below in your notebook and expand it.

### Word Cache For A Critical Review

| Acting/Characters | Plot | Setting | Special Effects |
|---|---|---|---|
| natural | fast moving | beautiful | annoying |
| unbelievable | boring | poor props | effective |
| realistic | suspenseful | | disturbing |
| clumsy | unrealistic | | |

2. Decide which words are positive and which are negative in describing a T.V. programme. Place a ' + ' or a ' − ' beside each word in your notebook chart.

3. Add your own words to each of the four lists on the chart and assign a ' + ' or a ' − ' to each new word. You may want to brainstorm with one or two other people in your class.

4. Write three or four sentences describing some of your favourite T.V. characters and programmes. Use some of the words in the word cache and underline the ones you use.

---

*Example:*
*Real Police Stories* is a **fast moving, suspenseful** show with **believable** characters, but **poor** special effects.

---

# What Should a Critical Review Do?

The people who make television shows pay a great deal of attention to reviews. Why?

A good review should do two things:

---

- It should give **general information** about the programme and the characters. The reader can then decide whether or not this programme is of interest to him or her.

- It should give an **evaluation** of the programme with evidence to support the reviewer's conclusion.

---

If you say, "*Life in The Big T* is boring and its characters are not true to life," you need to give examples telling the reader why you think this way. As part of your evaluation, you might compare the programme you are reviewing with another one.

---

## *Activity 9G    Looking at a Sample Critical Review*

1. Read the following sample review of *Life in the Big T* by student Sarah Miles.

2. After you have read it once, go back and answer the questions on the side.

---

| | |
|---|---|
| What information does Sarah include about the programme? | *Life in the Big T* is a detective/mystery show that airs each Wednesday at 21:00 h on Channel 9. It features Starla Delight in the role of nine-year-old Sylvia, Monty Moorhouse as her teenage brother Bart, and Lucy Luckless as Bart's girlfriend Tina. Each week, Bart and Tina get involved in solving a mystery or crime in their home town, Toronto (the "Big T"), while Sylvia usually gets in the way. Last week, for example, Bart and Tina witnessed a mysterious car theft. After some investigation and a lot of action-packed detective work, they gathered evidence that led to the arrest of the leaders of a well-organized car theft ring. |
| Why doesn't Sarah tell you everything about the story? | |
| Does this reviewer give enough evidence or examples to support her opinion? | |
| What are Sarah's major criticisms of this programme? | Although each episode of *Life in the Big T* has lots of mystery and adventure, the characters are weak and there is too much coincidence. It seems Bart and Tina's detective work depends more on luck than on skill. If a little more work went into the plot, and Bart and Tina were given more challenges to show what two youthful detectives could *really* do, the show would have more appeal. Also, Sylvia doesn't really contribute that much to the show. She should be given a more active role. |
| What suggestion does Sarah make for the producers of the programme? | |
| What comparison does Sarah make? | Perhaps the authors of the show could learn something from *The Hardy Boys* and *Nancy Drew* books and from mystery/detective shows such as *Cagney and Lacey* with their more believable plots and interesting character development. With some better plots, and more interesting detective work, *Life in the Big T* could be a very entertaining show. While the show has its moments, it is not consistently interesting and entertaining. |
| Is the ending to Sarah's review effective? Why or why not? | |
| What suggestions do you have to improve Sarah's review? | Sarah Miles, student |

# Writing A Review

Let's put your mind to work. It's time to write a critical review of a real T.V. programme.

## Activity 9H    Getting Ready: Prewriting

You have to write a review of a T.V. programme for Sandra Nails, a very critical T.V. executive who makes the whole T.V. station run like clockwork.

1. Remember your audience as you prepare to write.
   a. In a small group of 3 or 4 students, decide what kinds of information are most important to Ms. Nails when she makes decisions about which programmes to keep and which to cut.
   b. What kind of layout and language does Ms. Nails most appreciate?

2. Choose a television programme to review.
   a. Watch three programmes you are familiar with and might like to review.
   b. Of these three, choose the one you think has the most promise for an interesting review.

3. As you watch the programmes, make some notes about them. Write down observations about the plot, characters, setting, or any other aspect of the programmes.

4. On a date decided by the whole class, bring your notes to class.
   a. In small groups, discuss what you watched and what programme you chose to review. Read your review notes aloud.
   b. Listen to and evaluate other students' comments about your observations.

5. Remember that the audience for your review will be someone working with T.V. programmes. Decide if there is something else you should include in your review. Add to or revise your notes as necessary. Don't forget your discussions about television in the first part of this chapter (Activities 9A to 9D). You may wish to use some of the points concerning the influence of television on young people.

## Activity 9I   Drafting Your Review

1. Using your notes as a guide, write a first draft of your review.
   a. Include both general information and evaluation.
   b. Look back at Sarah's review on page 139 if you need further help with the structure of your review.

## Activity 9J   Talking With Others: Revising

1. Choose a partner to help you revise your work.

2. Read each other's reviews and write down some comments about the review's effectiveness. Use the following questions to guide your thinking.

**Revision Guide**

**Content:**

- What is the writer's **evaluation** and over-all opinion of the programme?

- How many **specific examples** has the writer used to support or explain criticisms?

- What other points could she or he add?

- Are there any points that should not be included? Why not?

**Form:**

- Do the opening and concluding sentences interest the reader? Do they introduce and conclude the topic effectively?

- What is an alternative way to order the material in your partner's review?

3. Tell your writing partner how Ms. Nails is likely to receive this review.

## *Activity 9K    Getting It Right: Editing*

1. Use the editing checklist below as a reminder of things you should check before you make your final draft.

2. You may wish to work with a writing partner and edit each other's reviews.

**An Editing Checklist**

- Start at the end of your review and read it backwards, one sentence at a time. Check to make sure that each sentence starts with a word that has been capitalized, ends with the right punctuation mark, and is not a fragment or a run-on sentence.

- Check your paragraph indentation. It should be at least two centimetres.

- Make sure you have capitalized all important words in any titles and that titles of articles are enclosed in quotation marks. Titles of books, plays, and television programmes are underlined.

- Check your spelling carefully. Ms. Nails *hates* incorrect spelling.

## Activity 9L    Listening Critically to a Review

1. Form groups of two or three students.

2. Each person will read his or her review to a partner or the group.

3. As you listen to each other's reviews, write down the writer's main points so you can discuss them later.

4. After you have listened carefully to the whole review, *summarize* in a sentence or two what the writer's opinion is and why the writer has that opinion.

5. Read your analysis to the writer of the review to check
   a. the accuracy of your summary
   b. how clearly the writer communicates his or her ideas.

## Activity 9M    To Ms. Nails: Publishing and Sharing

1. When you are satisfied with your revision and editing, prepare a final draft of your review for Ms. Nails.

2. Proofread your copy carefully and correct any errors you spot.

3. Find out the name of the manager of the T.V. station that airs your programme. Write a covering letter and send it along with your review.
   - Explain that as a viewer you wish to make your opinions known.
   - Keep your letter brief and businesslike, fitting your intended audience and purpose.

# Station Break

Television is an important mass medium. It affects your habits, lifestyle, and even the way you choose products or think about things.

Writing a critical review should help you to watch television more carefully. Like Archie in the cartoon below, you may find that television can be homework once in a while.

What we want is something
new. If it does anything,
so much the better.

**Semantics** is the study of words and their effect on people's behaviour. What words you choose when you speak or write can influence your audience in several ways. As Ben Wicks' cartoon above suggests, the word *new* is often all that is needed to make something sell. Words can be powerful persuaders. You live in a world of **a gentle hard sell**.

# A GENTLE HARD SELL

"It's sophisticated ... it's for today's real you!"

When you hear something like this sentence, you know someone is trying to persuade you. These words have been chosen carefully to attract your interest and tempt you to buy a product. Words like *sophisticated* and expressions like *today's real you* appeal directly to your emotions. They are weapons in a battle to convince you to act in a certain way. The **gentle hard sell** works through words.

In this chapter you will practise using words to help **persuade** your listener or reader. You will learn some interesting things about words and their meanings by trying the gentle hard sell.

# WORDS AND THEIR MEANINGS

## Language: A Complex Set of Symbols

Humans are unique! As a human being you have the ability to use **symbols** called **words** to refer to the world around you. You make the symbols represent things. The study of this amazing ability is **semantics**. One area of semantics is **general semantics**. It is concerned with how words affect people by making them think and feel in certain ways.

The first step in understanding the power of words as symbols is to understand the relation between words and their **referents**, what the words stand for.

You can describe the referent pictured here by a number of different words.

*mutt*

*mongrel*

*purebred*

*dog*

*cur*

*pooch*

*poodle*

Some of the words that represent the referent are **favourable**, some are **neutral** (they carry very little emotion or feeling), and some are **unfavourable**.

## *Activity 10A   Words and Their Referents*

**1. Copy the following chart into your notebook.**

| Favourable Words | Neutral Words | Unfavourable Words |
|---|---|---|
| purebred<br>pooch<br>poodle | dog | mongrel<br>cur<br>mutt |

2. Working with a partner, brainstorm to come up with as many words as you can for the referent in the picture. Record the words in the chart, classifying them as favourable, neutral, or unfavourable.

3. As a class, discuss what you have learned about words as symbols of referents.
   a. How many symbols can one referent have?
   b. How do different symbols produce different feelings about the referent? Give examples.

# Communication Is Sharing Meanings

To communicate with someone, both of you must share common referents. If a friend comes up to you and asks, "Have you seen my *kamooks*?," you might inquire if it has one hump or two. If you knew the *Chinook Jargon*, an old trading language of the Pacific Coast, you would immediately think of something like the picture on page 146. *Kamooks* means *dog* in Chinook Jargon.

Words in themselves have no meaning. **Words are symbols to which groups of people have given meaning so they can communicate.** Look at these words:

> Okook eena tl'kope *stick*.

There is just one word here to which English speakers can give meaning—the one in italics. However, the word *stick* when used here has a different referent for speakers of Chinook Jargon. The word *stick* means *tree*. In Chinook Jargon the whole sentence means *This beaver is cutting a tree.*

## Activity 10B   More About Word Referents

The following cartoon achieves its humour through confusion among words and their referents.

1. Read the cartoon and decide how the cartoonist created humour through words.

2. In two or three sentences in your notebook, explain what can happen when people do not share the same referents. Try to give your own examples.

## Activity 10C   Frogs Are Frogs

1. Read the following sentences. Each one contains the word *frog*.

> a. I sewed four *frogs* on my dress.
>
> b. This horse has an injured *frog*.
>
> c. Use a *frog* in that flower arrangement.
>
> d. You have a *frog* in your throat.
>
> e. Attach this *frog* to your belt so you have a place to carry your hammer.
>
> f. Tighten the *frog* on your violin bow.
>
> g. These railway tracks are equipped with *frogs*.
>
> h. A *frog* is an amphibious creature.

2. Use the sentences in question 1 to list as many referents, meanings, for *frog* as you can.

3. Use a dictionary, when necessary, to define each *frog*. Who might have made each statement?

4. What semantic conclusion can you reach about the word *frog*?

Humpty Dumpty in *Alice In Wonderland* said, "When I use a word, it means just what I choose it to mean—neither more nor less." You can see how his statement is often true. Not all words are as flexible as *frog*, but many words do have more than one referent.

## Activity 10D   Multi-Referent Words

1. Working with a partner, list in your notebooks at least ten words that have more than one referent.

*Example:*

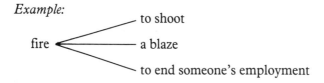

2. Some of the students should write their answers on the chalkboard. As a class, discuss their words. Do you have any other definitions for the words?

# Emotional Referents Are Important

The most interesting kind of referent a word can have often has to do with the **feeling** or **emotion** it arouses in the reader or listener.

Words with more than one emotional referent have changed the course of history. You have probably never heard the Japanese word *mokusatsu*, but look how it changed the world.

*Mokusatsu* has two emotional referents:

|  | *mokusatsu* |
| :---: | :---: |
| *favourable emotion* | *unfavourable emotion* |
| meaning: to wait, remaining quiet | meaning: to ignore with scorn and contempt |

In July, 1945, anxious to end World War II, the Japanese responded to a surrender or be crushed warning from the Allies. Their message contained the word *mokusatsu* in its *no comment* or *quiet* sense. They were requesting more time to discuss the terms of peace. Because of a translation mix-up, the *ignore* meaning came through: "The Japanese Cabinet *ignores* the demand to surrender." If the intended meaning had gotten through, the war might have ended through negotiations. The lives of thousands of people would have been saved.

Your words will probably not change history, but they must be chosen carefully to invoke the right emotional referent. Audiences are persuaded positively—or negatively—by word choice.

## *Activity 10E   Does a Rose by Any Other Name Smell as Sweet?*

1. In your notebook, write down answers to the following questions:
   a. Which would you rather be called: *fashionable* or *trendy*?
   b. Would you rather be involved in a *scheme* or *project*?
   c. Would you rather be called *sophisticated* or *stuck-up*?
   d. Would you rather be described as *thrifty* or *cheap*?
   e. Which is more appealing to you: *a frosty mug sensation* or *a glass of carbonated drink*?

2. With a partner, discuss why you made the choices you did.

3. Talk about how you respond to words like *trendy*, *stuck-up*, *cheap*, and *scheme*.

4. Samuel Hayakawa, a Canadian *semanticist* (someone who studies semantics), said that words can often be classed as purr-words or snarl-words depending on their emotional referents. Copy the following chart in your notebook. With your partner, place the words in question 1, parts a to e, into the two columns.

| *Purr-Words* | *Snarl-Words* |
| --- | --- |
|  |  |

5. Continue to work with your partner. Add at least three more pairs of purr-words and snarl-words to the lists. Share your answers with the class.

# Watch Out for Loaded Words

Words that have well-known emotional referents are known as **loaded words**. Speakers and writers use such words to persuade an audience. The **emotional meaning** attached to them is also called **connotation**. Connotations exist along side the **literal meaning** of words, the **denotation**.

Below are some examples of multi-referent words with their denotation and connotation.

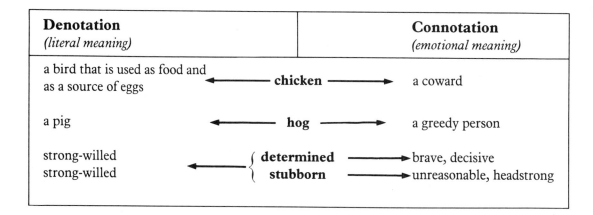

| **Denotation** *(literal meaning)* | **Connotation** *(emotional meaning)* |
| --- | --- |
| a bird that is used as food and as a source of eggs ◄— **chicken** —► | a coward |
| a pig ◄— **hog** —► | a greedy person |
| strong-willed ◄— { **determined** —► | brave, decisive |
| strong-willed { **stubborn** —► | unreasonable, headstrong |

## *Activity 10F    Connotations in Expository Writing*

1. Read the following short paragraph:

> A *young boy damaged* a *car* belonging to one of the city's *leading officials*. He was thoroughly *questioned*. In court he was sentenced by the judge who said that *children* like him need to experience being *inmates* in the *Juvenile Correctional Institute*. The judge also pointed out that the *man* who reported the *incident* should be rewarded for his contribution to *crime prevention*.

2. Rewrite this paragraph, substituting each of the italicized words with words from the word cache below. The words are listed in the order they should appear in the paragraph.

| | | | |
|---|---|---|---|
| ↓ hood | public servants | jailbirds | tragedy |
| vandalized | interrogated | slammer | law and order |
| limousine | brats | hero | |

3. Contrast the two paragraphs and write your answers to the following questions in your notebook.
   a. What is the major purpose of the writer of your revised version?
   b. What is the writer's attitude?
   c. What is the role of the *loaded words* or *word connotations* in each message?

# WRITING AND REVISING WITH PERSUASIVE WORDS

## Words of Varying Intensity

### *Activity 10G    It's a mistake! a setback! a calamity! a catastrophe!*

1. Arrange the following groups of words on an *emotional intensity scale*. For example:

> contented, happy, delighted, thrilled, ecstatic
> (least intense)                    (most intense)

a. unhappy, restless, discontented, miserable, wretched
b. important, necessary, urgent, crucial, pressing

Government approves tough new laws

Firm denies it acted illegally

Dangerous toys banned

November rainfall drenches 1852 record

Store-wide sales!

Mustangs overpower opposition

2. Using words that would rank on the *most intense* end of your scale, revise the following community notice so that it becomes more persuasive and arouses more anger and pity from its audience.

### To Householders

Citizens of our community are concerned because of the poor condition of city streets. The number of potholes is simply too great. Last week, twelve-year-old Otia Jensen hit one while riding her bicycle and fell to the ground, hurting her arm and shoulder.

Streets should be safe for all. This situation of poorly kept streets should not continue.

We invite all interested citizens to attend a meeting at City Hall, Room A, on Saturday, February 10, at 9:00 h.

Thank you,
Citizens for Action Committee

3. As you *revise* the notice, remember to

- keep your **purpose** for revision in mind.
- get your audience to respond emotionally, but don't overdo the emotional appeal.
- feel free to rearrange sentences and paragraphs if doing so will help achieve your purpose.
- read your draft as if you were the audience. Place an "X" beside any sentence that may need further rewriting.

4. Form response groups of three or four students.
   a. Attach a blank piece of paper to your draft.
   b. Each member of the group should read each draft and write down on the blank paper at least one incident of well-chosen persuasive words.
   c. Each group member should suggest at least one different choice of persuasive words.

5. Look at the group's comments about your draft. Think about any suggestions for change or improvement and use the ideas you think are worthwhile.

# The Right Impression

Suppose you have to write a paragraph for your school newspaper about the basketball (or field hockey or soccer and so on) team's loss of its big game to its greatest rival. Using what you know about words, their referents, and their connotations, you could lead your audience to see the team in a good light, a neutral light, or a bad light.

## Activity 10H    Team Suffers Spectacular Loss

Working with three or four classmates, write the story about the team's big loss.

1. Decide the basic details of the story as a group:

- time and place of the game
- scores at the end of each quarter or period; ("They were winning during the whole first half of the game!")
- stars of the team; make up names and their achievements.
- how the loss happened

2. Decide who your *audience* is—adults, students, or readers of the sports page of the newspaper. What is your *purpose* in writing—to persuade the audience either that the team is great but lost nonetheless, or that the players are hopeless bumblers?

3. Try the prewriting technique of *group writing*, a variation on brainstorming, to generate a word cache and some appropriate details for your story. Group writing allows you to work with others to come up with ideas in a short time.
   a. Take a blank piece of paper.
   b. Arrange your group so you can pass your papers to each other quickly and conveniently.
   c. On one side of your paper, write down your topic and begin a word cache that will help communicate your chosen point of view. Here are two possible beginnings:

| Words with a Positive Connotation | Words with a Negative Connotation |
|---|---|
| heroic | incompetent |
| valiant | bumbling |
| stunning | uncoordinated |

   d. On the other side of the paper, write down a possible opening for your story and two or three supporting details.
   e. Place your paper in a pile in the middle of the group.
   f. Pick up someone else's paper from the pile of papers and read what that person has written *on both sides* of the paper. Add some suggestions to it.
   g. Continue until everyone has had a chance to read and comment on all the papers.
   h. Return papers to their originators.

4. Read over the word cache and the ideas on your paper and mark anything you think you can use in your story.

5. Draft your story, always keeping your audience and persuasive purpose in mind.

6. Revise your draft using the points for revision found in Activity 10G, question 3 on page 153.

7. Return to the groups you used for group writing. As one person reads his or her story, the others should listen carefully for the loaded words that strengthen the persuasive purpose. Write down the persuasive words and, after each story is read, compare and discuss your lists.

# The Gentle Hard Sell

People who write advertising are experts at the kind of writing you have just been practising: **choosing words to create the right persuasive effect**. After you look at a few examples of what advertisers do with words, you will have a chance to sell a product of your own.

## *Activity 10I    Get Fit in One Easy Lesson*

1. Study the ad on page 156 for *Muscle Magic* to find out how the writers use language to make their product appeal to their audience.

2. In your notebook list the italicized words in the ad and explain why each is appropriate. For each italicized word, suggest a *neutral* word that means the same thing but would not be as effective in achieving the purpose of the ad.

3. Go back to the ad and write down in your notebook ten examples of *purr-words* and *snarl-words* that the ad writers have chosen to make the product more appealing.

4. In your notebook, write down a reason why
   a. the ad uses pictures of people.
   b. the ad uses the endorsements from *J.H.* and *A.K.*
   c. the ad uses terms like *muscle strength and tone, cardiovascular workout*, and *arms, legs, hips, thighs, upper body.*

5. Choose and write down five words from the ad that would rank high on a scale of emotional intensity.

6. What impression does the ad create by using words and phrases like *simple, easy, flexible, creative, fun*, and *practically overnight*? How do these words lead up to the ad's final slogan?

7. Discuss your observations about the ad with your class. Someone in the class should act as a *listener* who will summarize the class discussion.

# YOU TOO CAN LOOK LIKE THIS!

**It's simple and it's made for you.
Here it is guys and gals... for only 15 minutes a day!**

## MUSCLE MAGIC

*creative*

*flexible*

*builds muscle strength and tone*

*revolutionary*

*easy*

*provides cardiovascular workouts*

Let's get serious—looking good and feeling good opens doors... to *popularity*... to *success*... to *that special someone*.

With MUSCLE MAGIC you can't go wrong—and everything will be so right: arms, legs, hips, thighs, upper body. There's not a part of you that can't benefit from a simple 15 minute a day MUSCLE MAGIC workout.

**Arms**

**Legs**

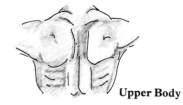

**Upper Body**

**Send this coupon to us today.**
Yes: I want to join the MUSCLE MAGIC crowd. Send me your free health guide and full-order forms for MUSCLE MAGIC products.

Name _____

Address _____

Postal Code _____

**A WORD FROM A LEADING HEALTH CONSULTANT**

MUSCLE MAGIC has one goal: a fitter, healthier, more alive you. And it's so easy with the MUSCLE MAGIC. The instructions are easy to follow. You'll feel and look better practically overnight. It's not just for athletes and it's loads of fun. In the time it takes to wash your hair you can be on your way to a healthier, happier future. MUSCLE MAGIC brings *real* results.

-J.H., Spartan Gym, London

"I discovered MUSCLE MAGIC two months ago. I've shed unwanted fat, firmed up my thighs, and I feel great. I recommend MUSCLE MAGIC to everyone.

-A.K., Saint John, New Brunswick

EXERCISE DOESN'T HAVE TO BE A SWEATBAND AFFAIR. LET **MUSCLE MAGIC** WORK FOR YOU.

## *Activity 10J    Persuasive Language in Advertising*

1. Find at least two ads in magazines or newspapers for three of these products: cars, motorcycles, soft drinks, sports equipment, or make-up.

2. List words that seem to appear regularly in these ads no matter what the product is that is being advertised.

3. Present your findings to your class, explaining briefly why these particular words are key words in the world of persuasive advertising.

## *Activity 10K    The Gentle Hard Sell: Prewriting*

1. Invent a new product of some kind to sell to your classmates. Your form will be a short speech.
   - Name your product carefully, whether it be a car, pencil, camera, computer, household robot, weight reduction formula, or anything else.

2. Make a word cache for yourself, deliberately using emotionally intense purr-words to add appeal for your product and snarl-words to make rival products seem worthless in comparison.

   *Note:* If you wish, work with three or four other students and their products, using the group writing technique from Activity 10H.

## *Activity 10L    The Gentle Hard Sell: Drafting*

1. Use the word cache that you created in Activity 10K, and any other ideas you may have, to begin to draft your speech.
   a. Use the jeans ad on page 158 as a model for selecting words to persuade.
      - Notice the use of purr-words. Can a pair of jeans really be *new* and *revolutionary*? Can they really be *sleek* and *huggy*? Can any jeans be the *ultimate jeans*?
   b. Write several sentences that tell how great this product is.
   c. Write several sentences that tell how well it works.
   d. Write several sentences that tell why no one should be without this product.
   e. Write two or three sentences that contrast it with the opposition—the products of different brands.

2. Read over the sentences that you created for question 1. Place an asterisk beside the six sentences that you think are the best.

# The ultimate jeans are here at last!

Move into the in-crowd with new, revolutionary SLIME-LINE jeans by *Now Look*, makers of clothes for Canada's "with it" teens.

Sleek, smooth—and oh, so huggy—SLIME-LINE jeans will fit your natural curves to a "t".

Why stick to those old baggy-in-the-knees pants that only have designs on the pockets going for them? Here's your chance to move on up to a newer, better YOU!

YES—PUT YOURSELF INTO THE PICTURE. GET YOUR NEW SLIME-LINES TODAY

3. Use these sentences as the beginning of your persuasive speech to convince someone about the value of your object.

4. Write your speech.
   a. Write a short, snappy introduction to catch the immediate interest of your audience.
   b. Provide a series of details to tell your audience about the value of your object.
   c. Create a strong ending that sums up the value of your object. A short, easily remembered slogan will do the job very well.

## *Activity 10M    The Gentle Hard Sell: Revising*

1. Read your speech over. Check it carefully following the guidelines for revision outlined in Activity 10G, question 3 on page 153. Make any changes you think are necessary.

## *Activity 10N    The Gentle Hard Sell: Editing*

1. Use the editing checklist below as a reminder of things you should check as you prepare to deliver your speech.

2. You may want to work with a writing partner and edit each other's speeches before you begin work on delivering your speech.

---

**An Editing Checklist**

- Have you made the best use of persuasive words that you can?
- Are all your sentences correctly structured?
- Have you handled sentence fragments wisely?
- Do your sentences emphasize the persuasive nature of your speech?
- Is spelling correct?
- Have you used punctuation correctly, so that it serves as an aid in speech delivery?

---

## *Activity 10O    Listening to the Gentle Hard Sell: Sharing*

1. Practise delivering your speech to your writing partner.

2. After everyone has had a chance to practise delivering his or her speech, listen to each speech, either with your whole class or in a small group.

**3. Keep the following points in mind:**

> **When giving the speech,**
> - let the inflection in your voice help sell your product.
> - know your speech well enough that you can maintain eye contact with your audience.
> - be enthusiastic.
>
> **When listening to the speech,**
> - listen carefully for examples of purr-words and snarl-words.
> - listen for key words that are emotionally intense.

**4. After listening to each speech, discuss why it was effective as an example of persuasive language. What specific words describing the advertised product and rival products do you remember?**

# Semantically Yours

Through the activities in this chapter, you have practised some of the key principles of general semantics: the study of words and their effects on people. For the most part, you have used advertisements as a model to see how words are used. Ads do this very well; they succeed or fail on whether or not they can make you believe in their product.

There is a visual aspect of advertising that hasn't been examined in this chapter. Words, together with a visual image, make up the world of ads. Consider the visual impact of ads after you have looked at Chapter 17, *Visual Literacy*.

For now, you need to think only about words themselves. They are fascinating and powerful. Precise and effective communication—whether oral or written—demands that you choose words carefully. The language of persuasion is a good example of such an important principle. You may not be in the business of creating ads, but you very often have to sell ideas. Your awareness of the principles of semantics will help you do this task more convincingly.

Sir Frederick Banting and Lord Moynihan

# THE SEEDS OF HUMANITY

| | |
|---|---|
| **Question**: | What do Alexander Fleming, Frederick Banting, Linus C. Pauling, and Lester B. Pearson have in common? |
| **Answer**: | Alexander Fleming, Frederick Banting, Linus C. Pauling, and Lester B. Pearson are all Canadians who have been awarded a Nobel Prize for their contributions to humanity. |

Each year on December 10, Nobel Prizes are awarded to individuals who have worked for the good of humanity in the fields of literature, science and peace.

The winner of the 1984 Nobel Peace Prize, Bishop Desmond Tutu of South Africa believes strongly in the equality of humans and constantly makes one point: "All races stand equal."

Buffy Sainte-Marie is concerned about the same theme. She expresses her thoughts in the song "The Seeds of Brotherhood." She says,

> There'll never be a better year
> For brotherhood to take its root,
> To bloom its blossom, and sprout its shoot.

## Your Writing Task

As you work through this chapter you will do the thinking, research, and prewriting necessary for a final writing assignment: a short essay on **Equality for All People**.

You will use reading, writing, listening, speaking, and thinking skills to explore your own thoughts on the subject of equality, as well as to collect facts, ideas, and opinions from outside sources.

Your final **essay** should be about two to three pages in length, and your audience will be your teacher and your classmates.

# ESSAY WRITING

The purpose of writing an essay is to express ideas in writing for others to read. There are two parts to this writing task:

* You need to collect information and ideas to write about.

* You need to organize the information you have collected and present it effectively.

*your own ideas*

*the ideas of others*

This chapter will take you through each of the following stages:
* collecting information and ideas from a variety of sources
* making notes on what you find
* interpreting your findings by organizing them into categories
* using your classifications to write a final essay

# THINKING AND TALKING ABOUT EQUALITY: PREWRITING

The following activities will help you explore your thoughts and your beliefs about the theme of the writing task—*Equality for All People.*

## *Activity 11A    A Thought Web*

1. Construct a thought web with *people* as the centre. See page 27 to remind yourself about thought webs.

2. When you are finished, compare thought webs with a writing partner. If your partner has any ideas that you like, borrow them to add to your own thought web.

### Activity 11B    Fast Writing

1. Write the following topic sentence in your notebook: *I believe that everyone is created equal, but we live in an imperfect world.*

2. When your teacher says "Go," write continuously about this idea for four minutes.
   a. Keep your pencil going at all times.
   b. If you can't think of anything to say, just keep writing the word *people* until ideas start to flow.

3. When you are finished, find a writing partner who is *not* the person with whom you worked in Activity 11A.
   a. Partner A reads his or her fast writing to Partner B.
   b. Partner B listens carefully. When Partner A has finished, Partner B should add at least one idea or set of words from Partner A's writing to his or her own work.
   c. Repeat steps a. and b. with Partner B doing the reading.

4. Use this activity to talk with each other about the writing task.

# LEARNING FROM OTHERS: TALK ABOUT IT

To find out new information for your essay, you have several options. Here are two of the more common methods:
- You can ask people for their opinions and ideas about your topic.
- You can read about it in books, newspapers, and magazines.

In the next activity, you will discuss the topic of *Equality for All People* with your classmates. You will listen to the opinions of others and think and talk about your own ideas.

### Activity 11C    Buffy Sainte-Marie

1. Form groups of four or five students to read the lyrics of Buffy Sainte-Marie's song, "The Seeds of Brotherhood." Have one group member read the lyrics aloud while the others listen. Reread the lyrics if necessary.

2. Starting with the first reader, go around the group. Each member should say something about this song. Don't stop to discuss any of the ideas. Your task here is to make sure that each person suggests a thought about the lyrics.

## The Seeds of Brotherhood

It's time to open your eyes,
Take a look outside, and all around,
To North and South, and up and down.
The weather is right, the time is here,
There'll never be a better year
For brotherhood to take its root,
To bloom its blossom, and sprout its shoot.

*Chorus*
Time to plant a brand new world,
Where promises keep and paths unfurl
To young and old, to boy and girl,
To rich and poor, to woman and man,
To black and white, and gold and tan.
To big and little, and fast and slow;
Oh, see how brotherhood can grow.
Let the sun shine in your face,
To ev'ryone of ev'ry race.

Open, open up your eyes,
It's time to find a place to hoe,
To find a place to plant your row,
Where the seeds of love can grow and grow;
Your heart's the perfect spot, you know.
It's time to clean your garden plot
Of sticks and stones and other old rot.

*Chorus*

Words and music by Buffy Sainte-Marie

3. Go around the group once more with each member adding a new thought or idea.

4. Throw the session open for a general discussion of "The Seeds of Brotherhood."

5. When the discussion is finished, write notes to yourself on loose-leaf paper to record the ideas presented in the group discussion. Keep these notes in a special folder for *Equality for All People.*

Activity 11C has helped you explore your own thoughts about the song as well as the thoughts of some of your classmates. By now, you should have some ideas on the topic of *Equality for All People* and a record of these ideas in your notes. In the next section, you will go further than your classmates' ideas to discover more information on the subject.

# RESEARCH THE TOPIC: READ ABOUT IT

People from other times, other cultures, and other continents have thought about your topic, *Equality for All People*, and have written about it. Books, magazines, newspapers, and reference materials all contain valuable information that can help you with your essay.

## Make Notes on What You Read

The purpose of the note-making system below is to have an easily accessible record of the information you read about.

---

### A Note-Making System

**Step 1:** Skim the material you are reading and make a note of the title.
- Look at any pictures, charts, diagrams, or illustrations. Read their captions.

**Step 2:** Read the summary or last paragraph closely. It often contains the important points covered in the chapter and will give you the key issues on which to focus your attention when you read the piece more closely.

**Step 3:** Reread the piece slowly one paragraph at a time. Decide on the main idea of each paragraph and write it down.

**Step 4:** Read over your notes to make sure you have included all the major points of the article.

---

*Remember*: As you read, it is *very* important to keep a record of all the sources from which you collect your information. You will need exact data about them when you write up your bibliography. Always note this information about your sources:

- Name of book, newspaper, or magazine
- Author's name
- Publisher and date of publication

## Activity 11D   Inequality Between the Sexes: An Opinion

This activity gives you practice developing your skills in note-making. Work by yourself to complete it.

1. Skim the editorial, "Our School System Fosters Inequality of the Sexes." Remember to keep the idea expressed in the title in mind.

# Our school system fosters inequality of the sexes

by DORIS ANDERSON

About this time of year, a lot of parents troop off hopefully and with some trepidation to "meet-the-teacher" nights at school.

Every year, as the parents of three boys, we went through this frustrating ritual. Every year, we had to listen to the same monotonous and baffling verdict about our brilliant, cherished offspring. "Oh, he's doing very well. But, of course, he can't compete with the girls."

It was certainly a shock to me, an introduction to a whole world I never suspected existed when I went through school. It seemed to me as a child that the boys were bored and that they didn't try as hard as the girls. I hadn't realized they were actually inferior.

But a lot of people have gone to a lot of trouble to document the extent of a young male's handicaps—six months to a year behind a young female in development.

Boys have more than three times as many speech and reading problems as girls. They are more apt to stutter. They are far more likely to be perceptually handicapped and they have more emotional problems.

Girls are better with their hands, of course. Boys tend to hog the computers and still have an edge in math and spatial ability (figuring out the relation of one object to another). But even that is changing, according to Esther Greenglass, a psychology professor at York University.

Boys aren't even as robust as girls, it seems. They are physically more frail and contract diseases more often. Yet, doltish creatures, they take more risks and have more accidents.

And, of course, they cause a lot more trouble in school and have to be disciplined more often than the better-behaved, more socially adept girls.

Hopefully, I believed all of this would change when my offspring hit high school. There, they would surely emerge from their long incubation in mediocrity and soar like the eagles I was convinced they were. But, no. The dreary recital continued. Boys dropped out of school more often. They still continued to cause more trouble, do more property damage and have to be disciplined more often.

How come, I asked myself again and again, is everything in the world I live and work in run by males who at one time must have been dumb-dumb boys? How come all the bright girls turn into drudges who do all the dull, dead-end jobs when they grow up? What turns all the bumbling blockheads into captains of industry, cabinet ministers, judges and bankers?

Even in professions in which women outnumber men, like

teaching, men outnumber women 8 to 1 as principals in elementary schools and 25 to 1 in high schools.

One clear reason is that in the early grades, women dominate the classroom. The whole atmosphere is female-oriented. My son spent the fall of Grade 2 studying ballet in preparation for attending *The Nutcracker*, which he had already been taken to each year by me since he was 3.

By the time high school comes along, there are more male teachers and some of the boys start to do better. The girls, on the other hand, have got another message through TV and even through school texts: If they are to catch one of these boys, they had better slow down and not appear too clever and frighten them off.

But what a self-defeating way to run the school system. Why make it impossible in the lower grades for boys to do much more than stumble along behind the girls? And what does this kind of early experience do to boys? No wonder we find men in business, politics and university faculties so happy to be out from under the pettifogging world of women that they never let a woman take a position in authority ever again.

And no wonder girls gradually get the idea that since males seem to be slightly dim-witted, yet are destined to run everything, the best route is to fool them and manipulate them—but never to be honest with them or to level with them.

And what a waste for the nation and human relationships. We're throwing away a lot of potential talent among women, since only a handful ever make it into top positions in business, politics and the professions. But far worse, we're locking ourselves into dishonest stances between the sexes that, if perpetuated, diminish us all.

*The Toronto Star*

2. Read the last paragraph. In one sentence, summarize the thought expressed there and write it in your notebook.

3. Read the entire article, one paragraph at a time, and pick out the main idea expressed in each paragraph. Write these main ideas down in your own words.
   *Note*: You will now have the main idea expressed in a single sentence, and several points selected from the paragraphs in the article.

4. Read over your notes and check that you have included the major points of the article.

## Activity 11E   Notes on Equality for All People

1. Use the same note-making system as you continue to research the topic of *Equality for All People*: the seeds of humanity.

2. Search in as many sources as possible for information and ideas about your subject.

3. Keep all your notes together in one place, perhaps a special folder or loose-leaf binder.

**Suggestions for Research**

- Go to your school library and check the subject card catalogue for titles of books related to your topic.

- Check encyclopedias for information on the topic.

- Ask your school librarian for help locating recent articles from magazines and clippings from newspapers.

- Check your local public library to see what information you can find there that is not available in your school library.

# More Practice Note-Making

Below is an interview with Mother Teresa by the British journalist Malcolm Muggeridge. Mother Teresa is a Catholic nun from Skopje, Yugoslavia, who gave up her life as a teacher to care for the poor and dying in Calcutta, India. In 1979, she was awarded the Nobel Prize for Peace because of her humanitarian work. Mother Teresa's nuns now work in twenty-five cities in India, Venezuela, Tanzania, and Rome.

As you listen to the interview, ask yourself the question:

> Through her words, her work, and her example, what is Mother Teresa saying about the equality of all humans?

## *Activity 11F    Mother Teresa: Listening to Make Notes*

1. **Close your textbook and listen carefully as someone reads the interview with Mother Teresa. The reader(s) should read the excerpt twice.**

2. **After the second reading, make notes on the important points in the interview.**

3. **Use your notes to answer the following questions.**
   a. **What kinds of people did Mother Teresa help?**
   b. **How did she help them?**
   c. **How would you explain Mother Teresa's views on the equality of humans to someone who has never heard of her work?**

4. **Add this information to your folder of materials on the topic** *Equality for All People.*

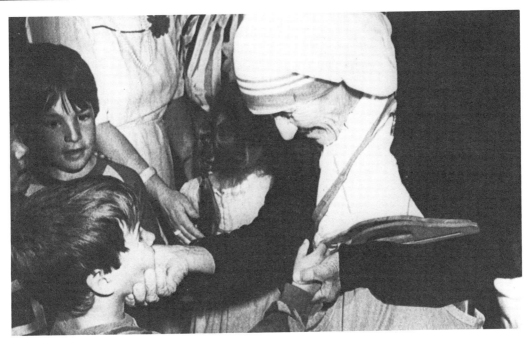

**Mother Teresa:**
In 1952 we opened the first Home for the Dying.

**Muggeridge:**
When you say Home for the Dying, you mean that these are people on the streets who have been abandoned and are dying?

**Mother Teresa:**
Yes, the first woman I saw, I myself picked up from the streets. She had been half eaten by rats and ants. I took her to the hospital but they would not do anything for her. They only took her in because I refused to move until they accepted her. From there I went to the municipality and I asked them to give me a place where I could bring these people, because on the same day I had found other people dying in the streets. The health officer took me to the temple, the Kali temple. It was an empty building; he asked me if I would accept it. Within twenty-four hours we had our patients there and we started the work of the home for the sick and dying who are destitute. Since then we have picked up over twenty-three thousand people from the streets of Calcutta, of whom about fifty per cent have died.

**Muggeridge:**
What exactly are you doing for these dying people?

**Mother Teresa:**
First of all we want to make them feel that they are wanted; we want them to know that there are people who really love them, who really want them, at least for the few hours that they have to live, to know human and divine love. That they too may know that they are the children of God, and that they are not forgotten and that they are loved and cared about and there are young lives ready to give themselves in their service.

**Muggeridge:**
What happens to the ones who don't die?

**Mother Teresa:**
Those who are able to work, we try to find some work for them; for others, we try to send them to homes where they can spend at least a few years in happiness and comfort.

Malcolm Muggeridge, "Mother Teresa," adapted from *Something Beautiful for God*

# ORGANIZING YOUR MATERIAL

When you have collected information for your report from a wide variety of sources, you will need to organize it into categories. This process is called **classification**.

Classification means sorting ideas and information into groups or families. The key to this process is finding an element that ideas or pieces of information have in common.

Once you have classified your material, you can see what content you have and how your ideas might fit together. You can decide in what order to place them. This examination will allow you to form paragraphs and to build the structure of your essay.

The material you have gathered for your report on the equality of all humans probably needs to be organized into three or four major categories. The next activity will help you to classify your information.

## Activity 11G    Classifying Information

Work with a partner to complete this activity. Do all writing on loose-leaf paper and make sure that both partners have a copy of any notes you make during this activity.

1. Read over the items below and then classify them into the following groups:
   - qualities necessary for equality for all
   - groups who are often treated unequally
   - results of unequal treatment

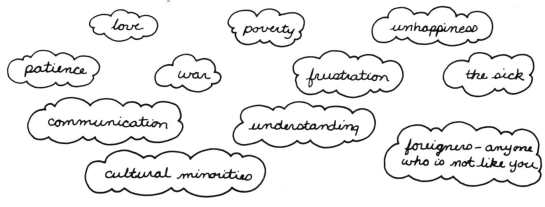

Be prepared to justify your decisions regarding your classification.

2. Keep your work in your folder of notes.

3. Using a process such as the one outlined above, classify your own notes on the topic of *Equality for All People*. You should come up with three or four major classifications for your subject.

# A FINAL ESSAY

Now that you have researched your topic and recorded and classified your findings, you are ready for the major writing task—your essay. The next activity will help you collect your thoughts on your topic.

## *Activity 11H    A Thought Draft*

1. Read over your entire collection of notes.

2. Write the title *Equality for All People* at the top of a blank sheet of paper.

3. Write everything you know about the subject. Do not be concerned about spelling or punctuation at this stage of the writing process. Don't worry about the order or sequence of your ideas. Your main objective is to get your ideas on paper.

Remember that, for this writing task, the audience and form have been determined for you. Your audience is your teacher and you will be presenting your completed essay for formal evaluation. The form of this writing assignment is a two to three page formal essay.

## *Activity 11I    Audience and Form*

1. Working with a writing group of three or four students, discuss these questions:
   a. What kind of sentence structure is appropriate for the audience for whom you are writing?
   b. What kind of vocabulary is appropriate?
   c. What can you do to communicate ideas most effectively to your audience?

2. How will your teacher look at your use of the essay form?
   a. What format will your reader expect to see in your essay? Discuss the details.
   b. What will your reader expect with regard to
      • punctuation
      • spelling

• paragraphing
• handwriting
• margins

Now that you have completed your research and classified and organized your findings, you are ready to begin to write a first draft of your essay. Use the ideas in your thought web as a pool of information for your first draft.

Before you begin, you need to think of an interesting sentence that will both attract your reader's attention and present a statement of your purpose in writing the essay. This statement is called a **thesis statement**.

> A **thesis statement** presents the reader with the issue being dealt with, the writer's stand on that issue and the reasons for his or her stand.

## Activity 11J    A Statement of Purpose

1. Working alone, write three different thesis statements for your essay.

2. Share your statements with a partner. Help each other by responding to the following questions orally. Discuss each partner's statements in turn.
   a. Does the statement present the issue to be dealt with in the essay? Indicate the exact words that do this.
   b. Does the statement present the writer's stand on the issue? Indicate the key words that do this.
   c. Does the statement give reasons for the writer's stand?

3. After listening to your partner's comments about your thesis statements, choose the one you think is best and use it as the opening sentence of the first draft of your essay.

## Activity 11K    The First Draft

1. Write the first draft of your essay.

2. Think of a good title for your essay and place it at the top of your piece of writing.

## Activity 11L    Revising and Editing

1. Exchange work with a writing partner and help your partner examine his or her work using the questions below as a guide.
   a. Does the essay have an interesting title? Suggest two other possible titles for it.

b. Does your partner have an interesting way to introduce this essay? Suggest to your writing partner another way to begin this essay.

c. Are there enough reasons and examples given to support each of the major points in the essay? Give suggestions for any additional information you think is necessary.

d. Is there a good conclusion to your partner's essay? If the essay simply ends, suggest a good conclusion.

3. Read over your partner's comments and consider them carefully. Then reread your essay and make any necessary revisions. Use the following questions to edit your work.

- Add: Do you need to add any additional information?

- Omit: Are there any phrases or sentences that could be left out or cut from your report?

- Substitute: Can you substitute any words, phrases, or sentences with better ones in order to communicate your ideas more effectively?

- Rearrange: Is the arrangement of sentences and paragraphs the best it could be to communicate your ideas?

4. Write a second draft of your essay. Use your partner's advice but be sure to make up your own mind about what you want to include and what should be left out.

## *Activity 11M    Bibliography*

When you present your final essay, you must include a bibliography, listing all the references and sources you used as you researched your topic.

1. Use the following example as a model to set up your bibliography:

---

**Bibliography**

Anderson, Doris, "Our School System Fosters Inequality of the Sexes," *Toronto Star*. September 29, 1984.

Muggeridge, Malcolm, "Mother Teresa," *Something Beautiful for God*. Toronto: Collins Publishers, 1977.

Smucker, Barbara, *Underground to Canada*. Toronto: Clarke, Irwin & Company Limited, 1977.

---

## Activity 11N  Proofreading

Work in a group of five students to go over the mechanics of your paper.

1. Student 1 reads over your paper and checks for spelling errors.

2. Student 2 checks to see that each sentence is complete and underlines any incomplete sentences or any that are joined with only a comma.

3. Student 3 checks for correct capitalization and punctuation, paying particular attention to the bibliography.

4. Student 4 checks for correct paragraphing.

## Activity 11O  Publishing and Sharing

1. If necessary, write a final copy of your essay. If you did not have to make many mechanical changes, your second draft may be good enough to submit.

2. Present your completed essay to your teacher for formal evaluation.

3. You could share your work with others outside your classroom by choosing one or more of the following suggestions:
   a. Give a copy of your essay to the editor of your school newspaper or yearbook and ask that it be published.
   b. Send your essay to your local newspaper and write a covering letter to the editor asking that it be published.
   c. Give a copy of your essay to your school librarian to display in the school library as a model for other students who have essays to write.

# It's Time To Open Your Eyes

In this chapter you have learned the steps involved in writing an essay, as well as finding out a lot of information on the topic *Equality for All People*. Remember the steps you went through to produce the final polished product.

> • You thought about your own ideas on the topic and expressed them orally.
>
>                         →

- You talked to others on the topic of equality and listened to ideas from others in your class.

- You researched various aspects of the topic and made notes of your findings.

- You went through the stages of the writing process, produced an essay, and presented it for formal evaluation.

These steps will help you write an essay in any of your school subjects.

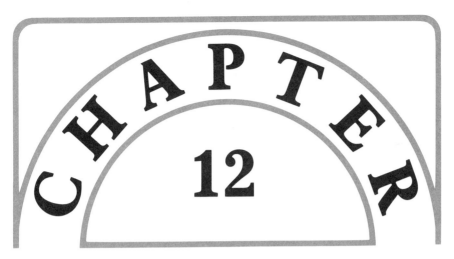

# THE VIDEO WORLD

Many people strongly believe that communication is changing in the modern world, and changing rapidly. You can receive a picture in your living room from all over the world in a matter of seconds. The satellites orbiting the earth have put every part of the globe in touch with every other part. Marshall McLuhan, a Canadian who studied the effects of electronic communication, has described our world as a **global village**.

Visuals or pictures are very much a part of this global village. Your grandparents used to listen to the top forty pop-music hits on the radio. You watch them as videos. Songs are no longer just songs. They are songs and pictures.

It is interesting to know something about visuals. How are they made? Who makes them? How do cameras work? What is a good video shot?

And behind all these questions is another question: Is print dead? Is it senseless to learn to write? This chapter will help you consider some of these questions.

# CAMERA SHOTS—READING THE VISUALS

Surprisingly, the magic lamp of video relies very much on written communication. Audio-visual productions almost always involve writing scripts. To understand these scripts you need to know something about types of camera shots.

Usually production crews, both inside and outside the studio, work from written, shooting scripts. Camera operators record on a camera card the shots they have to take. Abbreviations on the card tell the camera operator what shots the director wants. A director, for example, may want several shots of the same subject so that he or she can choose the clearest or most dramatic effect for viewers.

## Activity 12A   Possible Shots

1. **Read the illustration below to find out about various camera shots. As you read, write down each term and its abbreviation in your notebook. Doing this will help you to become familiar with the terms and their abbreviations.**

### CAMERA SHOTS

**Zooming In**. The camera operator changes shots without interrupting the flow of the scene. The scene may be shown like this:

The camera then **zooms in** so that the viewer sees only a small part of the scene like this:

**Cut to**. The camera stops and focusses on a new subject.

**Close-up (CU)**. A close-up examines the details of the subject very closely. The subject fills the screen.

**Medium Close-Up (MCU)**. This shot is half way between a close-up and a medium shot.

**Medium Shot (MS)**. The subject does not fill the whole screen, but you are able to examine details of the subject. The emphasis is on the whole subject rather than a detail of the subject.

**Medium Wide Shot (MWS).** This shot is half way between a medium shot and a wide shot.

**Wide Shot (WS).** The subject fills up much less of the shot; more of the environment can be seen. The emphasis is shared between the subject and the environment.

Medium close-up (MCU on script)

Close-up (CU on camera script)

Medium shot (MS on camera script)

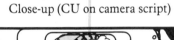

Medium wide shot (MWS on script)

Wide shot (WS on camera script)

2. In pairs, test each other's knowledge of camera shots and terms.
   a. Below is a wide shot of a Canadian mountain climber who was part of an eventful trek to the top of Mount Everest. With your partner, decide how much of the photo to include if you want
      - a medium wide shot
      - a medium shot
      - a medium close-up
      - a close-up

   b. With your partner, talk about the effects of different camera shots on a subject.

© Pat Morrow and *Macleans*

3. Work with a partner for this activity. You will apply your knowledge of terms and camera shots.
   a. One partner assumes the role of the director, and the other, of the camera operator.
   b. Find a scene in your classroom that the director wants to shoot.
   c. As the director tells the camera operator what kind of picture she or he needs, the camera operator labels the required shot.
   d. Take turns giving directions and labelling shots.

# THE FORM OF AN AUDIO-VISUAL SCRIPT

If you will look back to page 178 you will find a Dracula story but in scrambled order. Here is an audio-visual script that could be used to tell a camera operator how to shoot this story. This script gives you the first three shots in a six-shot sequence.

The following chart shows you what is needed in an audio-visual script.

| VISUAL | | AUDIO |
|---|---|---|
| The kind of shot for the picture? | Description of the shot | The sound that accompanies each picture. |

## Activity 12B   Following the Model

1. Look once again at the Dracula story on page 178 and the script on page 184.
2. Decide on the best order for the three remaining shots for this Dracula story on page 178.
3. In your notebook complete the audio-visual script for the adventures of Dracula. Use the sample script on page 184 as a model.

| | **VISUAL** | **AUDIO** |
|---|---|---|
| | MWS of a coffin on the ground in front of a stone wall. | Silence |
| | A claw-like hand slowly emerges out of the end of the coffin closest to the camera and, as lid is slowly lifted, eyes in the coffin become visible. | Creak of door |
| | Cut to a WS of Dracula in silhouette form walking across a moonlit field sparsely populated with leafless trees. | Eerie sound of wind, hoot of owl and the sound of snapping twigs as Dracula shuffles along |

# FILM DEVICES: TOOLS OF THE TRADE

Filmmakers use the techniques of composition, lighting, colour, movement, sound, and editing to create powerful responses in audiences.

## Composition

Composition refers to everything—the objects, people, and places—that is part of the camera shot. Feelings of happiness, heaviness, flight, despair, excitement, and so on can be achieved by the proportion and balance of what is within the camera shot. You can consider the following when thinking about the composition of a camera shot:

- the **distance** from which the shot is taken. The distance will change the size of the subject within the shot.
- the **angle** of the shot.

## *Activity 12C   Distance, Size, and Mood*

1. Look at the size of the objects and compare them to the size of the background in "Super, Natural British Columbia." What effect is achieved by the composition of this photo?

2. Is this an effective photograph? Why or why not?

SUPER, NATURAL
BRITISH COLUMBIA, CANADA

Tourism, British Columbia

## *Activity 12D   Being the Director*

1. Experiment with the photograph on page 186. Use four pieces of paper and frame the mouth, blocking out the rest of the photo.
   a. Compare your close-up with the original. What effect do you achieve through the close-up?

2. Continue to use four pieces of paper to experiment with other camera shots of this photo.

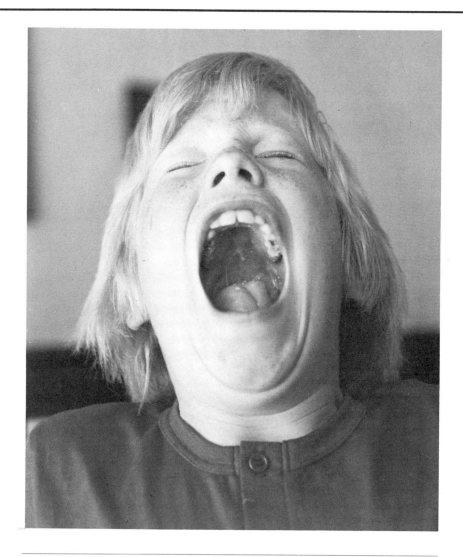

## *Activity 12E   Angle and Mood*

**Shots from different camera angles will create different moods.**

1. Look at the following photos of grain elevators for a few minutes. What mood do they evoke in you?

2. Describe in your notebook how the different camera angles created the mood of each picture.

3. Compare your ideas with the rest of your class.

4. What other camera angles could have been used? What moods would they have created?

# Lighting and Colour

You know that different colours make you think about different things. You are red with anger, green with envy, or yellow with fear. You react emotionally to colour.

Movie and television directors use your sense of colour to reinforce the mood created in a scene. For example, soft light, with little colour contrast, can help give a soft, romantic, nostalgic feeling to a shot. The colours are all very similar. There is nothing there to jar you or startle you.

Harsh lights, strong colour, and strongly contrasting colours will make you react differently. They can make you think that a scene looks hard, stark, and formidable. You may even react with terror. Strong colours can also give a cool, detached, modern feeling.

Lighting alone can convey particular feelings. A harsh, revealing, white burst of light will convey a feeling of naked, hard truth. Unexplained bursts of light in horror films can generate tremendous fear in the audience.

## *Activity 12F   Light Words, Colour Words*

1. **In your notebook, list all the sources of light you can think of in three minutes. As a class, compare lists and make one master list of everyone's ideas.**

2. **List all of the colours you can think of in two minutes. Then, as a class, compare your lists to make one master list.**

# VIEWING TELEVISION AND FILM

## *Activity 12G   Composition, Light, Colour*

1. Watch a television programme or film and record your observations about the film's techniques. Keep in mind the following questions.
   a. Did the distance between the camera and the subject vary?
   b. What effect(s) did the distance create?
   c. Was camera angle used effectively? Where? How was it used?
   d. How were light and colour used to create mood?
   e. Were there any unusual sources of light?

2. Discuss your observations as a whole class.

# VIEWING A POEM

## *Activity 12H   Creating Visuals*

1. Silently read "Erosion" by E.J. Pratt, a Canadian poet.

---

**Erosion**

It took the sea a thousand years,
A thousand years to trace
The granite features of this cliff,
In crag and scarp and base.

It took the sea an hour one night,
An hour of storm to place
The sculpture of these granite seams
Upon a woman's face.

E.J.Pratt

---

2. With a partner, read the audio-visual script based on Pratt's poem. Imagine the visuals and sound effects as you read the script.
   a. Have one partner read aloud one frame of the audio side of the script.
   b. Then the other partner should read the accompanying visual.
   c. Continue alternating until the end of the script.

## Audio-Visual Script for "Erosion"

| Visual | Audio |
|---|---|
| **MWS** Aerial shot from the top of a cliff looking down at waves pounding into the base of the cliff. There is green vegetation on top of cliff. | **Sound Effects**: sound of waves of the sea crashing into cliff and the cries of gulls<br>**Announcer's Voice**: "It took the sea a thousand years," |
| **Cut to WS** at sea level of cliffs in early winter. The cliffs are dull brown. Some snow is visible in the upper crevices of the rocks. The tide is out. | **Announcer's Voice**:<br>"A thousand years to trace" |
| **Zoom in** to the lower part of the cliff to the jagged edges and erosion lines formed by the sea. | **Announcer's Voice**:<br>"The granite features of this cliff, in crag and scarp and base." |
| **Cut to** a WS of a raging sea at the last stage of sunset. Slightly left of centre is a barely visible light house with a flashing lamp. | **Sound Effects**: low sound of fog horn and wind<br>**Announcer's Voice**:<br>"It took the sea an hour one night," |
| **Cut to** a MS of three men dressed in black rain coats and hats struggling to hang on to the sides of a small boat as it is tossed wildly by the sea. | **Sound Effects**: howling wind and slashing rain<br>**Announcer's Voice**:<br>"An hour of storm to place"<br>**Sound Effects**: men's voices shouting: "Hang on! Hang on! The cliffs! Look out for that rock!" |
| **Cut to** a MWS of the sea water withdrawing from a rock sculptured by the sea. | **Announcer's Voice**:<br>"The sculpture of these granite seams" |
| **Cut to** a MS of the back of a woman's head. She is standing in front of a storm-lashed window holding a coal oil lamp. As she turns, **zoom** in on her face lined by worry. Freeze on her hollow eyes. | **Announcer's Voice**<br>"Upon a woman's face." |

3. Choose a poem or section of a poem or song about ten lines long that would be suitable to use in an audio-visual script. (You may like to write your own poem or song and use it.)

4. Using the script for "Erosion" as a model, write your own audio-visual script.
   a. For most lines, you should provide one visual per line.
   b. Consider what sound effects you could use to support your visual presentation.
   c. Make certain that you consider pauses, since silence in a visual presentation can be very effective.
   d. Make certain that you give yourself an audio lead on your audio script. That is, begin with a few seconds of music to give yourself enough time to synchronize your visual with the audio presentation.

# YOUR OWN SCRIPT

When you complete the activities in this section, you will produce your own audio-visual script. The first three activities take you through the prewriting stage of the writing process. But, in addition to considering the ideas of your story, you also have to pay attention to the visual and audio part of your script. Indeed, you have to weave all three components—story, visual, sound—into a single unit. The remaining activities take you through the other stages in the writing process.

It's rather odd when you think about it! The world of video—television and film—is based upon writing. And the same process that produces a school essay will produce the television spectacular.

## *Activity 12I    Writing a Script from Visuals*

1. Examine the pictures on page 191. Decide on an order for them so that they tell a story. You can arrange the pictures in various ways depending on the story you want to tell.

2. Copy this chart into your notebook. Then write the number of the pictures in the order you want to tell your story. For example, if picture 8 comes first in your sequence, write 8 in the first box of your chart.

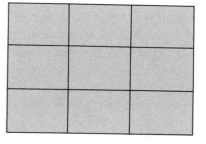

3. In each square, describe the sound or the words you want to accompany the corresponding picture.

4. As a whole class, decide what kind of shot each picture is: a close-up (CU), a medium close-up (MCU), a medium shot (MS), a medium wide shot (MWS), or a wide shot (WS). Record this information in the chart you drew in question 2.

## *Activity 12J    The Audio-Video Script Form*

This activity will help you write an audio-video script for the story you created in Activity 12I.

1. Using your completed chart as a guide, describe the first frame of your story.

2. Before you record the next shot, decide what instructions you will have to give the camera operator. Will the camera operator have to zoom-in or zoom-out? Will the camera move at all? Will the camera cut to another object or person? Be clear about what the camera operator will have to do to catch the shot you want.

3. Continue this procedure until you have included the nine shots and the sound or words that should accompany each one.

## Activity 12K   Who Is the Caller?

Your final task is to describe a frame in which you reveal the caller in the story you constructed in Activity 12I.

1. You should consider the following as you create this added frame.
   a. Think about the composition of the shot. How will you use your knowledge of composition to create an effective shot?
      • Will the shot be a close-up to create intensity, or a wide shot to create detachment?
      • What camera angle would contribute to the mood you want to create?
   b. How can you use colour and light to create the effect you desire?
   c. Where should you insert the next shot in the sequence of frames to create the most dramatic effect?

2. Once you have reached the decisions about the new frame and inserted it into the script you created in Activity 12I, add the sounds or words you want to accompany this frame.

## Activity 12L   Revising Your First Draft

1. Share the script that you created in Activity 12K with a writing partner. Use the following questions to help make suggestions about each other's first draft.
   a. Is each shot identified accurately?
   b. Are the instructions to the camera operator included between the shots?
   c. Is each shot fully described?
   d. Is the sound or words accurately recorded? Can you make suggestions about the words used in any dialogue?
   e. Is the frame describing the caller placed in the most dramatic place?

2. Use your partner's suggestions to revise your script.

## *Activity 12M    Sharing and Publishing*

1. Form small groups and review each other's scripts. Decide on one script that could be made into a video.
2. As a group, create the video based on this script.
3. Share your work on *Monday Afternoon Videos*.

# And That's a Take

In this chapter, you have learned about the techniques of television and video. You have examined how a camera operator or director can use composition, light and colour to create moods. As you used the script form you learned how writing is important to the video world. As well you have seen how the video world can be used to make a poem more vivid. Finally, you created your own version of a script from a series of pictures by writing both the audio and visual parts of it. As they say on the set when the scene is completed: "And that's a take."

1

2

3

4

5

6

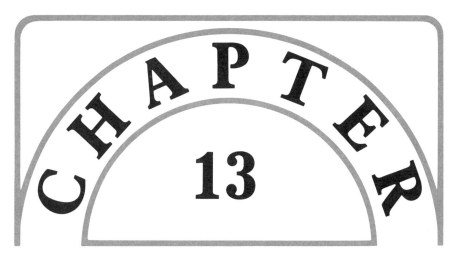

# CELEBRITIES

---

# CELEBRITIES OF THE PAST

The people in the photographs on the opposite page are famous Canadians. Look at them closely before you do the following activity.

---

### *Activity 13A    Past Celebrities*

1. In your notebook write down the names of the celebrities you can identify.

2. To check your answers and to learn more about these famous Canadians, turn to the description of them on page 209.

---

In this chapter you will be asked to think of heroes of today and to write about one of them.

## Your Writing Task

Your writing task for this chapter is to create a message about a famous person, a celebrity of your choice. In this piece of writing you want to communicate your impression of this celebrity by letting your classmates know both your thoughts and feelings about him or her.

You have a choice in the form for your writing. You can present your message as an audio-visual script, which you learned to write in Chapter 12. Or you can write a report about this celebrity, using your writing skills to interest your audience.

Let's summarize your writing task.

> **Audience**: your classmates
> **Form**: a one minute audio-visual script or a two to three paragraph report
> **Purpose**: to communicate feeling and information
> **Impression**: to be decided
> **Details**: to be decided

# STAGE 1: PREWRITING

The activities in this section will help you think about your subject, the celebrity, and explore it in many different ways. When you have finished the activities, you should have enough information to write either a script for a one-minute audio-visual production or a two or three paragraph report.

## *Activity 13B    Your Kind of Celebrity*

1. Read the list below of categories of people. Rewrite it in your notebook in a different order. Begin with the category that interests you the most and end with the category that interests you the least.

| | |
|---|---|
| Politics— | politicians, officials, leaders |
| Science and Industry— | scientists, inventors, experts |
| Sports and Art— | musicians, athletes, actors, actresses, writers, cartoonists, artists, comedians, dancers |
| Working for Others— | people who have made sacrifices or who have been courageous |

2. As a class, discuss the reasons for your order.

## *Activity 13C    Possibilities*

1. Form groups of three or four students.

2. Each group should think of names of people in each category— Politics, Science and Industry, Sports and Art, and Working for Others. Write down each group member's ideas in your own notebook. As a group, spend about two minutes on each category.

3. Each group should appoint a recorder. She or he will read out the group's list to the class at the end of the group's discussion.

4. As each recorder reports, add any names that interest you to your own list.

## *Activity 13D    A Thought Web*

1. From the list you created for Activity 13C, choose the one person who interests you most.

2. In a thought web, record what you already know about your subject. Your thought web could include

   • words that categorize the celebrity. For instance, he or she might be an athlete, a rock star, or a political leader. Think of at least three ways to categorize your celebrity.

   • words that show qualities or features you associate with your subject. Think of at least five adjectives or phrases that describe your celebrity.

   • words that show time or place associations. Think of at least two times and places you associate with your celebrity.

   • words that describe things you associate with your subject. Think of at least three things you associate with your celebrity.

Activities 13B and 13C have helped you gather ideas and make decisions. You have decided on a subject, your celebrity, gathered ideas in your thought web, and made some decisions about what you can say about your subject.

As you gather ideas at the prewriting stage, you are constantly thinking about the decisions you have to make. Here are some decisions you make at this stage.

### Prewriting Decisions—In the Control Room

| WHO you want to read, see, or hear it— AUDIENCE | WHAT FORM you want to use | WHAT IMPRESSION you want to create |

| | | |
|---|---|---|
| WHAT DETAILS you want to use | WHAT you want to say | HOW you want your audience to feel |

Two of the decisions have already been made for you. They were included in the statement of your writing task for this chapter:

> Your Audience—who you want to read, see, or hear your writing.
>
> Your Writing Task—what you want to communicate to your audience

And, just as a reminder, your writing task is to communicate your impression of your celebrity to your audience, your classmates. You can use either a script for an audio-visual production or a two or three paragraph report.

Consider how you want your classmates to feel and think and what you want them to know. You will want them to agree with your impression of your celebrity and feel the same way you do about him or her.

Now it's time to make the next decisions:

- **What impression** do you want to create?
- **What details** do you want to use?
- **What** do you want to say?
- **What form** do you want to use—an audio-visual script or a two or three paragraph report?

The next activity will help you decide on the impression you want to create.

## *Activity 13E   An Impression*

1. **Reread the thought web that you created about your celebrity in Activity 13D.**

2. **Choose three adjectives or phrases from the web that summarize your impression of your subject.**

3. **Use these words to write one sentence in your notebook to present your impression.**

Now that you have selected your celebrity and decided what impression you want to create, you need details to convince your audience to agree with you. You gather details by doing some research.

## *Activity 13F    Details*

1. **From the list of research methods below, select and use at least two methods to gather more ideas about your celebrity.**

---

- Talk to another person or group.
- Listen to discussions or radio programmes.
- Read books, newspapers, and journals.
- Watch films or television.
- Look at pictures.
- Sit by yourself and think.
- Write notes to yourself.

---

2. **As you gather ideas using the two methods you chose in question 1, consider which form you will use. If you choose to write an audio-visual script, go to Activity 13G. If you choose to write a report, go to Activity 13H.**

## *Activity 13G    Prewriting—The Audio-Visual Script*

**Here are some questions to help you think about your script.**

1. **What personal information do you know about your celebrity that could be used to explain him or her to your audience? For example, do you know the celebrity's age, past, family, special interests or hobbies, opinions, or lifestyle?**

2. **How could you best reveal the facts you know—an interview with the celebrity, an announcer's voice describing the celebrity, or a combination of the two, accompanying the visuals?**
**You can also consider the following as you do research for your visual script.**

---

- What ideas for visuals can you get from other media?
- Can you find pictures in magazines, or remember and accurately describe visuals you've seen on films or television?

→

---

- If you were to set up a television interview with your celebrity, how would you arrange the set?
- Where would you interview the celebrity?
- What would your celebrity wear? What would you wear?
- How would you use colour and lighting to set the scene effectively?
- What questions would you ask the celebrity?
- What answers do you think the celebrity would give?
- In what other settings or situations would you like to videotape your celebrity?

3. Decide how you will present your visual ideas. You have a choice in how to indicate the shots you will use in the final film. You may want to
    - use pictures from magazines to illustrate your final images. (You will need twelve images.)
    - draw some of the visuals and use commercial pictures for the rest.
    - use very accurate word pictures. This choice is particularly useful if you cannot find suitable pictures to present the impression and information in the way you want to. (With this choice, you are not restricted by what pictures are available or your drawing skill. Your imagination can run free.)

Go to Activity 13I

## Activity 13H  Prewriting—The Report

Here are some questions to help you think about your report.

1. What personal information do you know about your celebrity that could be used to explain him or her to your audience? For example, do you know your celebrity's age, past, family, special interests or hobbies, opinions or lifestyle?

2. What is the best way to get these facts into your report in an interesting way?
    a. What information would make the best introduction—something that would interest your reader immediately, a kind of hook to catch his or her interest?

b. What is the best order to present the information you have about your celebrity? Should you use chronological order—the order in which events happened? Or can you find another way to categorize events and present them in your way?

c. Can you add any personal anecdotes or thoughts to the report?

d. What can you use in your report to give it a solid conclusion that will stay in your reader's memory?

3. Perhaps you could do some library research on your celebrity.

a. When you are gathering information, remember to follow the note-making system on page 167.

b. Make a list of questions about your celebrity to which you would like to find answers.

4. Once you have gathered your information, review the sentence you wrote in Activity 13E. Do you still agree that you want to create this impression about your celebrity? If not, rewrite the sentence.

5. Think once again about the order in which you could present your material. The following classifications may be useful:
- my celebrity's early life
- my celebrity's present life
- my celebrity's talents
- my celebrity's future ambitions
- my celebrity's accomplishments
- my celebrity's personal traits such as age, family, and so on
- my celebrity's pastimes

Go to Activity 13J

---

# STAGE 2: WRITING

Once you have gathered ideas and decided how you will present them, you are ready for the next stage of the writing process: **the drafting stage**.

## *Activity 13I    The Audio-Visual Script*

1. Read the impression you recorded in Activity 13E. Now that you have researched more information about your celebrity, do you still agree with your statement? If not, rewrite your impression.

2. Use this impression as the first entry for the audio side of the audio-visual form. See page 184 to remind yourself of this form.

3. Remember this impression as you gather or describe the *twelve visual* shots. Each visual should last at least five seconds to fill the sixty seconds.

4. If you are gathering visuals from magazines or drawing them, number the visuals and cross-reference them on the audio-visual form. Below is an example of how to cross-reference:

|  | Visual | Audio |
|---|---|---|
| Mackenzie King | Close-up shot of Mackenzie King | "Mackenzie King remains one of Canada's most important historical figures." |

5. If you are describing the visuals, you may want to refer to pages 184 to 187 in Chapter 12 to review how you can use composition, light, and colour to make your shots as effective as possible.

6. Once you have the visuals arranged in an order you want, write the audio script to match the visuals. You should plan to have each audio statement last at least five seconds.

Go to  Activity 13K

## *Activity 13J  Writing a Report*

1. Look again at the thinking you did in Activity 13H. Make a decision about the information you want to include in your report and the order in which you want to present it.

   a. As you write, remember you are trying to persuade your audience of your views. Include any interesting facts you found in your research.

   b. Try to make your report as personal as possible. Personal anecdotes and memories usually make this kind of writing more interesting.

2. If you have trouble getting started with this task, try the fast writing technique. On a piece of scrap paper, write anything and everything that you can about your celebrity. Just keep your pen going for about ten minutes. When you have finished your fast writing, search through it for anything that you can use.

3. Use the impression statement that you wrote in Activity 13E to create a title for your report.

Go to  Activity 13L

# STAGE 3: REVISING AND REWRITING

## *Activity 13K    Back to the Cutting Room*

1. Share your work with a partner who has also written an audio-visual script. Here are some things to consider when you examine each other's visual script.
   a. After reading the first entry, look at the other visuals. Do they create the impression described in the first entry?
   b. Has the writer told you what kind of shot to use—CU, MCU, MS, MWS, WS?
   c. Could details be added to show the angle of the shot?
   d. Ask your partner about the colour and lighting of objects within the visuals.

2. Below are some questions to ask each other as you check the audio scripts:
   a. Does the audio script enhance the visuals?
   b. Will each audio fit into five seconds? If not, what changes can you suggest?
   c. Is there any description of visuals in the audio column that should be in the visuals column?
   d. Are there any possibilities for dialogue?

3. Now write a second draft of your script.
   a. Study your partner's responses. Remember, it is your writing. Choose to use only those responses with which you agree

and ignore the rest. Your partner's comments are advice only, not law.

    b. Decide what changes you want to make to your first draft, using your partner's suggestions and any new ideas that you may have discovered during the *revising stage*.

Go to  Activity 13M

## Activity 13L    Back to the Desk

1. Exchange work with a writing partner who has also written a report.

2. Use the following guide to help your partner's ideas *SOAR*.

S   *Substitute*—   Suggest other words or phrases that accurately describe your partner's enthusiasm for her or his celebrity.

O   *Omit*—   Point out anything that could be left out because it is not related to the rest of the information in the report.

A   *Add*—   Suggest any information you know about the celebrity that could be added to the report.

R   *Rearrange*—   After reading your partner's classifications, decide whether the facts are in the most effective order.

Exchange work again so you each have your own report.

3. Study the suggestions made by your partner. But remember, it is your writing. Choose to use only those suggestions with which you agree. Ignore anything that you don't like.

4. Decide what changes you want to make to your first draft, using your partner's suggestions and any new ideas that you may have discovered during the revising stage.

Go to  Activity 13N

# STAGE 4: EDITING AND PROOFREADING

---

## *Activity 13M    Fine Tuning the Script*

---

1. Once you have finished your second draft, exchange it with your writing partner.

2. Ask your partner to edit your script, using the following questions to guide his or her thinking:

   a. Is the speaker identified?

   b. Is the end punctuation accurate: periods, question marks, exclamation marks? Do the punctuation marks tell a reader when to pause while reading the audio script?

   c. Is the same tense used throughout?

Go to Activity 13O

---

## *Activity 13N    Fine Tuning the Report*

---

1. Once you have revised and rewritten your report, exchange your writing again with your writing partner.

2. Ask your partner to edit your work, being careful to check for mechanical mistakes such as

   • capitalization
   • spelling
   • punctuation

Go to Activity 13P

# STAGE 5: SHARING AND PUBLISHING

---

## *Activity 13O    Airing Your Script*

---

You can present your work in a number of ways. Here are some suggestions.

1. If you described the visuals script, you could make an oral presentation to your class with the help of a partner. You read out the visual description while your classmates try to visualize the shot. Your partner then reads out the audio script for each visual.

2. If you collected or drew the visuals, you could create a bulletin board display of your script.

3. If you collected or drew the visuals, you could tape it on a video machine to present to your class.

4. You could read each other's scripts in small groups.

---

## *Activity 13P    Sharing and Publishing Reports*

---

You can present your work in a number of ways.

1. Have a look-alike day. Come to class looking like your celebrity. Read your report to your class as you think your celebrity would deliver it.

2. Make an audio-tape of your report, complete with sound effects. Present your audio-verbal report to your class.

3. Put together a Reader's Theatre session based on your reports. Several students get together and decide how their reports fit together. Then the reports are read as a group to the audience. Again, sound effects and choral reading or choral background can be effective.

4. Send your report to your celebrity. See if you can get a response.

5. Put together a class *Celebrity* magazine, based on the movie magazines that you read.

| | Video | Audio |
|---|---|---|
| | WS. A shower of sparks from fireworks against a dark sky. | Three loud booms from the explosions of fireworks. |
| | Cut to your personal logo. | Announcer's Voice: This has been a _____ production brought to you through **the writing process**. |
| | Cut to starry sky. | |
| | Letters appear from the bottom of the screen and move over the starry sky. Based on ideas gathered by—**prewriting**. First produced by—**writing. Revised and edited**—with the help of a partner. **Published** for a viewing audience. | Silence |

# The Credits

Chapter 13 has been about celebrities and you have thought about someone you admire. The chapter also provided you with the opportunity to review the writing process—a system to use as an aid in composing written work.

**The Writing Process**

Prewriting

Writing

Revising and Rewriting

Editing and Proofreading

Sharing and Publishing

As a system, the writing process is a guide, not a rigorous, step-by-step procedure. For example, you may find yourself editing your work during the early prewriting stage. Or your efforts at revision may send you back to do more thinking about your topic. Such a mingling of the stages of the writing process is normal and something that professional writers often do.

As you progress through secondary school, you will find that your knowledge of the writing process will help with your writing tasks in all subjects. It is a good system to know, particularly if you make it work for you.

---

**Answers for Mystery Celebrities on Page 194**

1. Lucy Maud Montgomery, writer
Her story, *Anne of Green Gables*, was rejected by four publishers before it was finally published. Eventually the novel became world famous and has been translated into ten languages.

2. Emily Carr, painter, writer
Born in 1871 in Victoria, British Columbia, Emily Carr painted the woodlands, Indian villages and totem poles of her province. Her paintings are exhibited in every major Canadian collection. Her book *Klee Wyck* won the Governor-General's Award in 1941.

→

3. Tom Thomson, painter
Two of his paintings are titled *The West Wind* and *The Jack Pine*. These two paintings are the most frequently reproduced of all Canadian paintings. Thomson drowned mysteriously in Canoe Lake in Algonquin Park, Ontario, on July 8, 1917.

4. Nellie McClung, lecturer, teacher, writer, ardent advocate of women's rights in Canada
Her work in Manitoba on behalf of the suffrage struggle led to the women's suffrage.

5. Thomas D'Arcy McGee, politician, poet, historian, orator of international reputation
He was a founding father of Confederation. McGee was assassinated in 1868 in Sparks Street, Ottawa, by Patrick Wheland. McGee had denounced a political group called the Fenians; Wheland was a member of the Fenian group.

6. Justice J.H. Sissons, judge of the first territorial court of the Northwest Territories
He performed the job for 11 years until he was 75 years old. He believed he should carry justice to everyone's door and held court in every kind of shelter—an iglu, an airplane, a priest's manse, and a warehouse.

*The Sprinter,* Ken Danby

# CHAPTER 14

# THE END OF THE TRACK

*The Sprinter*, by Ken Danby, is a study in concentration. The runner knows exactly what he is doing, why he is doing it, and how to do it well. He is determined, his mind set on his goal.

Look at him closely. Study his eyes, his nostrils, his set mouth, the clenched fists at the ends of muscular arms and shoulders. Head down, dirt flying beneath his feet, he looks as if he will charge right through you. He does not see you; he sees only his goal at the end of the track.

But he does not run alone. Any performer—and an athlete *is* a performer—needs an audience as a stimulus and an incentive. The sprinter's audience may be other runners, the spectators in the stands, or a coach with a stopwatch. But you can be certain that any sprinter knows who the audience is and why it is important.

A writer, too, is a performer who needs an audience. You do not write alone in a vacuum; you write so that someone will read your work. This chapter deals with **audience**—identifying possible audiences for your writing, choosing an audience, analyzing your audience, and writing with a specific audience in mind.

# AT THE START

The sprinter in the Danby picture probably has positive views about running. It takes years of training to achieve the muscle tone you see in his arms and legs. He enjoys what he's doing. He runs for a purpose; he's physically fit and works to maintain that condition.

# Your Writing Task

Not everyone is as dedicated to running as this athlete is, but most people have views about running and other physical activities. Some opinions are positive; some are negative. Let's see what your views are, as you write a personal commentary about physical activity. You can write about running itself, about a track event that may or may not involve running, or about physical fitness in general. And you have to write your commentary for a specific audience. Your finished work should be two or three pages long.

## *Activity 14A   What Do You Think?*

1. In your notebook write continuously for five minutes outlining your opinion of the physical activity idea of your choice. You can take a positive approach and describe what you like or admire about the physical activity, or you can take a critical approach pointing out what you dislike about the activity. Or you can mix your ideas and write about both the good and bad points.

The views you express and how you express them are influenced by your *audience*, the people for whom you are writing. In the writing you just did for Activity 14A, you probably did not consider who your audience was. No one suggested you should. But now it is time to consider it.

## *Activity 14B   Possible Audiences*

1. In your notebook, directly following the writing you did for Activity 14A, list three audiences who might be interested in your views. Here are some suggestions.

   • a physical education teacher
   • a nutritionist
   • a peer not interested in physical activity
   • a coach of a team

2. As a class compare the possible audiences you listed in question 1. Note the number and variety of audiences who might be interested in your views.

3. Add to your own list any ideas that interest you from the class list of possible audiences. You now have a piece you have written and a list of possible audiences for your writing. Keep them handy. You'll use them again in the section *Making Your Move*.

# SETTING UP

Although there are many audiences to whom you can direct your views, a writer usually addresses only one audience at a time. Each time you write you choose the most appropriate audience for your writing. The audience you decide to address will influence how you present your views. Writing to your school principal involves different language from the language you use to write to an eight-year-old. This section will help you become more aware of how audience affects what you say and how you say it.

## *Activity 14C   Listening for Audience*

1. With your textbook closed, listen as your teacher reads the sentences in the box.

2. For each sentence, answer the questions below:
   a. Who is the speaker?
   b. Whom is the speaker talking to? That is, who is the speaker's audience?
   c. Which words tell you who the audience is?

3. Be prepared to explain the reasons why you chose the audience you did.

---

1. The biggest problem for students in high school is to develop an effective set of study habits.
2. Move over, ya big lug!
3. I'd like two deluxe cheeseburgers, please, one order of french fries, one of onion rings, and two vanilla milkshakes.
4. Excuse me. Will you please sit over there?
5. We've looked all over. We can't find her. The kitty will come back when she's ready. Now, let's not cry.

---

## *Activity 14D   Looking for Audience*

1. Study the ads on pages 214 and 215. Each one is directed to a specific audience.

2. In your notebook write the name of the ad. Then suggest the audience to whom you think it is directed.

3. Give three reasons why you think your suggestion is the intended audience.

4. **As a class, discuss the audience to whom you think the ad is directed and the reasons for your choice.**

**Should clothing that performs this well look this good?**

At Brooks® the answer is an unqualified "Yes."

Because for us, runningwear that looks great but can't perform just doesn't make it.

So sure we've got some pretty exciting new styles and colors. But they're all made of materials that work. Like our newest nylon Feathermesh. For breathability it's probably the next best thing to your very own skin.

Then there's our reflective yarns. Great to look at in the daytime. Highly visible at night.

**PERFORMANCE FACTORS**

Less visible but supremely important are our performance features. Those details that can make the difference between a pleasurable run and an uncomfortable experience.

Features like our "knit to fit" short liner that eliminates chafing and minor skin irritation.

Or our side vents at leg and arm holes for freer movement.

Plus convenience features like an inside key pocket and Scotch Release® Fabric Treatment for easy care and washability.

**LOOK FOR BROOKS®**

Our runningwear must meet the same exacting standards as our running shoes. For quality and for performance. Which is why athletes who know the name "Brooks®" look for our label or signature wherever fine athletic equipment and clothing are sold.

**≯BROOKS®**

*High performance from the ground up.*

# Bill Rodgers introduces a suit for the other 23 hours of the day.

The fabric has polyester in it for durability.

The fabric has nylon in it for stretchiness.

Our built-in stretch brief.

Convenient pockets.

The fabric has cotton in it for absorbency.

Most runners hit the road for about an hour a day. Which leaves a lot of time to play softball, throw frisbees, or ride bicycles. So we've designed clothes  for those activities. Our new active wear suit. It's comfortable. And very stylish. Even if you don't plan on running in it, you should run out to get one.

*Bill Rodgers & Company, 86 Finnell Drive, Weymouth, MA 02188 (617) 335-2740*

## Activity 14E    Making a Selection

Below are some sentences with three possible audiences for each one.

1. Read each sentence and choose the audience to whom you think it is directed.

2. In your notebook write down the audience and explain why you think the speaker was directing his or her words to that particular audience.

   a. *Speaker*: sports commentator

   > **Here we are again. A minute left in the game, the Toughies are down by two and twenty metres from field goal range. Hang on to your seats! It's not over yet!**

Possible audiences:
- fans in the stadium watching the football game
- fans at home watching the game on television
- fans reading a newspaper account of the game

b. *Speaker*: doctor

> **The x-rays show a stress fracture of the fibula. Treatment: 1) immobilization by cast for three weeks; 2) physiotherapy for three weeks. Am I correct?**

Possible audiences:
- patient
- medical student
- x-ray technician

c. *Speaker*: politician

> **Remember the last election? The opposition party promised to hold the line on taxes. And what did they do when they took office? What was the first thing they did? That's right! They raised taxes! Now I ask you...**

Possible audiences:
- voters
- cabinet members
- newspaper reporters

d. *Speaker*: flight captain

> **We're encountering some turbulence over the Winnipeg area. I'm requesting permission to change course to take advantage of calmer weather at higher altitudes. Ensure that all seat belts are fastened and smoking materials extinguished.**

Possible audiences:
- air traffic control
- passengers
- flight crew

3. As a class discuss your choices in each situation and the reasons for your choice. What clues in the language of each speaker tell you who the audience is?

4. Rewrite the dialogue for one of the examples in question 2 so that it is appropriate for one of the other audiences listed in the question.

# Addressing an Audience

Read the summary below of the story of a Canadian relay team.

Canada won the 4 × 100-metre relay for women in the 1928 games.

## The Race

Canada's women's relay team won a gold medal in the 1928 Amsterdam Olympics. That year, 1928, marked the first time women's track and field events were included in Olympic competition. As they entered the 4 × 100-metre race, each woman, for her own reasons, was anxious to win.

Bobbie Rosenfeld had lost the gold medal in the 100-metre dash. A very close finish resulted in a judge's decision deciding the winner, and Bobbie placed second. The 4 × 100-metre relay was her last chance for a gold medal.

Myrtle Cook, Canada's record holder over 100 metres, had been disqualified in the Olympic 100-metre final after two false starts. She was anxious to prove her running ability in the relay race.

Ethel Smyth placed just behind Bobbie Rosenfeld in the 100-metre final. She took the bronze medal.

Florence Bell, at eighteen, was the youngest member of the team. Because of a bad start, she was eliminated in the first heat of the 100-metre race. She was anxious to make up for her poor showing.

## *Activity 14F   The Difference an Audience Makes*

1. Work in groups of three or four for this activity. Reread the story of the 1928 Canadian women's relay team.

2. Each member of your group retells the relay team's accomplishment for one of the audiences listed below. Each person should choose a different audience.

3. Here are the audiences from which your group can choose.

   • In the role of Florence Bell's mother, write a letter to Bell's grandfather telling him of his granddaughter's achievement. The grandfather is quite forgetful and has trouble remembering things.

   • In the role of a Canadian newspaper reporter covering the 1928 Olympics, write an article for the front page of your newspaper back home.

   • In the role of Baron de Coubertin, a member of the 1928 Olympic organizing committee who opposed including women's track and field events, answer an Amsterdam reporter's questions about the results of the women's 4 × 100-metre relay race.

   • In the role of a member of the U.S. women's relay team, describe to the other American athletes the 4 × 100-metre race that your team was supposed to win but didn't.

   • In the role of a co-worker in the chocolate factory where Myrtle Cook worked, describe the relay team's victory to other co-workers.

   • Your own choice

4. Individually in your notebook write your account of the relay team's achievement for the audience you have selected.

*Note*: Keep in mind the facts you want to tell your audience. You can add names and facts to make your writing more realistic.

5. After all group members have finished writing, reassemble to share your work.

6. Use the following guidelines as you help each other look at what you have written.

   a. When you read your work aloud, first tell the group who you are as the writer and who your audience is.

b. Read your writing aloud a *second* time. Ask the other group members to answer these questions orally about your work:
- Which facts included in your writing are of interest to the intended audience?
- Which words and phrases seem especially suitable for your audience? Why?

7. Repeat question 6 until all group members have had an opportunity to present their work for group comment.

# MAKING YOUR MOVE

Now it's time to return to your own views on physical activity.

## *Activity 14G    Choosing an Audience*

1. Reread the views you wrote about running, track, or physical fitness in Activity 14A and the list from Activity 14B of audiences who might be interested in reading your views.

2. Add any additional audiences you can think of to the list.

3. Ask yourself the following questions about the audiences you have listed.
   a. Who would be *most* interested in hearing what I have to say?
   b. Who would find my ideas most helpful?
   c. Who would gain most from my thoughts and ideas?
   The answers to these questions will help you select the most appropriate audience for your ideas.

4. Select the best audience to hear your views about running, track, or physical fitness. Write your choice in your notebook.

You have views on running, track, or physical fitness that you can share. You have an audience with whom you want to share them. At this point, it's useful to examine what you know about your audience.

---

### An Audience Profile

1. For whom exactly am I writing?

2. What does the audience **know** about my subject?

3. What does the audience **believe** about my subject?

→

---

4. Will my audience agree or disagree with my views?

5. What is my audience's position? That is, what authority or status or occupation does my audience have?

6. How, if at all, can my audience act upon my views?

7. Why is my audience reading my writing?

## Activity 14H    An Audience Profile

1. **Read the questions about audience in *An Audience Profile*.**

2. **As a class, answer these questions about one possible audience for your views on physical activity.**

## *Activity 14I    Analyzing Your Audience*

1. Make sure you have written down in your notebook the idea you are writing about—running, track, or physical fitness—and the audience for whom you are writing.

2. Answer *An Audience Profile* questions about your chosen audience in your notebook. How will the answers help you present your views to the audience you selected in Activity 14G?

# FULL STRIDE

The answers to *An Audience Profile* provide you with a fairly complete description of your audience. This information will help you write your views on physical activity—with an audience clearly in mind.

## *Activity 14J    Expressing Your Views*

1. Reread the information you've gathered so far in preparation for your writing. You have a subject to write about—running or track or physical fitness. You've selected an appropriate audience (Activity 14G) and you've considered your audience carefully (*An Audience Profile* in Activity 14I).

2. Now, in your role as a grade-nine student with views to share, write, expressing your thoughts on physical activity, for your intended audience.

# FINAL LAP

You've written your views on physical activity with a particular audience in mind. How well have you matched your writing to your intended audience? Let's find out.

## *Activity 14K    Revising Your Writing*

1. Get together with a writing partner and exchange your written views.

2. Read your partner's writing and answer the questions below in your partner's notebook.
   a. Who is the intended audience?
   b. What do you know about the audience from reading the writing?
   c. Underline the clues in the writing that tell you who the intended audience is.

3. Return the writing and your answers to question 2 to your partner.

4. Read your partner's ideas about the intended audience for *your* writing. How closely does her or his opinion match your intentions?

5. If the match is close, that is, if your partner can tell from reading your writing who your audience is, congratulations! Add a title to the writing and go on to the editing and proofreading activity (Activity 14L).

6. If the match is not as close as it might be, discuss your writing with your partner. Where and how can you change the writing so that the intended audience becomes clearer? Rewrite your views as you and your partner decide is necessary. Add a title.

## *Activity 14L    Proofreading*

1. Read your writing through once to check for these concerns:
   • spelling
   • capitalization
   • punctuation
   • complete sentences

2. Read the sentences one by one as if you were reading from a list rather than from a complete piece of writing. This will help you ignore everything in the writing except the one thing for which you are checking.

3. Make the corrections as you find the errors.

## *Activity 14M    Publishing and Sharing*

After you have written your final copy, you are ready to consider sharing it.

1. You wrote for a specific audience. If possible, have that audience read your writing and respond to the views you expressed.

2. If it is not possible to have your intended audience read your writing, try one of these suggestions:
   - Ask your physical education teacher to read your writing and respond to it orally.
   - Send your views to the sports editor of your local newspaper. The paper might be interested in publishing the views of high-school students.
   - If your school publishes a newspaper, submit your writing to the editor for possible publication. Who knows? Maybe other students are interested in agreeing or disagreeing with the views you expressed.
   - Role play intended audiences for each other. Respond orally to your partner's work in the role of the audience for which it was intended.

# SECOND WIND

Long distance runners report that after they reach a certain distance or time in their running, they feel as if they could run forever. They catch their *second wind*.

## Activity 14N   Second Wind

1. Using the same subject you chose for the major writing in this chapter—running, track, or physical fitness—write your views again, but this time for an audience of eight-year-old children.
   - How can you say what you have to say to an audience quite different from the one you originally selected?

2. Read your second piece of writing to an eight-year-old. Ask this child if he or she understood what you said. Eight-year-olds will quickly let you know whether or not your writing matches its audience!

## At the Finish Line

This chapter focussed on writing for an audience—identifying, selecting, and analyzing a specific audience, as well as choosing language suitable for that audience. At the end of the track, a runner finishes one race but invariably begins to train for another. At the end of a writing, a writer finishes one piece and uses what he or she has learned about writing to apply to the next writing task.

# ENDINGS

The school year is almost over. It's time for you to put this year behind and move on to new things and new pursuits.

But, before you go, you may want to leave a record behind to tell future generations that you were here and what you were like. "Kilroy was here!"

The next activity will help you create such a record. This project will help your class get started on a **year-end documentary**. In this documentary you will give an account of what happened to the students in your class during this past year. This record can be placed in your school **archives**, a storage place for historical documents.

## *Activity 1   We Were Here*

1. Plan a half-hour documentary on *Our Classroom* and record it on audiotape or videotape, if available. The class will have to work in groups in both writing committees and production committees.

2. Follow the steps below to form writing committees.
    a. Form small-group writing committees of about three members.
    b. Choose a topic for the group to develop, such as
       * personal interest stories
       * the pick of our poetry
       * television programmes
       * the day that...
       * our achievements this year
       * reactions to current events
       * class anecdotes
       * un-achievements
       * your own topic
    c. Plan a five-minute segment, your *small-group production*. The actual time may vary depending upon the number of students in your class.
    d. Make certain that each member of your class has a chance to contribute something to the production.

3. Follow the steps below to form the production committees.
    a. Appoint one member from each small group to a central

committee. This committee will create the introduction and the links between small-group productions.

b. Appoint another member of each small group to a second central committee that will write the conclusion.

c. Appoint a third member from each small group to a third central committee that will plan the broadcast production.

  • Who will act as the anchorperson for the broadcast and read the script that ties all of the small-group productions together?

  • If the small groups do not suggest lead-in music, who will make the decision about music between small-group productions?

  • If you do a video broadcast, what visuals will be required and who will make them?

4. Put your production together and donate a copy to your school library so that your year-end class documentary becomes part of your school archives.

## *Activity 2    In Retrospect and Prospect*

Think about what you have learned about communication during the past year. Write notes to yourself by responding to the following guide questions.

1. About This Year—Retrospect

  a. What communication goals did you set for yourself at the beginning of this course? How successful were you in achieving these goals?

  b. What was your most successful *writing* experience? What was so successful about it?

  c. What did you learn about informal *talks* and formal *speeches* during this course?

  d. In what ways has this course made you more aware of the skill of *listening*?

  e. What is your opinion of *visual literacy* and the skill of *viewing*? How important is this skill in your life?

2. About the Future—Prospect

  a. List for yourself three things to do next year to make certain that you continue to grow as an effective communicator.

  b. Write a note to yourself about the importance of developing your skills as a writer.

- **Johannis Wallis**, in 1674, made up the rule about the use of *shall* and *will*. This rule states that you have to use *shall* with the first person but *will* with the second and third person.

> I shall go
> you will go
> he/she/it will go
> we shall go
> you will go
> they will go

Contemporary usage accepts *will* in all situations.

Why did Wallis state this rule? Because he thought it was inefficient for a language to have two words meaning the same thing, he set up a rule that made *shall* and *will* different.

- **Geoffrey Chaucer** used *double negatives* all the time in his writings. So did **William Shakespeare**. But, in 1762, **Bishop Lowth** decided that two negative words in a sentence made the sentence positive. He wanted to make language as systematic as mathematics. Yet anyone knows that in this sentence, "*Jodi can't hardly lift the box*," the lifter is having trouble. And no one has trouble accepting the following sentence, even though it contains a double negative, "*His attempts to rescue the horse from the sale were not wholly unsuccessful.*"

- School grammar, presented in Resource Chapter 20, suggests that English is made up of words that can be classified as parts of speech: nouns, verbs, pronouns, adjectives, adverbs, prepositions, conjunctions, interjections. How did this classification develop?

A century or more ago, Latin was the common language among scholars. A common language allowed a Danish scholar to communicate with, for example, a Rumanian scholar. Since Latin can be classified into eight parts of speech, scholars assumed that it was the best way to classify English words. And so the practice stuck.

Recent study of language has suggested that the parts of speech are not the only way that words in the English language can be classified. For example, words can be classified according to the units of sound of which they are composed.

# RESOURCE CHAPTER
# USAGE

The world of language is a strange one. People are very concerned about language, and often criticize others for the way they use it.

Let's see what kind of sense you can make out of some of the rules of language.

## Activity 15A    Rules of Usage

1. Study the examples given on the opposite page.
   a. What does this information tell you about the way people use words?
   b. Who sets the rules telling you how you should or should not use words?

2. As a class, make up a list of rules that tell you how to write and speak correctly.

## Activity 15B    Some Word Problems

1. Decide which sentence in each group below is an example of correct English.
   a. I always do my homework.
      I do always my homework.
   b. I always am ready for action.
      I am always ready for action.

Resource Chapter

c. I forget always the correct formula in math.
I always forget the correct formula in math.

d. I can understand never your crazy English grammar.
I can never understand your crazy English grammar.
I never can understand your crazy English grammar.

2. As a class, decide, if you can, why you accept some sentences and reject others.

3. Think about the correct answer in each of the following situations:

a. You knock on your principal's office door and hear the reply: "*Who is there?*" What do you say?
- It is I.
- It is me.

Why?

b. You are practising for a soccer match. The coach calls a locker-room huddle. In explaining one play, the coach asks the team, "*Which group has the ball now?*" What would you say?
- I think that it's them.
- I think that it is they.

---

I can understand never your crazy
English grammar.

He and me went to the store.

I don't got my book.

They don't have nothing to say about the accident.

To better understand language, you need to know something about two terms: **grammar** and **usage**.

What does it mean when people tell you that you have bad grammar? Usually, they do not mean that you have bad grammar at all. Instead, they are saying something about your *usage*. But wait. This story is getting too complicated. Let's look at the separate parts.

# GRAMMAR AND USAGE

## About Grammar

Grammar is an explanation of the way sounds and words work together to communicate meaning. In other words, grammar describes the way words work as a system. Those who are concerned about grammar are concerned only with how the system works. They are not concerned with the values that people place on words.

This sentence will probably make you react negatively.

> Me ain't did nothing.

"Yech, bad grammar!" you'll cry. But wait a minute. Is this really bad grammar? The system works, doesn't it? There is a subject, a predicate, and an object. Everything is in the right order and the right place. And the sentence communicates a meaning. If we are concerned just with the way the system works, then we could say that this sentence is correct; it is an example of good grammar.

> Words + Words + Words
> + Phrases + Clauses
> = Syntax

Grammar is concerned only with the way words, phrases, and clauses—in other words, **syntax**—work together to communicate meaning.

# About Usage

Let's look once again at the test sentence.

> Me ain't did nothing.

This sentence has problems. You are used to everyone telling you that this sentence is wrong—your parents, your friends, your teachers. And no doubt they have a bit of scorn in their voices as they point out the error of your linguistic ways.

The problem is that language doesn't work entirely by itself. It is more than grammar and the workings of a grammar system. Language also affects or has an impact on others. How the listener receives it is an important element of language. This impact is called **usage**. It is a phenomenon or feature of language that often makes it difficult to understand. The rules of **appropriate usage** are never fixed. They vary from place to place and from time to time.

When you use words, they are sent out to someone else—your audience. This audience receiving your message passes judgment on your usage, although they usually call it your grammar.

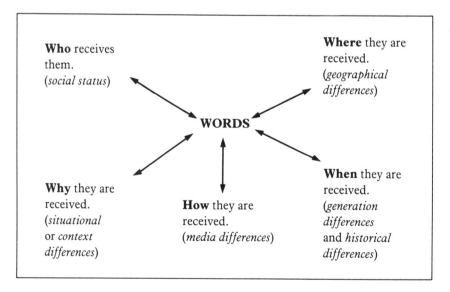

## Appropriate Usage

The illustration above leads to one conclusion: Words are appropriate, or good usage, when they are understood by the audience for whom they are intended.

Let's go back again to the test sentence:

> Me ain't did nothing.

The usage in this sentence cannot be considered good or bad. Usage can only be appropriate or inappropriate to the audience and context in which it is used. Therefore, this sentence might be **appropriate** in one situation (with listeners who accept the sentence) and **inappropriate** in some other situation (in a formal essay or report).

## *Activity 15C    Some Usage Problems*

1. How would you complete this sentence:

Everyone can do the job for $\begin{cases} \text{himself.} \\ \text{herself.} \\ \text{himself and herself.} \\ \text{themselves.} \end{cases}$

As a class, discuss your answers. Argue for your particular choice.

2. It was considered perfectly correct to use a double negative construction in English until 1762 when Bishop Lowth applied the laws of mathematics to language. He said that two negative words make a positive statement.
   a. Would anyone ever misunderstand you if you were to say
      • I don't have no pencil.
   b. If people understand this sentence, then what is the matter with using it? As a class, discuss your answers.

# USAGE—WHAT'S SO IMPORTANT?

Explaining that usage is appropriate rather than correct makes your task both easier and harder. You really cannot be said to use bad words, or have bad usage. Rather you can only use words inappropriately—the right word in the wrong place. This question of place can make things difficult for you or for any speaker or writer.

The illustration below oversimplifies the different kinds of usages. But it is useful to help you understand what words are and how they work.

**A Description of Usage**

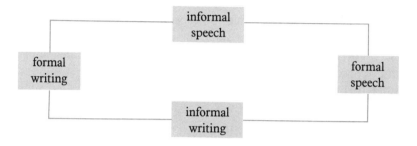

# Standard and Non-Standard Usage

One of your main tasks in school is to learn what usage is expected in formal speech and formal writing. This kind of usage is sometimes called **standard usage**, or edited Canadian English. There is formal, standard written and spoken English, as well as informal, standard written and spoken English.

Besides standard usage, there is **non-standard usage**—usage that is objected to, and even scorned, by some speakers. The test sentence, "Me ain't did nothing," fits into the second category. Non-standard usage presents a problem only because of the kind of reaction it receives from the audiences who hear it.

Most audiences who read your written work will expect standard, edited Canadian usage. A similar expectation often exists when you speak as well. For this reason, it is rather important that you master standard usage. Once mastered, you can use it if and when you have to.

*Activity 15D   Usage and You*

1. Think about the way you use words—your usage.
   a. Do you use standard usage with some groups and non-standard usage with others?
   b. With which groups do you use each kind of usage? Why?

2. Make a list of non-standard usage that you use.

The chart on page 233 outlines some of the usage forms that you should try to master. This chart points out that you know two kinds of usage now—standard and non-standard. If you know both the standard and non-standard forms, you can choose which form to use on a particular occasion. In other words, you will know the appropriate word for the situation and audience whom you are addressing.

| Standard and Non-standard Usage | |
|---|---|
| **NON-STANDARD FORM** | **STANDARD FORM** |
| **Verbs: endings** | |
| She *has ran* the campaign. | She *has run* the campaign. |
| Josh *seen* it. | Josh *saw* it. |
| We *had went*. | We *had gone*. |
| The page was *tore*. | The page was *torn*. |
| I am all *wore* out. | I am all *worn* out. |
| He *come* with us. | He *came* with us. |
| I *done* the job. | I *did* the job. |
| I *drunk* to your health. | I *drank* to your health. |
| They *have went* home. | They *have gone* home. |
| **Verbs: agreement** | |
| *One* of the girls *are* here. | *One* of the girls *is* here. |
| *Each* of the players *are* an expert. | *Each* of the players *is* an expert. |
| You *was* their first choice. | You *were* their first choice. |
| He *don't* go to school here anymore. | He *doesn't* go to school here anymore. |
| **Verbs: other** | |
| I *ain't* finished my lunch yet. | I *haven't* finished my lunch yet. |
| I *don't got* a pencil. | I *don't have* a pencil. |
| Georgette *ain't seen* the movie. | Georgette *hasn't seen* the movie. |
| *Learn* us a new song. | *Teach* us a new song. |
| **Pronouns** | |
| *Him and me* went to the basketball game. | *He and I* went to the basketball game. |
| It's a secret between *him and I*. | It's a secret between *him and me*. |
| *You and me* can go. | *You and I* can go. |
| **Adjectives** | |
| *This here* book is mine. | *This book* is mine. |
| *Them there* answers are correct. | *Those answers* are correct. |
| *Them folks* are very friendly. | *Those folks* are very friendly. |
| **Double negatives** | |
| They *don't* have *nothing* to say about the accident. | They *don't* have *anything* to say about the accident. |
| I *don't got no* pencil. | I *don't have* a pencil. |

# Appropriate Usage

The following activities in this chapter will help you master the concept of appropriate usage. In some activities, you will be expected to pick the appropriate usage in a particular context. In other activities you will practise writing standard, edited Canadian English—the kind of English expected in most school situations. Indeed, one of the major tasks of this textbook is to help you understand and use standard usage.

## *Activity 15E    Situation 1*

1. Form groups of three or four students to talk about your responses to the following situation.

You have just moved to a house in a new neighbourhood. You personally would much rather be back home where everything is normal but your parents had to move, so here you are. And you have decided to make the best of it.

The neighbour next door, who is somewhat elderly, is busy washing the family car. This neighbour smiles and says, "Hello, new in the neighbourhood?"

How would you reply and why?
a. "Yea, I suppose so."
b. "Yes. We've just moved in."
c. "Right on. We've just dug in here."
d. "Most certainly. We have just recently inhabited these premises."
e. your own statement

## *Activity 15F    Situation 2*

1. On your own, read the following story.

You are late for soccer practice, and your coach gets pretty snarky if you aren't there on time. You are trying hard to get a place on the all-star team, so you don't want to make the coach angry. To get there on time, a twenty-year-old friend of your sister has volunteered to drive you. This friend takes your family car and off you go. You are rather edgy and keep asking the driver to go faster.

To gain time, this friend cuts down an alley behind some old stores. The alley is rather narrow and not easy to drive down at the best of times. Your sister's friend is not driving very fast, but it is still too fast for a narrow alley like this one.

Just before you get to the end of the alley, a delivery truck backs out from a driveway suddenly. There was no way the driver of the truck could see you, and no way for the driver of your car to see it. Smack! Crrrunch! The collision couldn't be avoided.

The front end of your family car is badly crumpled. Water is dripping onto the ground and the radiator is hissing as steam escapes. The truck has a very slight dint in its side, just in front of the rear wheel.

2. Form groups of three to five students. Each group should prepare a response to one of the communication situations in the box below and on page 236.
   a. Take about ten minutes to discuss the situation. Consider who would be talking, what would be said, how it would be said, what words would be used, and what tone of voice would be used.
   b. Make a group list of the words and phrases that the speakers would probably use in each situation.
   c. Choose one member of the group (or more if you have planned a dialogue) to present your conversation to your class. You should plan to be spontaneous; that is, improvise the dialogue, rather than reading it from a prepared script.

3. As a class, talk about each presentation. What differences in usage did you find among the groups?

4. Repeat questions 1 to 3 with each group choosing a different communication situation.

## Communication Situations

1. After the accident, you are late for soccer practice. What happens when you meet the coach?

2. You tell the story to your friends on the soccer team in the locker room after practice.

3. You describe the accident to the police officer investigating the accident.

4. You describe the accident to the insurance agent in the agency office three days after the accident.

5. You talk about the accident later that same day with your sister's friend, the unfortunate person who was doing you a favour by driving your family car.

6. You tell the story to your parent(s) who is quite upset about the accident.

7. You use the accident as the subject of a talk in your speech class.

You frequently have to change your use of words to match the expectations of the audience receiving your communication. You must do this whether your message is oral or written. The next activity gives you practice in adjusting your usage to the intended audience.

## *Activity 15G    What Sells... Audience*

1. On your own, read the *Peanuts* cartoon on page 237. You should be able to identify with Linus's predicament: writing on the theme of *Returning to School after Summer Vacation*.

2. How would Linus's use of language change if his audience changed?
   a. Rewrite Linus's report to communicate with one of the following audiences:
      • one of your grandparents
      • a very cool DJ on a local radio station
      • the superintendent of your school system
      • the premier of your province
      • a person who does not usually use standard usage (edited Canadian English)
      • a penpal from the southern United States
      • the president of your local Elocution Society
      • your own choice

3. Share some of your answers as a class.
   a. As each writer reads his or her rewritten cartoon, the other class members should try to determine Linus's intended audience.

4. Talk about how each writer used different word choices, or usage, to match the intended audience.
   a. Did the writer communicate effectively with her or his intended audience? Why or why not?

Theme: On Returning to School after Summer Vacation.

No one can deny the joys of a Summer vacation with its days of warmth and freedom!

It must be admitted, however, that the true joy lies in returning to our halls of learning.

Is not life itself a learning process? Do we not mature according to our learning? Do not each of us desire that he

9-6

YES, MA'AM? OH... WHY, THANK YOU..I'M GLAD YOU LIKED IT..

AS THE YEARS GO BY, YOU LEARN WHAT SELLS!

b. What are some specific words that told you for what audience the cartoon rewrite was intended?

Much of the writing you do in school is for more formal situations such as reports and business letters. For this kind of writing, you need to know standard usage. You may find, however, that you want to convey to your readers how a group of people actually speaks—particularly a group that tends not to use standard usage as the community norm.

Below is a passage from a short story by Gertrude Story. Ms. Story writes about a family with a German background, the Schroeders, who lived on a farm in Saskatchewan about the time of World War II. The excerpt describes Mrs. Schroeder's reaction to her sister-in-law's American husband who lost both legs in battle.

> "Well, just look at them out there," Mama said. "See the way he fidgets? I bet you he's telling her he don't like the way she's got his shawl folded. I bet you he's telling her he don't like the weight of the apple blossoms falling on his lap. Look, look!" Mama said, moving out of the way and making room for him [Papa] at the window, "What did I tell you? There she is fussing, brushing something off his lap. Oh, I just don't know," Mama said, "some men would be by now at least trying the crutches but he—he won't even so much as try."
>
> "He's a injured man," Papa said. "A person has to remember, he's a injured man." Papa didn't come to the window, though Mama stood there holding back the window curtains for him. "He took a awful wallop to the body, sure, but who's to tell how hard it hurt him in the mind."
>
> Gertrude Story, "War"

In her story, the author has used both standard and non-standard usage. She mixes the two to capture the feeling of the German farm family—not only the way they speak but their very way of life.

## Activity 15H   Authors Do It

1. On your own, reread the passage from Gertrude Story's short story.

   a. In your notebook, write down the words and phrases that are examples of non-standard usage. You can also include examples of syntax (the way words are put together) as examples of non-standard usage.

2. Discuss your answers as a class and talk about the effect of non-standard word choices and syntax on the story. Consider the reason(s) why the author made these choices.

3. On your own, find examples of non-standard usage from books you are reading or have read. Be prepared to share them with your class and to talk about the reasons why the author made those particular choices.

So far in this chapter, you have learned the distinction between standard and non-standard usage. It should be clear by now that standard usage contains some arbitrary rules, rules that dictate how you communicate in some situations.

Yet, because you have a certain mastery over the English language, you know many answers without resorting to rules. You know the answers because you are a native speaker of English. If, however, English is not your first language, then you might have to consciously learn these rules.

The next activity will demonstrate to you just how many rules of English usage you actually know.

## *Activity 15I    You Know the Rules*

1. Read through the words and phrases in the box below.

| | |
|---|---|
| in my liking | in my opinion |
| to my view | to my way of looking at it |
| to my opinion | in my view |
| different from | different than |
| different with | different to |
| different by | |
| I disagree with your opinion. | |
| I am speaking against your point of view. | |
| I am disagreeing with you. | |

2. Divide them into two categories: acceptable English usage and unacceptable English usage.

3. As a class, discuss what forms of usage you accept and do not accept as native speakers of English. What does this activity tell you about the way language works? about usage?

## Activity 15J   Which Is Right?

1. As a class talk about the following sentences. Decide which ones you accept as good English sentences and which ones you cannot accept.
   a. Him and me don't got no pencil.
   b. Throw the cow over the fence some hay.
   c. Essay I tomorrow in hand will my.
   d. Lazy, soft love eats ravenously.
   e. The coach expectorated on the ice.
   f. For us to have agreed with you would not have been a surprise.

2. Give reasons for your choices.

# LANGUAGE DIFFERENCES

It is too simple to define all language differences as either standard or non-standard usage. Other factors are involved in the differences in the way people use language.

## Jargon

Almost every group of people develops its own way of communicating within the group—electricians, nurses, football teams. Each group uses words that have special meanings for that group. This use of words is called **jargon**. Sometimes the meanings of jargon words differ from the standard meanings. Other times, they have only one meaning but it is specialized and known only to the group. A group's jargon will change from place to place and time to time. If you understand the jargon of one sports team, for example, you will not necessarily understand the jargon of another team.

## Activity 15K   Jargon

Form small groups of three or four students and select one of the following topics as a group project.

1. Search for examples of jargon among specific groups.
   a. Each member of your group should choose a different group to study, such as an occupation, a sports team, or a hobby club.

b. Spend some time with that group. Make a list of words used within the group that are easily understood by members of the group, but not by those outside the group.

c. Meet to share ideas and compare your findings. Prepare an oral report that your group can deliver to the class.

2. With your small group, listen to three or four different sports announcers.

a. Note how each sport has a special jargon, as well as how each announcer has an individual special jargon.

b. Prepare to report your findings orally to your class.

3. Watch television for one evening with your ear tuned to hear the jargon used in the various programmes. Report your results to the class.

# Slang

Jargon is sometimes referred to as **slang**. However this term is used more frequently to describe words that come and go within popular speech. Slang words are in-words that have not been classified as standard usage. Some slang words disappear quite quickly; others hang on for years, always remaining slang; still others gain acceptability, moving from slang to standard usage.

For example, the word *tête* in French used to be a slang word, coming from the Latin word *testa* which means *earthen pot*. *Tête* has remained in French as standard usage. Shakespeare used the expression *beat it* to mean *leave*; this phrase remains today as an example of slang. The word *uptight* was once a definite slang word but its usage is changing. It may be on its way to achieving permanence as standard usage.

## *Activity 15L    Slang*

Your class should divide into small groups of three or four students. Each group should research one of the following problems.

1. a. Listen to some students in your age-group in your school. Make a list of the slang they use.

b. Listen to people who are about five years older than you. List their slang.

c. Talk with four or five people who are about five years older than you. Ask them to tell you about the slang they used when

Resource Chapter

they were your age. Compare and contrast this list with the slang that you use.

d. Interview four or five people who are about the same age as your parents. Ask them to tell you about the slang they used when they were your age. Compare and contrast this list of slang with the slang that you know and use.

e. Interview four or five people who are about the age of your grandparents or older. Find out what slang they used when they were your age. Compare this list with the slang that students your age use.

f. Spend some time with a group of children about five or six years younger than you. What slang are they using? How do children acquire slang?

2. Choose an excerpt from a novel or short story that you have studied. Rewrite it using current slang. Read your results to the class.

3. As a class, talk about the values and limitations of slang.

4. See if your class can start a new slang expression. Choose your expression and make a secret pact as a class to use the expression and not tell anyone that you invented it. See if you can get others to use your expression.

# PRACTICE WITH STANDARD USAGE

Use the next activity to practise standard usage. This activity will make you aware of some of the concerns to keep in mind when you are called upon to use standard, edited Canadian English.

## *Activity 15M   Standard Canadian Usage*

1. For each sentence on the following page, choose the word in parentheses that best conforms to standard usage and write your answer in your notebook.

2. Check your answers in a dictionary or a glossary of standard usage and be prepared to explain why the form you chose is the preferred usage.

*Set A*

a. Agatha was elected president because she (had run, had ran) a strong campaign.

b. Bruno was able to give a complete report because he (had went, had gone) to the library to check out his sources.

c. Elda (seen, saw) the reason why they (come, came) late.

d. Chen (don't, doesn't) realize the importance of his special oratorical skills.

e. Josh (sat, set) down to (learn, teach) his dog to beg for a treat.

f. Do-Quyen thought that (Joe and me, Joe and I) were able to help her with the special project.

g. They don't have (anything, nothing) to say about Frederico's win in the local music festival.

h. Bohdan was unhappy because you and (I, me) couldn't go with him.

i. José kept the secret between Leena and (me, I).

j. Jan has (drunk, drank) to our good health.

---

*Set B*

a. As we sat in the circus tent, we watched the lions (preform, conform, perform) their tricks.

b. Jarmila knew that her library book was (do, dew, due) at the end of the week.

c. After the results are listed, (we'll, well, wheel) have a better understanding of what to do next.

d. Iona went to (their, they're, there) ceremony.

e. The group went to hear the (imminent, eminent, immanent) lawyer talk about contracts for sport stars.

f. The group wanted to (improve, impress, imprint) the inspector with its efficiency.

g. We went to the big city because we thought our (prospects, proceeds, process) for success would be greater.

h. After the parade, the soldiers gathered to pay a special tribute to the (colonial, kernel, colonel, cornel).

i. Jacqueline received her mark and walked slowly down the (aisle, isle).

j. On our field trip, we came across a historical (cite, sight, site).

---

*Set C*

a. Hasan wore a green cloak that (complemented, complimented) his brown uniform.

b. Last year, we had the opportunity to work with the local (counsel, council) to talk about issues involving young people.

c. After listening to a disturbing radio programme, Ingrid decided to choose the topic of (piece, peace) for her major speech.

d. Guy wanted someone to explain the (principle, principal) reason for the group's decision.

e. Gina noted that the strange object in the sky appeared to be (stationary, stationery), showing no signs of movement.

f. Hans went with his mother to (canvas, canvass) their district for the Heart Fund.

g. Every member decided to choose (his, his or her, their) own candidate for the election.

h. Jonathan placed the ball (beside, besides) the bat.

i. Pierre had to take the dog's (conscription, prescription, proscription) to the pharmacy.

j. Lying on a beach in January is a most (pheasant, peasant, pleasant) dream for a Canadian.

---

*Set D*

a. The laws governing the stars in the heavens are almost (indefensible, indefinable, indefatigable).

b. Milk, eggs, honey, and wheat are some of the (opponents, components) of this traditional meal.

c. The Norse made their way across Europe, (raising, rising, razing) the countryside as they went.

d. Piero took lessons on the trumpet but they did not have much (affect, effect) on his playing.

e. No one (was, were) aware of Natasha's awards.

f. Milan knew which dog was his and which one was (there's, theirs).

g. The ghost on the wall was just an (illusion, allusion) of their inner fears.

h. Olga, Roman, and Micheline divided their winnings equally (among, between) themselves.

i. Miroslav (lay, laid) the basket on the wooden table and decided (to lie, to lay) down for a short while.

j. After we listened to the premier's speech, we (inferred, implied) from the remarks that there would be an election next year.

# Word Scan

This chapter has surveyed the topics of usage and non-standard usage. The knowledge that you have acquired about words most certainly doesn't make the task of writing any easier for you. But you can now make one additional choice in your writing and speaking—to choose the usage appropriate for the audience whom you are addressing.

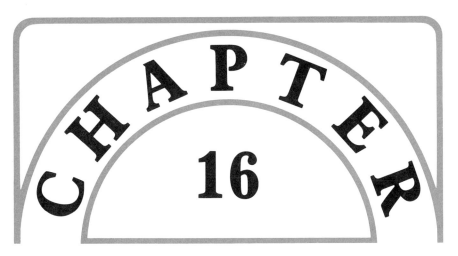

# RESOURCE CHAPTER
# LISTENING

You are involved in some kind of communicative act every minute of the day. Researchers have studied how much time people spend on the various communication skills as they go about their lives. The chart below shows their findings, the amount of time the average person engages in each communication skill.

| Time Spent in Communication | |
|---|---|
| *communication skill* | *per cent of time spent engaged in this activity* |
| listening | 46% |
| speaking | 30% |
| reading | 15% |
| writing | 9% |
| [Viewing has not been accounted for in this survey.] | |

The information in this chart shows you how important the skill of listening is since you spend almost half of your time listening.

To understand this communication skill, you need to consider the differences between two terms: **hearing** and **listening**. The term *hearing* suggests the physical act of receiving sounds from a source. *Listening*, on the other hand, involves understanding the meaning of the noise that you collect with your ear. *You hear with your ear; you listen with your mind.*

Resource Chapter

## *Activity 16A    I Hear; I Listen*

1. For one day, keep track of the amount of time you spend on each communication skill: listening, speaking, reading, writing, and viewing.

   *Note*: It is possible to be engaged in more than one communication skill at the same time, for example, viewing and listening.
   a. Construct a chart or graph such as the following example to display your results.

### Time Spent with Each Communication Skill

|           | 7:00 h–8:00 h | 8:00 h–9:00 h | 9:00 h–10:00 h | 10:00 h–11:00 h | etc. |
|-----------|---------------|---------------|----------------|-----------------|------|
| listening |               |               |                |                 |      |
| speaking  |               |               |                |                 |      |
| reading   |               |               |                |                 |      |
| writing   |               |               |                |                 |      |
| viewing   |               |               |                |                 |      |

   At the end of each hour, enter the time you spent on each skill, using multiples of five minutes.

2. As a class, tabulate the results. Are the class results similar to those given in the chart on page 247? How does the addition of viewing change your results?

3. Classify your results according to time spent in class and time spent out of class. Do you use different communication skills in school than you do outside of school?

4. As a class, talk about your results and what they mean.

5. In your notebook, write a paraphrase of the statement: "I hear with my ears; I listen with my mind."

   *Note*: Paraphrase means to explain a statement in your own words so that you make its meaning perfectly clear.
   a. Share your response with the class.
   b. Do you *view* with your mind as well? Talk about this idea as a class.

6. Look for statements about listening in books, magazines, and cartoons. Share what you find with your classmates.

No doubt the results of your survey suggest that the skill of listening is one of the most frequently used communication skills. It probably rivals viewing for first place. For this reason, it makes sense to spend time considering this skill and learning how to become a better listener.

# TYPES OF LISTENING

Not all listening situations are the same. As a result, you develop different kinds of listening abilities. This chapter discusses four different types of listening:

- for understanding and evaluating
- for discriminating stimuli
- for appreciation
- for helping a friend

## Listening Accurately to Understand and Evaluate

Let's begin with the type of listening you often engage in at school: *listening to understand and to evaluate*. The first task of this type of listening is to acquire information. Acquiring information involves receiving facts and ideas—without judging them. Once you have acquired the information and understood it, you are in a position to make judgments about it or to evaluate the facts and ideas you have heard.

### Activity 16B    Accurate Listening

1. With your textbook closed, listen as someone reads the listening questions below and write the correct responses in your notebook.
   a. Write these five numbers in your notebook: 6, 18, 12, 49, 37. Circle the largest number.
   b. If you circled 37, write *cat* in your notebook; if you did not, write *dog*.
   c. If Sir John A. Macdonald was born before former Prime Minister Pierre Elliott Trudeau, write *Canada Day* in your notebook. If not, write the name of your school.
   d. If Winnipeg lies east of Thunder Bay, write *Lake Superior* in your notebook; if not, write *Lake Huron*.

e. If Ottawa is situated on the St. Lawrence River, make an *x* in the upper left corner of your page. If not, place an *equal sign* in the upper right corner.

f. If Margaret Laurence is a well-known Canadian writer, write *Montreal* backwards on your page. If she is not, write *Montreal* forwards on your page.

g. If you are male, write *The Two Solitudes* on your page; if you are female, write *Who Has Seen the Wind?*

h. If you can catch Atlantic salmon on the Pacific Coast, write the name of the present prime minister in your notebook. If not, write the name of a long river that flows to the Arctic Ocean.

i. If Alberta and Saskatchewan border on salt water, write *Chicoutimi, Quebec* in your notebook. If not, write the larger of these two numbers: 24, 18.

j. If Madame Jeanne Sauvé is the first woman governor general of Canada, print your last name in your notebook. If not, draw three circles horizontally on your page.

k. If the Beatles were a Canadian rock group, write the name of your English teacher in the bottom right corner of your page. If not, print your surname in the upper right corner of your page.

l. If the Olympic Stadium is in Montreal, write the name of Canada's smallest island province in your notebook. If not, write the name of the last province when all the provinces are put in alphabetical order.

2. In a small group, make up some accurate listening quizzes using question 1 as an example and try them on members of your class.

## *Activity 16C    Beauty Contest*

1. Listen carefully while someone reads the opinion statement about beauty contests in the box on page 251.

2. After you have heard the opinion statement once, answer the questions below.

   a. What is the writer's opinion about beauty contests?

   b. What details from the statement support your answer?

3. Listen while someone reads the passage a second time. Then change or add any information you think is necessary to your initial answers.

4. Discuss your answers in class. Then evaluate this opinion state-ment. Which supporting details in this argument are statements of fact? Which are statements of opinion? How does the writer of the written statement add an emotional overtone to it?

---

**Beauty Contest**

In my opinion, beauty pageants should be abolished from our TV screens. Many people still watch this rubbish that goes under the name of entertainment. Several times a year we are subjected to these contests in spite of the fact that some countries have banned them. If you feel as I do, make your opinion count: next time you see a beauty pageant on TV—turn it off!!!!

---

Often someone will give you a series of directions and expect you to carry them out. When you leave for school in the morning, for example, your parent might say something like

---

*When you get home from school tonight, let the dog out. Then peel six potatoes and put them on the stove to cook. When you are done, phone me and I'll let you know if there is anything else I want you to do. If the dog barks, let her in.*

---

Surprisingly you can remember all of this even after several hours. How do you do this? First, you have to listen to the message. If you don't hear it correctly, you will make mistakes—and let the potatoes out and peel the dog. Then, you have to store the information in your memory so you will know what to do when you get home.

The next activity will give you some practice in listening to remember details.

## *Activity 16D    Now Hear This!—You Mean Listen?*

1. Working on your own, write a series of directions in which you give several related direction statements, but no more than five. Make your statements short and clear. You can also use props that are readily available in your classroom. For example, you might make up something like
   a. Put your left hand on top of your head.
   b. Cross your right leg over your left leg and smile without showing your teeth.
   c. Turn your head so that you are looking at the main door of the classroom.

Resource Chapter

2. Form groups of four or five students. Take turns reading your directions to each other and being the listener. For each series, read all directions at one time. Once the listener has heard all the directions, he or she carries them out.

3. As a small group, talk about this activity.
   a. Were the direction statements clear?
   b. What kind of direction statements caused listeners the most trouble?
   c. Did the order in which the directions were given seem to make it easier or harder for the listener to remember the series of direction statements?

4. Working together as a group, compose a set of direction statements for another group to carry out. Your directions must give every member of the other group at least one direction to carry out.
   a. Take turns with other groups reading and following direction statements.
   b. As a class, talk about the results of this activity.
      • Did the groups create good, clear directions?
      • Did the groups listen carefully to follow the directions?

*Variation*: If you can complete these activities easily, increase the number of directions you give to the listener(s).

## Listening to Discriminate Sounds

You often need to distinguish sounds when you are listening. Slight changes in sound can change the meaning of a word. There is only one sound that is different, for example, between the two words /lass/ and /last/. To understand the different meanings of the two words, you have to discriminate between the sounds.

### *Activity 16E    Distinguishing Words*

1. Select ten words from the following list and write them in a column on a piece of paper. Choose only one word from each set.
   a. affect, effect
   b. adapt, adopt, adept
   c. ate, hate
   d. budge, fudge, drudge, judge
   e. disillusion, dissolution

f.  exalt, exult
g.  forbidding, forbidden
h.  witch, which
i.  misting, missing
j.  misted, misled
k.  sins, since
l.  cemetery, seminary

2.  Work with a partner. Read your list and ask your partner to copy the words you have selected. Make certain that your partner can't see your list, but has to listen to you. Reverse positions and have your partner dictate his or her words to you.

3.  Correct each other's lists. How good were you at distinguishing words?

4.  Repeat this activity with a set of words that you make up.

    *Variation*: When dictating your list, sit back to back so that your partner cannot see you reading the list of words.

## *Activity 16F    Distinguishing Voices*

1.  Form small groups of about five students. As a group, prepare a sound tape with each member of the group reading a selection of poetry.
    a.  Each student should choose about ten lines of poetry for his or her reading.
    b.  Prepare an audiotape of each group member reading his or her selection.
    c.  Half of the group's members should read normally and the other half should try to disguise their voices.
    d.  When you are preparing your audiotape, be sure to leave time between each reading. You might include a short musical interlude of about twenty seconds between each. The music can set the mood for the poem to follow.

2.  Exchange tapes with other groups and try to identify the readers of each poem.

3.  As a class talk about this activity.
    a.  How successful were you in identifying voices?
    b.  What clues allowed you to identify voices? Which ones caused you to make mistakes?
    c.  Was it easier to identify the natural voices or the disguised voices? Why?

## *Activity 16G    Distinguishing Sounds in Your Environment*

1. Form groups of about five students and prepare an audiotape of environmental sounds. Select about a dozen sounds from your environment such as someone walking, a door closing, someone skipping.
   a. Be sure to leave about twelve seconds between sounds as you record them. You might also give each sound a number.

2. Exchange tapes with other small groups and try to identify the sounds.

3. As a class talk about what clues you used to identify each sound.

   *Variation*: Turn this activity into a contest. Each group prepares an answer sheet for its tape, making enough copies for every student in the class. Exchange tapes among all the groups to see which group is able to correctly identify the greatest number of sounds.

# Listening for Appreciation

Sometimes the purpose for listening to something is for enjoyment or appreciation. This enjoyment may come from letting the words flow over you without much thought. Or it may come as a result of careful listening to catch specific details. The activities in this section ask you to listen carefully to catch the precise details of written work.

## *Activity 16H    "Perspective"*

1. Listen while someone reads the poem "Perspective" to you twice.

2. After you have heard the poem a second time, answer the following questions:
   a. What scene is described in the poem?
   b. How does the poet describe the hayloft? the hay?
   c. What are the four reasons the poet gives to explain why it was always the father who said, *"time for a rest"*?

3. What does the title of the poem mean?

**Perspective**

My mother in the hayrack
pitching the hay up
into the black box of the loft
where my father's pitchfork took it,
tossed it to the back;
a synchronism asserting itself
through the dry slither of hay,
the pivot of her fork, his fork,
the fulcrum of arm and necessity

until my father's voice—never hers—
saying, *time for a rest*,
and why should I still need to know

if it was because he tired first
or if it was not her right to choose?
And tugging up lately in myself,
like fresh forksful of hay,
a third possibility,
that she refused to give in first,
and a fourth,
that he knew this
and stopped for her sake—
unnerving me
with the increasing complexities
of their lives.

Leona Gom

## Activity 16I  Listening to Poetry

1. Find a poem that suggests a vivid picture, something a listener
   can easily visualize.
   a. Read it to a small group or the whole class. After listening to
      the poem, ask the listeners to draw a picture describing the
      scene. Talk about the results. Can you understand from the
      picture what the listener has heard? Is it what you expected
      the listener to hear?

2. Find a short poem or a section of a poem that has a very strong
   rhythm or beat to it.
   a. Read it with expression to your small group or class.
   b. Then ask the listeners to write a line of their own, using the
      same rhythm.
   c. Compare lines to see if other writers have used the same
      rhythm.

## Activity 16J  Dialogue

1. Find a passage from a novel or short story in which two characters are speaking.
   a. Read your passage to a small group, omitting any words or
      phrases that tell what these characters are like.
   b. Ask the students to tell you what the characters are like by just
      listening to the dialogue.

Resource Chapter

# Listening to Help a Friend

When you listen to something like a speech or a television commercial, you listen critically, to evaluate and form an opinion. But when you talk with friends, you do not necessarily judge what they say. Rather, you try to really hear what they are saying, to make certain that you understand. You are completely non-judgmental as you listen. Often what you do is let your friends speak while you act as a sounding board to allow them to discuss their problems, opinions, or ideas.

One of the basic skills in non-judgmental listening is the **paraphrase**. You say back to your friends what you understand they have said to you. This skill tells your friends that you have heard and understood, and encourages them to go on. The next activity gives you practice in paraphrasing.

## *Activity 16K    Helping Friends*

1. **Form pairs and decide who will be Student A and who will be Student B.**

2. **Student A thinks of a topic that he or she has strong opinions or feelings about.**

   *Examples*:

   > • **unemployment**
   > • **world hunger**
   > • **the environment**
   > • **war**
   > • **classical music**

   Student A then talks to Student B about this topic for one minute.

3. **At the end of Student A's talk, Student B paraphrases it. Student B's task is to summarize, without comment or judgment, what Student A said—to give both the content and the feelings.**

4. **Repeat this activity with Student B presenting the one-minute talk.**

   *Extension*: Repeat several of the more successful talks and paraphrases in a *gold-fish bowl*. That is, different pairs of students volunteer to do their talk and paraphrase as the whole class watches. Often the speakers sit in the centre of a circle, with the other members of the class watching. When the talk and paraphrase are finished, the whole class talks about the one experience. You might ask such questions as these: Did the listener do a

Sometimes friends want to talk over a problem with you. In such cases it is your role to listen to what they are saying. Often you don't have to give answers, but only provide your friends with a chance to talk about what is concerning them. In other words, your friends will find their answers not from what you say but from what they say. You may occasionally give an idea of your own but, more important, you should help your friends find their own conclusions. The box below gives you some hints that will help you be a good listener for a friend.

---

### Listen to Help a Friend

- Be sure to look at your friend and maintain eye contact.

- Give non-verbal signals that you are listening such as nodding your head.

- Give your friend verbal signals that you are listening by saying such things as "I see," or "Yes," or "Go on," or "I know how you feel."

- Ask questions that show you are listening and understand what your friend is saying.

- Occasionally paraphrase or say in your own words what your friend is saying. Paraphrasing lets your friend know that you are listening and understanding.

- Concentrate on letting your friend talk and say whatever is important to him or her. This is not really your conversation.

---

## *Activity 16L  For a Friend*

1. On your own, think of a topic or problem that interests you. Write rapidly about your topic for three minutes in your notebook. Explore as many possible angles of this topic as you can. Try to state at least four different points about it. For example, you could write about

    technological society
    the future
    community needs
    careers
    a problem of yours that you are willing to discuss with others

2. Divide into pairs and decide who is Student A and who is Student B.

3. Student B will begin to talk about his or her chosen topic. However, he or she should only volunteer two points about the topic initially.

4. Student A should listen to student B. She or he must use the techniques given in the box above to get Student B to say more about the topic. Student A should paraphrase Student B's comments and then ask questions to get Student B to say more about his or her topic.

5. Student B should keep track of all the points being brought out by making brief notes on each point.
   *Note*: Questions 3 and 4 should not take longer than five minutes to complete.

6. With your partner compare the points brought out in the discussion with those Student B had originally written down in question 1.
   a. Was Student A able to get Student B to talk about all the points he or she had written down in question 1?
   b. Was Student A able to get Student B to discover additional points not considered in question 1?
   c. Was Student A a good listener?

7. Repeat this activity with Student A talking and Student B listening.

   *Extension*: Use the *goldfish bowl technique* to watch two or three listening sessions. Appoint some members of the class to record the questions used by the listener. Others should note the paraphrases, and still others should keep track of the verbal and nonverbal signals used by the listener.

## Putting It All Together

### *Activity 16M    Listen and Write*

1. With your textbook closed, listen as someone reads Passage A, "Outlaw," by Sinclair Ross to you twice.

2. With your textbook still closed, write in your notebook as much

of this passage as you can remember. Include as many of the words and sentences from the passage as you can.

3. Open your textbook and compare your version to the original below.

4. Over the next few weeks, repeat this activity with the remaining passages B to D below. Or use paragraphs from other books you are using in class, such as your literature or social studies textbooks.

## Passage A

She was beautiful but dangerous. She had thrown one man and killed him, thrown another and broken his collar bone, and my parents, as if they knew what the sight of her idle in her stall was doing to me, never let a day go by without giving lurid details, everything from splints and stitches to the undertaker, of the painful and untimely end in store for me should I ever take it into my fool young head to try to ride her.

Sinclair Ross, "Outlaw"

## Passage B

Passage B is taken from "The Foxes of Beachy Cove." In this paragraph, Harold Horwood, a Newfoundland writer, describes the annual run of the caplin that seem to flood the beaches.

The beaches that the caplin left behind were littered with the debris of their living and of their dying. But the sea has its own ways of cleansing its shores. First came the gulls and the terns in wheeling flocks, squabbling and calling, inviting their fellows to share the feast, then trying to drive them off when they arrived. The tiny rock crabs and sand spiders ate the scraps. When the feast was done, a spring tide came in, washing the sand, the pebbles, the water-worn boulders, then retreating slowly past the line of the kelp on the offshore shallows. When dawn broke once more, the beach lay clean and empty and scoured, as though the drama of life and birth and death had never been played out on its rocks.

Harold Horwood, "The Foxes of Beachy Cove"

## Passage C

The sun burned a hole in the sky and sent its thermal rays into the bare fields between the trees. The air was tense and still, as if every living organism was hoarding its strength for something vague but promised by the quiet day. Now and then Marcel Boudreau stopped his labors between the rows of yellowing leaves that topped the potato plants, and

Resource Chapter

looked above the boundary of spruce and fir trees into the north-west sky.

Around the small cleared patch of farmland the wooded hills that skirt the Gaspé Coast had the appearance of a dirty patched fur rug laid in massive folds by some forgotten giant hand. From the ridges of the hills to the narrow valley in which the homestead lay, the thick forest growth was yellow interspersed with the still heavy green of the coniferous trees.

Hugh Garner, "Red Racer"

### Passage D

When the mountains beyond the city are covered with snow to the base, the late afternoon light falling obliquely from the west upon the long slopes discloses new contours. For a few moments of time the austerity vanishes, and the mountains appear innocently folded in furry white. Their daily look has gone. For these few moments the slanting rays curiously discover each separate tree behind each separate tree behind each separate tree in the infinite white forests. Then the light fades, and the familiar mountains resume their daily look again. The light has gone, but those who have seen it will remember.

Ethel Wilson, "Hurry, hurry"

## *Activity 16N    Review*

1. **What kind of listening activity is involved in each of the following situations? Here is a list of the four possible listening activities:**
   - **understanding and evaluating**
   - **discriminating sounds**
   - **helping friends**
   - **appreciating**
   a) **You listen to a lecture by a police officer on proper attitudes toward driving.**
   b) **You listen to a poet read from his or her own work at a poetry reading.**
   c) **You listen to the Prime Minister on television.**
   d) **You listen to a politician deliver a campaign speech.**
   e) **You listen to the radio as you do your homework.**
   f) **You attend a rock concert in a big city.**
   g) **You listen as a friend talks about the death of a favourite pet.**
   h) **You listen as a stranger gives you directions to the home of a new friend.**
   i) **As the conductor of an orchestra, you listen to check whether or not an instrument is tuned correctly.**

j) You listen to hear your dog bark to tell you it wants to be let into your house.

2. On your own, write a set of directions in which one vital piece of information is missing. For example,

   To get to the next service station, you drive two kilometres down this highway. Turn when you see the sign for Truro. There are Esso and Gulf stations just beyond the entrance.

   a. Working in small groups of three or four, each member reads his or her set of directions aloud. The other members of the group listen to discover the missing detail.

3. Each group prepares a set of directions, with two vital facts missing. The set should be more complex than the directions you created for question 2.

   a. Plan a group reading of your directions. Each member should read at least one direction.

   b. As each group reads, the other groups listen for the missing information.

4. Prepare an audiotaped lecture of about six minutes on a topic that interests you.

   a. Prepare a quiz of comprehension questions based on your lecture and distribute it to your classmates.

   b. Play your tape for the class. The students should listen without looking at the question sheet. When the tape is finished, they should answer the questions.

   c. Correct the answers and talk about the results. What about your lecture made it easy for students to answer the questions? What made it hard? What have you learned about delivering a lecture so that you make it easier for the audience to listen to it and remember the details?

   *Variation*: For some audiotapes, let students look at the prepared questions as the tape is presented. Does knowing the questions improve the number that students can answer correctly? Why?

5. Bring a selection of music and play it for the class. Tell the class what they should listen for in the music so that they can listen more appreciatively.

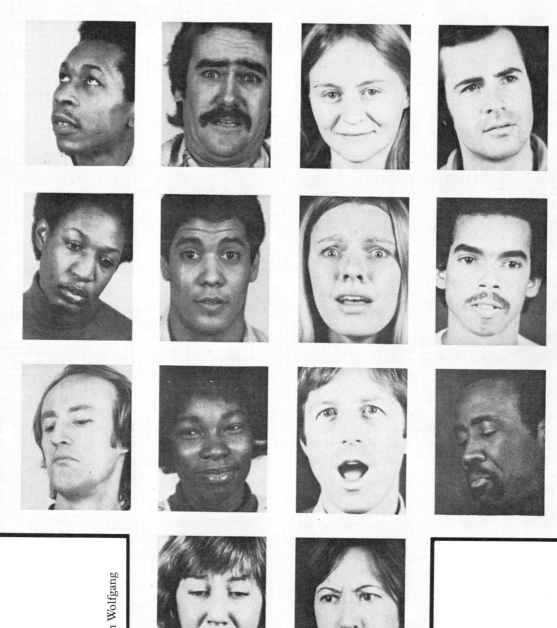

*Face Test, Aaron Wolfgang*

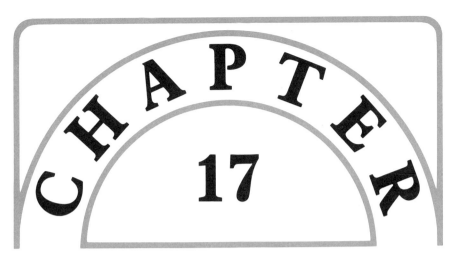

# RESOURCE CHAPTER
# VISUAL LITERACY

Stop for a moment and think about how you receive information from your environment. Certainly you listen quite a bit, and you read. But a lot of the information you receive comes from viewing. Here's a list of places in your environment from which you receive visual information.

| | |
|---|---|
| • photographs | • signs |
| • billboards | • films |
| • television | • comics |
| • slides | • cartoons |
| • architecture | • sculpture |
| • paintings | • posters |

## Activity 17A    Viewing

1. As a class, add other sources to this list from which you receive visual information.

2. Discuss how each source communicates information visually.

3. Form small groups to make a visual display of one of these sources. Show how it communicates information visually.

The purpose of this Resource Chapter is to help you explore the idea of visual literacy and to consider how some sources in your environment communicate visually.

Resource Chapter

# NON-VERBAL COMMUNICATION

A very significant part of your visual environment is **non-verbal communication**—the messages people send out without speaking.

## Activity 17B    Face Test

1. Study the faces on page 262.

2. In your notebook, write down the emotion that each face expresses. (You can check your answers on page 279.)

3. In small groups, practise making facial expressions to communicate different emotions. Try to express as large a range of emotions as possible.

4. As a group, make up a *face test* for the rest of your class. Use your own facial expressions as the test.

## Activity 17C    Body Test

1. In small groups, practise communicating non-verbally through your body stance—the way you stand or sit.

2. Create a group *body-stance test* to quiz the rest of your classmates by posing in a *still-photograph picture* in which members of the group take various body poses. The combination of the poses should make a statement or a story about something.

People usually stand at a certain distance from each other. The distance varies depending on the circumstances. If they know each other well, or if they are arguing, they tend to stand closer together. People who are uncomfortable with each other will stand further apart. The amount of space around people with which they are comfortable varies from one culture to another and different cultures have different reactions to the distance between people.

## Activity 17D    Stand Off

1. Watch a television programme or short film with the sound turned off.

2. Keep track of how far apart the characters are in relation to each other. Use this information to determine the characters' emotional involvement.

3. Be prepared to talk about your conclusions in class.

---

### *Activity 17E    Colour Me Beautiful*

1. As a class, list the emotional responses people often associate with various colours. For example, red—danger.

2. Look at the way colour is used in your environment.
   a. Examine the colours in your classroom and school. Why were these colours chosen?
   b. Do you like to wear clothes of a particular colour? Why?
   c. Watch a film or television programme to see how the director uses colour to communicate meaning. Look particularly at the dress of the characters.
   d. What is your favourite colour for a car? Why?

3. Talk about your responses as a whole class.

---

# VISUAL THINKING

Most of the time you think with words because you live in a verbal world. Other times, however, you think with shapes and images. You sometimes use this skill when you watch television or film, or read poetry or fiction.

In Chapter 11 on report writing, you practised the skill of classification by finding ways to cluster words and ideas together. The next activity asks you to do the same thing with visual symbols.

---

### *Activity 17F    Visual Classification*

1. Study the symbols in the following illustration.

2. How many ways can you think of to group or cluster these symbols?
   *Remember*: To classify these symbols, you must find a common characteristic, or attribute, that each symbol in the cluster has.

3. Share your classifications with your class and explain the common attribute that each classification has.

## Activity 17G  Visual Memory

1. For thirty seconds, study the box below.

2. Then close your book and continue with some other task for at least ten minutes.

3. Without looking again at the box below, turn to page 268 and decide which box is identical to it. Record the number of your choice in your notebook.

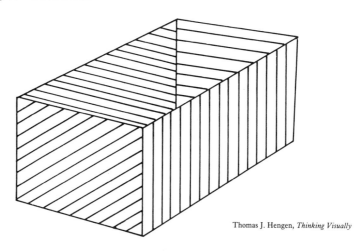

Thomas J. Hengen, *Thinking Visually*

4. Look on page 279 to check your answer. How well were you able to remember the visual details?

5. Create your own visual memory puzzles for your classmates.

People who write advertisements for TV and magazines often appeal to their audience through visual images. To do this they depend upon the viewer's ability to understand and remember visual pictures, or **images**.

Let's suppose an advertising agency has been hired by a new company to create a TV commercial to sell white socks—plain old socks that you wear on your feet. Anyone can wear these socks—male or female, from aged ten to seventy or more. The only thing at all unique about these socks is a coloured ring around the top.

To design an effective advertisement for these socks, the agency has to display them in a setting that makes the potential buyers feel good about the socks and have a pleasant memory about what they saw. (A catchy sound track would help the overall impact, too.)

In other words, the agency would have to analyze its audience and find a TV image that would appeal equally to all audiences from ten to seventy or more. The advertising writer would have to first prompt this audience to classify the visual image, then associate it with something pleasant and finally remember it.

This process may sound like a far-fetched task, but it's not. Advertising agencies create advertisements like this example all the time. The only difference might be that they appeal to a smaller age range of people.

## *Activity 17H   Look at Advertisements...*

1. Analyze ten television advertisements by noting the product sold in each one and the main visual image(s) associated with it.

2. Collect four advertisements from four different magazines. Be prepared to show them to your classmates and point out the product being sold in each one and the main visual images created to sell it.

3. As a class, make a list of the common items advertisers use as visual images to sell products to young people.
   a. Analyze your list to determine the five most common visual images advertisers use to sell products to teenagers.
   b. What is the appeal of these five visual images?

Writers of poems, plays and novels also use visual images in much the same way that advertising writers do. They can't show you objects visually, of course, but they do mention and describe people, objects and settings in their works. Readers react to their descriptions, forming a visual memory that they associate with the visual description.

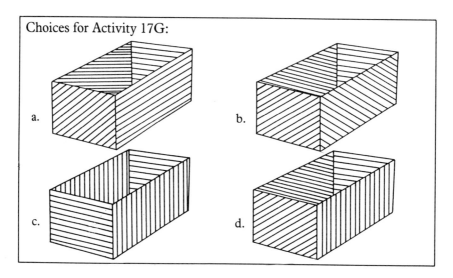

Choices for Activity 17G:

a.

b.

c.

d.

## *Activity 17I   Look at Books...*

1. What would be your mental association if you read an introductory paragraph for a short story that mentioned
   a. a loaded gun lying on a coffee table
   b. daffodils and blue water
   c. spiders
   d. tall, dark trees with hanging vines
   e. sheep
   f. a pin cushion

2. Each member of your class should choose to look at one piece of literature with each person choosing a different piece. You could limit your choice to those literary works that the whole class has read.
   a. Read only the first hundred words and list the main items mentioned. Look for descriptions of objects, scenery, the clothing people wear, and so on.
   b. Skim the whole writing quickly to remind yourself about its plot or main ideas.
   c. Be prepared to explain to your class the relationship, or lack of it, between the item(s) you listed in part a. and the main intent of the literary work.

3. As a class, talk about your findings. What can you decide about the way authors use images in their writing?

4. Your class should divide into two groups. One half will be assigned Set One and the other, Set Two.

    a. On your own, write an introductory paragraph for a short story. Your paragraph must contain at least six of the words listed in your set of words.

| Set One: | | | |
|---|---|---|---|
| midnight | rain | thunder | mud road |
| blackness | wind | wolf | shadow(s) |
| **Set Two:** | | | |
| sun | noon | field | green grass |
| stream | breeze | deer | singing birds |

    b. Listen as several students assigned Set One read their paragraphs.
       • What is the overall feeling or mood created by each paragraph?
       • Based on the opening paragraph, what do you think the rest of the short story will be about?
       • Is there a common pattern for all of the paragraphs written for Set One?
    c. Repeat part b. for the paragraphs written with the words in Set Two.

5. As a class, summarize the ideas you have presented about the relationship between *setting*—the description of place, things and characters—and the plot of a short story.

# CARTOONS

Almost everyone is attracted to a good cartoon. Cartoonists not only amuse their audience, they frequently comment on contemporary social concerns. Cartoonists often have more impact with a simple drawing than writers have with many words. Cartoons are interesting for not only what is said in them but how it is said.

## *Activity 17J   Social Cartoons*

1. What does the following cartoon say about life in modern society?

2. How does the cartoonist make this statement? Is the cartoonist in favour of increasing the use of computers in society? How do you know?

"But I don't *want* to be a computer programmer!"

3. a. What comment does this cartoon make about life today?
   b. Do you agree with the cartoonist's view of modern life?

## *Activity 17K  Non-verbal Cartoons*

Some cartoons use no words whatever to deliver their message.

1. Look at the cartoon below. Do you find it funny? Try putting this cartoon into words. Does it still retain its humour?

2. Can you put this cartoon into words and still retain its humour?

   a. What social comment is this cartoon making?

   b. Do you think this cartoon is effective in commenting on a modern problem?  →

Resource Chapter

Political cartoonists are a special kind of cartoonist. They comment on the political affairs of a nation. Often they have more impact on public opinion than the editorial writers do who use only words.

## Activity 17L   Political Cartoons

**The cartoon below appeared in April, 1984, just before the Summer Olympic Games in Los Angeles.**

1. **Study this cartoon and then decide on the political situation behind it.**
   a. **What is the cartoonist saying?**
   b. **What political message is this cartoon saying?**

2. **Look at the following cartoon and decide on its message. Do you think it is an effective cartoon?**

## Activity 17M    Political Cartoons—A Comparison

The first cartoon (a.) on page 274 was published in the magazine *Grip* on September 30, 1876. It was created by J.W. Bengough, an important cartoonist in Canadian history.

1. What do you think this cartoon is about?

2. The second cartoon (b.) on page 275, published in *The Hamilton Spectator*, June 12, 1984, comments on the retirement of Prime Minister Trudeau. What statement does this cartoon make about Mr. Trudeau?

3. Compare the Bengough cartoon from 1876 with the Blair cartoon from 1984.
   a. Why does the Bengough cartoon contain more detail than the Blair cartoon?
   b. Why are the faces in the Bengough cartoon more realistic than the one in the Blair cartoon?
   c. Which cartoon do you consider to be the more successful? Why?

CONFEDERATION!
The Much-Fathered Youngster.

b.

So much for the traditional image of retirement......

# PAINTINGS

Just as cartoons comment on ideas, paintings express thoughts and feelings. With paintings, however, the technique of the artist plays an important part.

## *Activity 17N   Paintings*

1. Study the following painting by A.Y. Jackson.
   a. What does it tell you about the Quebec countryside where Jackson painted it?
   b. What was Jackson's attitude toward *Charlevoix County*? How do you know?

*Winter, Charlevoix County*, A.Y. Jackson

*Modern Times*, Nathan Petroff

2. Look at Petroff's painting, *Modern Times*. This painting was completed in 1937, at the bleakest point of the Great Depression of the 1930s.
   a. Describe the subject of this painting. What is she doing? Why? How do you know?
   b. Does she express an attitude of hope or of despair? How do you know?
   c. What kind of statement is *Modern Times* making about the people most affected by the depression? What might be their attitude to this painting? Why?

# PHOTOGRAPHS

The photograph on the next page has a most unlikely subject—an old building in the middle of a prairie winter. But still there is much pleasure in this photograph.

## Activity 17O    A Winter Look

1. Look carefully at the photograph on page 278 for about two minutes as you answer these questions.
   a. Why did the photographer place the old building toward the left side? What is the effect of having the building there?
   b. What is below the old building? How does it appear in the photograph? How does this part of the photograph affect you?

Resource Chapter

Peter Wilson/*Saskatoon Star-Phoenix*

   c. **What is the sky like? How does this part of the photograph contrast with the rest of it?**

   d. **What is the effect of the sun in this photograph?**

2. **What impression of a prairie winter does this photograph suggest?**

3. **Have a second look at the response you wrote for question 1. Do you still agree with what you wrote?**

## *Activity 17P   A Visual Response*

1. **Choose one of the two paintings from Activity 17N or the photograph from Activity 17O as the visual image that you would like to think about further.**

2. **Look intently at this picture for several minutes.**

3. **In your notebook, write about this picture. You cannot write more than one hundred words. Use as much description and imagery in this writing as you can.**

4. **Edit and proofread your writing to make it as mechanically correct as possible. If necessary, you may want to rewrite your work.**

5. Next, communicate visually the same thing that your writing is saying. You might do this in one of several ways.
   a. Use a camera to take a picture(s) that communicates your feelings and ideas.
   b. Draw a picture yourself with pencil or perhaps pastels. Your work could be realistic or abstract.
   c. Construct a collage of images collected from old magazines and newspapers.
   d. Cut or tear coloured paper into shapes and use them to construct your visual response.

6. As a whole class or in small groups, examine students' responses.
   a. Are students more successful at responding in writing or with visual images?
   b. Do some students in the class respond better in writing than they do visually? Do some respond better visually than they do in writing?

7. As a class, talk about your visual responses. How important is it for students to have the opportunity to respond visually?

# Look Again

This chapter has helped you look at your environment visually. You will no doubt agree that there is a great deal of information there; all you have to do is learn to look for it.

In this chapter, you considered several aspects of visual communication: non-verbal communication (remember the face test at the beginning of the chapter), visual thinking, several kinds of cartoons—non-verbal cartoons, social cartoons, political cartoons—as well as the visual components of paintings and photographs.

You should now be able to consider this part of your visual environment with more appreciation than you did previously. Perhaps you can use your new information to look more closely at other aspects of your visual environment.

**Answers to Activity 17B**

| Happy – H | Anger – A | Answers from left to right: I, F, H, I, |
| Sad – SA | Contempt – C | SA, SU, F, A, C, H, SU, C, SA, A |
| Fear – F | Interest – I | |
| Surprise – SU | | **Answer to Activity 17G:** d. |

a.

b.

Can you identify these athletes from Canada's Sports Hall of Fame?

c.

d.

a. Terry Fox   b. Helen Vanderburg   c. Hilda May Binns   d. Nancy Greene

# RESOURCE CHAPTER
# SENTENCE COMBINING 1

# HE SHOOTS! HE SCORES!

## A Look at the Basic Sentence

*"He shoots! He scores!"* These two sentences are the shortest, yet most powerful of any in Canadian sport. When you hear them, you are filled with joy or disappointment—depending on which team you are cheering for.

How would you react if you heard an announcer describe a professional hockey game like this:

> He, with one skillful about-face and tremendous effort, shoots the puck at the heavily defended goal! He, with great luck and a mighty swing of his stick, positively scores!

It's not quite the same as *"He shoots! He scores!"*, is it? There's nothing wrong with the grammatical structure of the longer version. But in this example, the short version is more appropriate.

Long or short sentences are not correct in themselves. Rather, the length of a sentence depends on what you are saying. When you write, you must make choices about the kinds of sentences you need.

Resource Chapter

# Subjects and Predicates

Sometimes, the **basic sentence**—the simple subject and predicate—is the most appropriate choice.

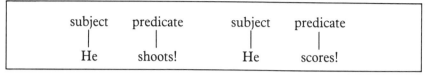

The subject and the predicate of a sentence are the basic building blocks of writing.

## *Activity 18A    Subjects and Predicates*

**In this activity, you will work with some sentences about outstanding Canadian athletes.**

1. **Match the subjects on the left with the correct predicates on the right.**

2. **Write the complete sentence in your notebook, drawing a line between the subject and the predicate.**

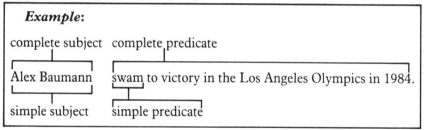

| Subjects | Predicates |
|---|---|
| 1. Harry Jerome | a. held the world bantamweight boxing title in the early twentieth century. |
| 2. Johnny Coulon | b. have been called one of the most remarkable and successful basketball teams the sport has ever known. |
| 3. The Edmonton Grads | c. accumulated 29 goals and 35 assists in his rookie year with the NHL. |
| 4. Marilyn Bell | d. was Canada's swiftest sprinter in the 1960s. |
| 5. Guy Lafleur | e. was sixteen years old the night she swam across Lake Ontario. |

## *Activity 18B   Subjects and Predicates—Again*

1. Turn to the photographs of Canadian athletes on page 280.

2. In your notebook, write one sentence about each picture. Make certain that each sentence has a subject and a predicate.

3. Divide each sentence into its complete subject and complete predicate. Draw a single line under the simple subject of each sentence and a double line under each simple predicate.

# Expanding the Basic Sentence

Good athletes practise for hours and hours so they can make the right moves at the right time. In the same way, you can practise writing sentences so that you know how to build the right sentence for every occasion.

In this section, you will practise many different ways to expand a basic sentence. Once you have mastered the various methods, you can always build exactly the kind of sentence you want.

One of the easiest ways you can expand a basic sentence is by using **joining words**, or **conjunctions**. Conjunctions link together the ideas expressed in two basic sentences.

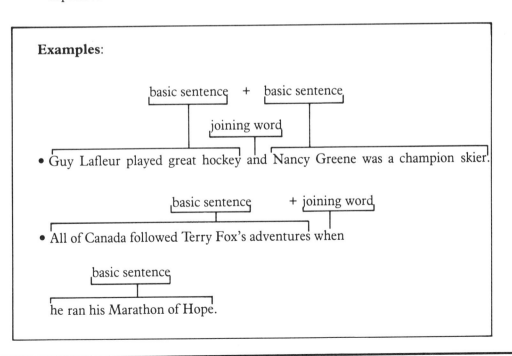

**Examples**:

basic sentence   +   basic sentence
              joining word
• Guy Lafleur played great hockey and Nancy Greene was a champion skier.

          basic sentence   + joining word
• All of Canada followed Terry Fox's adventures when

    basic sentence
he ran his Marathon of Hope.

Four basic types of joining words are listed below.

---

### Set A—coordinating conjunctions

- and
- nor
- for

- but
- yet

- or
- so

### Set B—correlative conjunctions

- both...and
- not only...but also

- either...or

- neither...nor

### Set C—subordinate conjunctions (adverb)

- after
- before
- since
- when
- until

- although
- except
- than
- where
- as

- because
- if
- though
- while
- unless

### Set D—subordinate conjunctions (adjective)

- who

- which

- that

---

As you proceed through this chapter, you will work with each of these sets of joining words. Right now, you'll start with Set A.

Look at the two basic sentences below:

---

- Helen Vanderburg is a synchronized swimmer.
- She achieved international fame in her sport.

---

You have a choice as a writer. You could add these two sentences to a paragraph you are writing exactly as they are written here. Or you could combine them. To give you specific practice using joining words, try adding one word from Set A:

---

- Helen Vanderburg is a synchronized swimmer.
- She achieved international fame in her sport.

                                               (combine...and)

---

This signal system tells you to join these two sentences using *and*.

*Rewrite*:

> Helen Vanderburg is a synchronized swimmer **and** she achieved international fame in her sport.

You can also make sentence combinations using joining words from Set C.

> • Helen Vanderburg won eight gold and five silver medals.
> • She was twenty years old.          (combine...before)

This combined sentence is the result.

*Rewrite*:

> Helen Vanderburg won eight gold and five silver medals **before** she was twenty years old.

It's time now for you to practise sentence combining, using joining words from Set A and Set C.

## *Activity 18C    She shoots! She scores!*

In this activity, you will be working with coordinating conjunctions (Set A) and subordinating conjunctions (Set C).

1. Use the combining signals to join the following basic sentences. Rewrite them in your notebook.

    a. She shoots!
       She scores!        (combine...and)
    b. She shoots!
       She scores!        (combine...but)
                          (combine...yet)
    c. She scores!
       She shoots!        (combine...when)
                          (combine...because)
                          (combine...whenever)
                          (combine...as soon as)
                          (combine...after)

2. Rewrite the sentences in part c. by changing the two parts around to create a different *syntax* or order of words.

*Example*:

> *She scores when she shoots* could become *When she shoots, she scores.*

3. In your notebook, write a statement explaining what this sentence-combining exercise teaches you about sentences and sentence parts, or syntax.

## Activity 18D    *More Practice*

1. Following the combining signals, write each sentence in your notebook.
   *Note*: The signal ✕ indicates you leave out the crossed-out word in your rewrite of the sentence.

*Example*:

> - Helen Vanderburg practised her swimming five hours a day.
>
> - ~~She~~ ~~practised~~ seven days a week
>
>                                    (combine...,)    Use this punctuation in your sentence.
>
> - ~~She~~ ~~practised~~ eleven months a year.
>
>                                    (combine..., and)
>
> - She was training for championship meets.
>
>                                    (combine...when)

*Rewrite*:

> Helen Vanderburg practised her swimming five hours a day, seven days a week, and eleven months a year when she was training for championship meets.

a. Helen Vanderburg did weight training.
   ~~She~~ attended dance classes.     (combine...and)
   She practised her swimming.     (combine...while)

b. Helen Vanderburg began synchronized swimming at the age of eleven.
She won her first individual gold medal at the Olympics in 1984.
(combine ... and)

c. Helen had to practise swimming instead of going to parties with her friends.
She was a teenager. (combine ... when)

d. In 1975 the Calgary YWCA Aquabelles team won the Canadian team title.
Helen and her teammates earned a trip to Mexico City.
(combine ... and)
The Pan American Games were being held in Mexico City.
(combine ... where)

e. They took the Silver Medal in Mexico City.
The next year they won the Silver Medal at the Pan Pacific Games in Japan. (combine ... and)

f. In synchronized swimming ▲ the most difficult task is staying under water for long periods.
You spend almost fifty percent of your time under water.
(combine ... ▲, where ... ,)

*Note*: The **caret** ▲ tells you where to place the joining word.

## Other Ways to Combine Sentences

There are other ways to combine basic sentences. They include the following structures:

> • prepositional phrases     • adjective clauses
> • appositive phrases

**Prepositional Phrases**
Here are examples of prepositional phrases:
- He shoots *behind the net.*     (preposition + noun)
- She scores *in every game.*     (preposition + noun)
- He scores *against him.*     (preposition + pronoun)
- She scores *into the waiting net.*     (preposition + adjective + noun)

The first word in a prepositional phrase is always a preposition. Prepositions signal that a phrase will follow. You have to be careful because some prepositions can also be used as joining words or conjunctions. But this 'problem' will be discussed more later.

Here is a list of prepositions:

- after, against, along, among, around, at
- before, behind, below, beneath, beside, besides, between, beyond
- despite, down, during
- except, for, from
- in, inside, into, like, near
- of, off, on, onto, out, outside, over
- round, through, throughout, to, toward
- under, underneath, until, up, upon
- with, within, without

## Activity 18E   Prepositional Phrases

1. Using the signals, combine the following groups of sentences. Write your answers in your notebook.

2. The signal *prep* indicates you should use a prepositional phrase in your rewrite of the sentences.

*Example*:

Canadians distinguished themselves.

They were *at the 1984 Olympic Games*

The games were *in Los Angeles*.   (combine...prep)

(combine...prep)

*Rewrite*:

Canadians distinguished themselves *at the 1984 Olympic Games in Los Angeles*.

a. Canadian swimmers, boxers, divers, cyclists, and paddlers became champions.
   They became champions of world standing.
   (combine...prep)
   They became champions during the fifteen days of the 1984 Olympic Games.   (combine...prep)

Now, try the following questions with no delete signal ✕ and no caret ▲.

b. The medals won continued the record begun by speedskater Gaetan Boucher.
The medals were won at the Los Angeles Games.
(combine ... prep)
Boucher won at the 1984 Winter Olympics.
(combine ... prep)
The Winter Olympics were in Sarajevo, Yugoslavia.
(combine ... prep)

c. At the 1984 Summer Olympics, Canada made an outstanding impression.
Canada ended up with 10 gold, 17 silver, and 16 bronze medals.
(combine ... prep)
The impression was on the world athletic scene.
(combine ... prep)
Canadian athletes were proud.
(combine ... and)

## Adjective Clauses and Appositive Phrases

**Adjective clauses** and **appositive phrases** modify or describe nouns and pronouns in either the subject or the predicate of a basic sentence. They can give a sentence the texture it needs to make it sound complete or better. Look at the example below.

> Louis Cyr, *who was Canada's famous strong man,* was born in 1863.

Adjective clauses begin with *who, that, which,* and sometimes *whom.* These words are the **joining words** listed in Set D on page 284.

The following chart shows you how to use these joining words.

| Join Word | Used To Replace |
|-----------|-----------------|
| who | people |
| that | people or things |
| which | things |
| whom | people |

Shortened adjective clauses become **appositive phrases**.

adjective clause

Louis Cyr, who was Canada's famous strong man, was born in 1863.

appositive phrase

Watch what happens when this sentence is reduced to its basic statements:

- Louis Cyr ▲ was born in 1863.

- Louis Cyr was Canada's famous strong man.
                                    (combine . . . app ▲)

*Note*: The joining signal **app** stands for appositive phrase. Appositive phrases are usually set off from the rest of a basic sentence with commas.

Louis Cyr, *Canada's famous strong man*, was born in 1863.

*Note*: Some adjective clauses are also set off by commas. They are called **non-restrictive adjective clauses**. They add extra information to a basic sentence, information that is not essential to understanding the meaning of the sentence.

non-restrictive adjective clause

- Louis Cyr, who was Canada's famous strong man, was born in 1863.

The information is not needed to understand the meaning of the basic sentence.

Adjective clauses that are needed to complete the meaning of the basic sentence are called **restrictive adjective clauses**. They are not set off with commas.

restrictive adjective clause

A famous strongman who is shown in the photograph was born in 1863.

This information is required so that you can completely understand the basic sentence.

At the peak of strength, Louis Cyr stood 179 cm tall and weighed 143 kg. His chest circumference was close to his height, being 153 cm. Legs were 84 cm around the thighs and 68 cm at the calf; biceps 61 cm and forearms 48 cm; waist 114 cm and neck 56 cm.

## Activity 18F    Adjective Clauses and Appositives

1. Combine each of the following groups of sentences in two ways.
   a. First, create an adjective clause.
   b. Second, create an appositive phrase.

2. Write your sentences in your notebook and label the adjective clauses and appositive phrases.

*Example*:

> Louis Cyr ▲ was known as the strongest man in the world.
> Louis Cyr was almost as wide as he was tall.
>
> > a. (combine... ▲who...)
> > b. (combine... ▲app...)

*Rewrite*:

> adjective phrase
>
> a. Louis Cyr, *who was almost as wide as he was tall,* was known as the strongest man in the world.
>
> appositive phrase
>
> b. Louis Cyr, *almost as wide as he was tall,* was known as the strongest man in the world.

a. Louis Cyr ▲ is still known as a strong man.
   Louis Cyr was a Québecois.
   > (combine... ▲who...,)
   > (combine... ▲,app...,)

b. Louis Cyr ▲ performed amazing feats of strength.
   Louis Cyr was known as the Canadian Samson.
   > (combine... ▲, who...,)
   > (combine... ▲, app...,)

Now try the following without any combining signals.

c. Cyr could do a backlift of 1755 kg.
   Cyr was a short man.
   Cyr weighed 127.4 kg.

d. Cyr could lift 224 kg off the ground.
   He could lift this weight with one finger.
   Cyr was a human dynamo.
   Cyr had 61 cm biceps and a 152 cm chest.

Louis Cyr, the strong man from Quebec, certainly surpasses even most Olympic weight lifting contenders today. Look at some more of his feats of strength as you work further with adjective clauses, appositive phrases, and prepositional phrases.

## Activity 18G    Review: Adjective Clauses, Appositive Phrases, Prepositional Phrases

1. Using the joining signals given, combine the following basic sentences.

2. As the activity progresses, there will be fewer combining signals. Near the end, you will find yourself making all of your own combining choices.

*Note*: There is a new signal added in this activity, $\boldsymbol{P}$ . It tells you that a pronoun should be substituted for a noun.

a. Louis's mother could carry a 90 kg sack ▲.
   The sack was filled with flour.
                                    (combine . . . that)
   She carried the sack on her shoulder.
                                    (combine . . . ▲prep)
   Louis's mother was also a strong person.
                                    (combine . . . app)

b. ▲ Louis became a farm worker.
   $\boldsymbol{P}$ Louis was twelve years old.      (combine . . . ▲when)
   Louis could do any chore the older farmhands could do.
                                    (combine . . . who)

c. Louis Cyr ▲ helped establish order and quiet.
   $\boldsymbol{P}$ Louis served as a police officer.
   Louis served in Montreal.
   Louis served in a very rough neighbourhood.
   Louis was a peace-loving man.      (combine . . . ▲app)

d. Louis once resisted the pull of four 485 kg horses.
   Louis regularly carried around his wife.
                                    (combine . . . and)
   His wife worked with him.         (combine . . . who)
   They worked in a restaurant.
   They owned the restaurant.
   He carried her with one hand.

e. Louis remains the envy of weightlifters.
   The weightlifters are all over the world.
   Louis was once accused of being possessed by the devil.
   He had superhuman strength.

f. Louis directed his own circus.
   The circus had 35 performers.
   This was before he retired from competition.

g. People always went home excited.
   People came to see Louis.
   They were excited about his strength.
   His strength was amazing.

a.

b.

Can you identify these athletes from the 1984 Summer Olympics?

c.

d.

a. Lori Fung   b. Larry Cain   c. Sylvie Bernier   d. Alwyn Morris and Hugh Fisher

# RESOURCE CHAPTER
# SENTENCE COMBINING 2

Athletes train hard to achieve their accomplishments. They spend many long hours training, repeating drills over and over again. They set goals for themselves. Once they have achieved one level, they are ready to go on to the next. Most athletes are proud to achieve a personal best in a competition, even if they don't win.

These chapters on sentence combining are your training sessions as you learn to manipulate the structures that make up sentences. Chapter 18 gave you practice with some rather simple structures. This chapter takes you to the next level of difficulty. In it you will work with noun clauses and the verbals: participles, gerunds, and infinitives.

As you work through this chapter you will meet other famous Canadian athletes: the Edmonton Grads, Nancy Greene, Harry Jerome, and Alex Baumann. All of these athletes have reached a world-class level in their events, an achievement that required much work and self-discipline.

## Noun Clauses

**Noun clauses** are used when a group of words is needed to express the subject or object of a sentence. Here's an example.

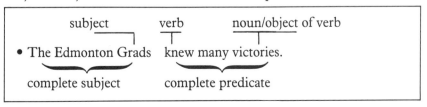

Resource Chapter

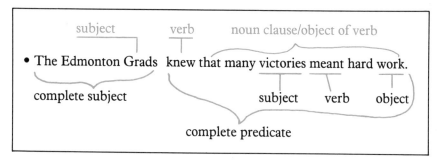

In the second example, the whole clause—*that many victories meant hard work*—serves as the object in the sentence. It is a noun clause. Because it acts like a noun, it could also serve as a subject, as the next example points out.

> noun clause/subject of verb    verb
>
> That many victories meant hard work  was  common knowledge to the Edmonton Grads.

Look at the basic statements that make up this example.

> The Edmonton Grads knew *something*.
>
> Many victories meant hard work.    (combine...that)

Rewrite the example.

> The Edmonton Grads knew that many victories meant hard work.

*Note:* The joining signal *something* indicates that a noun clause is the subject or object.

## Activity 19A    Noun Clauses

1. Combine the following sentences about the Edmonton Grads who ruled the basketball courts from 1915 to 1942. The signal *something* will help you add noun clauses to the basic sentence.

2. Write your answers in your notebook.

The Edmonton Grads in 1922.

*Example:*

> Many people forget *something*.
> The Edmonton Grads were a team of women basketball players in a
> sports world dominated by men.        (combine...that)

*Rewrite:*

> Many people forget that the Edmonton Grads were a team of women
> basketball players in a sport world dominated by men.

  a. *Something* is an amazing fact.
     The Grads played 522 games and lost only twenty.
                                      (combine...that)
  b. It is hard to imagine *something*.
     The Grads were never beaten in twenty-seven games during
     four different Olympic Games.    (combine...how)

c. *Something* is a testimony to their top-notch skill.
   The Grads played nine official games against men's teams.
   (combine...that)
   ~~They~~ lost only two of them.          (combine...and)
d. *Something* marks the coach of the Grads as a great Canadian.
   The coach of the Grads became Lieutenant-Governor of Alberta.          (combine...the fact that)
e. Dr. James Naismith ▲ once said *something*.
   "The Grads have the finest basketball team that ever stepped on a floor."          (combine...∅)
   ~~Dr. James Naismith was~~ the inventor of basketball.
   (combine...▲,app...,)

*Hint*: The null signal ∅ means no joining word is necessary.

## Activity 19B   Review

You can use the information in this activity to build a paragraph about Nancy Greene, a champion Canadian skier.

1. Combine the groups of basic sentences any way you choose. *Remember*: Each group does not necessarily have to become one sentence. You be the referee!

2. Collect or organize your sentence groups into a paragraph. As you build your paragraph, you may want to make additional changes to your sentences to make them fit together as a unit.

*Example:*

> Nancy Greene went from skiing for fun on the slopes of Red Mountain to win a World Cup in skiing.
> She also won a Gold Medal in the 1968 Olympics.
> She did all this in ten years.

*Possible rewrite:*

> In ten years Nancy Greene went from skiing for fun on the slopes of Red Mountain to winning a World Cup in skiing and a Gold Medal at the 1968 Olympics.

a. Nancy started competitive skiing as a member of her high school team in Rossland, British Columbia.
*Chatelaine* once described Nancy as looking "like everybody's favourite babysitter."

b. Her tough style earned her the nickname *Tiger*.
Her style was aggressive.
Tiger was invited to be a substitute on the British Columbia Junior Ski Team.
She was invited in 1958.

c. She placed third in the slalom at the Canadian championships that winter.
She placed second in the downhill.
She was a force to be reckoned with.
She was fourteen years of age.

d. Two years later, Nancy was inspired to win a Gold Medal.
Her Olympic teammate Ann Heggtveit inspired her.
Heggtveit won a Gold Medal in the slalom.

e. Her 1967 World Cup win edged her closer to her big goal.
Her win was by seven-one-hundredths of a second.
Her dream came true the next year.
She became the second Canadian in Olympic history to win a Gold Medal for skiing.

f. She capped off that victory.
She went on to capture another World Cup.
She had nine straight victories.

g. Nancy married Al Raine.
She married him in 1969.
Al Raine was coach of Canada's National Ski Team.
They have been heavily involved with the development of Whistler Mountain Ski Area.
Whistler Mountain is north of Vancouver.

# TONING UP YOUR SENTENCE MUSCLES WITH VERBALS

They may not be as difficult to master as the slap shot in hockey, but **verbals** open up more choices for you as you create sentences. Verbals are made out of verbs. When verbs become verbals, they can perform new jobs in a sentence.

Resource Chapter

# Sentence Combining with Verbals: Participles

Some verbals act like adjectives and describe subjects or objects. These verbals are called **participles**. The following chart describes how you derive the participle forms from verbs.

| Infinitive | Present Tense | -ing form or Present participle | Past Tense | Past Participle |
|---|---|---|---|---|
| to run | run | running | ran | run |
| to ski | ski | skiing | skied | skied |
| to be | am | being | was | been |
| to burn | burn | burning | burned burnt | burned burnt |

The following sentence-combining rule will show you how to use participles in a sentence.

*Example*:

> • Harry Jerome ~~was~~ running as quickly as he could.    base sentence
>
> Harry Jerome sprinted to victory.    base sentence
>
> (combine ... part/base #1)

*Note*: The signal, **part/base #1**, tells you to act on the first base sentence to form the participial phrase.

*Rewrite*:

> Running as quickly as he could, Harry Jerome sprinted to victory.
>
> participle    participial phrase

*Example*:

> • Nancy Greene was skiing her fastest.
>   Nancy Greene won the World Cup by seven-one-hundredths of a
>   second.                              (combine...part/base #1)

*Rewrite*:

> Skiing her fastest, Nancy Greene won the World Cup by seven-one-
> hundredths of a second.
>
> participle   participial phrase

*Example*:

> The skier was injured in the final turn.
> The skier made it to the finish line.
>                                   (combine...part/base#1)

*Rewrite*:

> Injured in the final turn, the skier made it to the finish line.
>
> participle   participial phrase

## *Activity 19C    Combining Participles*

1. **Use the signals to combine the following sentences about Canadian achievements at the 1984 Summer Olympic Games.**

2. **Underline the participial phrase in your rewritten sentence.**
   a. Linda Thom was showing calmness and courage.
      **Linda Thom won her gold medal in pistol shooting.**
                                   **(combine...part/base #1)**
   b. Lori Fung was showing her superb gymnastic ability.
      **Lori Fung captured the all-around women's championship in
      rhythmic gymnastics.**           **(combine...part/base #1)**

c. S~~ylvie Bernier was~~ engaged in a dramatic duel on the spring-board.
   Sylvie Bernier edged out Kelly McCormick of the United States for the gold medal.          (combine . . . part/base #1)

d. L~~arry Cain was~~ earning points for Canada.
   Canoeist Larry Cain won the 500-metre singles event.
                                                  (combine . . . part/base #1)

   L~~arry Cain~~ took a silver medal in the 1000-metre race.
                                                  (combine . . . and)

e. H~~ugh Fisher and Alwyn Morris were~~ bringing home a gold medal in kayaking.
   Hugh Fisher and Alwyn Morris had little difficulty proving Canada's skill in this event.          (combine . . . part/base#1)

3. Rewrite the following sentences to learn about the success story of Canadian diver, Sylvie Bernier, at the 1984 Summer Olympic Games.

   a. S~~ylvie Bernier was~~ raised in Ste-Foy, Quebec.
      Sylvie Bernier is a superb diver▲.
                                                  (combine . . . part/base #1)

      S~~ylvie Bernier~~ is only 157.5 cm.     (combine . . . ▲, who . . .)
      S~~ylvie Bernier~~ weighs only 50 kg.
                                                  (combine . . . and)

   b. S~~ylvie Bernier was~~ showing her skill at the Canadian-U.S.-Mexican ▲ meet a full year before the Los Angeles Olympics.
      ~~It was a~~ diving m~~e~~et.          (combine . . . ▲ part)
      Sylvie Bernier was ready for the biggest challenge of her life.
                                                  (combine . . . part/base #1)

   c. S~~ylvie Bernier was~~ concentrating in previous meets on the scoreboard instead of her dives.
      Sylvie Bernier was determined to overcome this problem.
                                                  (combine . . . part/base #1)

   d. S~~ylvie was~~ occupied by the music on her tape recorder be-tween her dives.
      Sylvie forgot all about the pressure of the scoreboard.
                                                  (combine . . . part/base #1)

   e. S~~ylvie~~ had taken the lead on the third out of ten dives.
      Sylvie held first place throughout the competition.
                                                  (combine . . . part/base #1)

   *Note*: The verb *had taken* will have to change its form in this example.

f. Sylvie was honoured as the first Canadian diver to win an
Olympic gold medal.
Sylvie was surprised *at something*.
(combine ... part/base #1)
She was even in the top three.     (combine ... that)

# Sentence Combining

Look again at the verb chart on page 300 and find the infinitive form of the verb. It is the form of the verb with *to* in front of it: to sing, to dance, to play, to walk. Words and phrases can join with the infinitive to form an **infinitive phrase**:

> to sing a song sweetly
> to dance in a marathon for three days
> to play basketball at recess
> to walk in the Marathon for Millions promotion

You will find infinitive phrases as part of the structure of some sentences. Here is how the above examples might look if they were included in sentences:

> He tried to sing a song sweetly.
> They struggled to dance in a marathon for three days.
> To play basketball at recess was his only hobby.
> To walk in the Marathon for Millions promotion, the participants needed dedication and courage.

The signal **inf/to** in the following activities tells you to change a base sentence to an infinitive phrase before you proceed with the combining activity.

## Activity 19D    Infinitives

1. Using the joining signal, combine the following sentences about swimming achievements at the 1984 Summer Olympic Games.

2. Write your answers in your notebook and underline each infinitive phrase.

Resource Chapter

Alex Baumann of Sudbury, Ontario

*Example:*

> • *Something* was a long-standing goal of Ontario swimmer Alex Baumann.
> A̶l̶e̶x̶ (is) an Olympic champion. (combine...inf/to)

*Note:* **The bracket reminds you to find the infinitive form of this verb.**

*Rewrite:*

> • *To be an Olympic champion* was a long-standing goal of Ontario swimmer Alex Baumann.

a. *Something* was a great honour for Alex.
Alex (held) the Canadian flag.  (combine ... inf/to)
The 438-member Canadian Olympic team entered the Los Angeles Coliseum.  (combine ... as)

b. Alex went on▲.
He (broke) his own world record.
(combine ... inf/to)
He broke the record during the games.
(combine ... prep)

c. Alex's fellow swimmer Victor Davis managed *something*.
He (slashed) 1.24 seconds from his world standard.
(combine ... inf/to)
He (won) the 200-metre breaststroke.
(combine ... inf/to)

d. Victor said *something*.
He wanted *something*.  (combine ... ∅)
He would set a new world record.
(combine ... inf/to)
The record would last a long time.
(combine ... that)

# Sentence Combining with Verbals: Gerunds

Some verbals can stand on their own in sentences, acting as subjects or objects. Verbals doing the job of nouns are called **gerunds**. The signal for you to create a gerund is **ger/-ing**.

Here are some examples of gerunds and gerund phrases.

---

- *Swimming for long distances* was Marilyn Bell's sport.
  (gerund as subject, with a prepositional phrase)
- *Skiing at a world-class level* made Nancy Greene famous.
  (gerund as subject, with a prepositional phrase)
- Harry Jerome loved *running competitively*.
  (gerund as object, with an adverb)

---

## *Activity 19E    Gerunds*

1. Using the joining signals, combine the sentences below about Canadian achievements in rowing at the Los Angeles Olympics, 1984.

2. Write your answers in your notebook and underline each gerund phrase.

*Example:*

---

*Something* is hard work.
T~~hey~~ (paddled) their canoe.          (combine ... ger/-ing)

---

*Remember:* The brackets around the verb remind you to change its form.

*Rewrite:*

---

*Paddling their canoe* is hard work.

---

a. *Something* was the ambition of Toronto twins Mike and Mark Evans▲.
   M~~ike and M~~ark wa~~nted~~ ~~to~~ (win).   (combine ... ger/-ing)
   M~~ike and M~~ark w~~er~~e members of Canada's canoeing team.
                         (combine ... ▲ app ...)

b. *Something* was quite easy for them.
   T~~hey~~ (qualified) for their event.    (combine ... ger/-ing)

c. *Something* was the hardest part of the race.
   T~~hey~~ (held off) a final sprint by the American rowers.
                         (combine ... ger/-ing).

d. *Something* brought rowers Tricia Smith and Betty Craig a hard-earned silver medal.
   Tr~~icia and B~~ett~~y~~ (failed) to catch the Romanian team.
                         (combine ... ger/-ing).

e. *Something* almost cost Tricia and Betty their chance to compete.
   T~~hey~~ (veered) into another boat during a practice session.
                         (combine ... ger/-ing)
   T~~hey~~ com~~pet~~ed in the race.        (combine ... prep)
   T~~hey~~ com~~pet~~ed for the championship.
                         (combine ... prep)

---

## Activity 19F    Review: Combining Sentences with Verbals

As you do this activity, you will create a Hall of Fame tribute to Marilyn Bell, the swimmer who conquered Lake Ontario in 1954.

1. Use all the joining signals you learned in this resource chapter to combine the following sentences.

2. Write your answers in your notebook.

   a. *Something* is a feat.
      She (swam) across Lake Ontario.   (combine . . . ger/-ing)
      The feat doesn't enter many people's minds.
                                        (combine . . . that)

   b. Marilyn Bell (endured) this awesome challenge.
      Marilyn Bell became a sixteen-year-old wonder.
                                        (combine . . . part/base #1)

   c. *Something* earned Marilyn the honour of *something*.
      She (swam) almost 50 km in both light and darkness.
                                        (combine . . . ger/-ing)

      She (completed) a remarkable feat in the history of Canadian
      sport.                           (combine . . . ger/-ing)

   d. ▲ Marilyn often felt *something*.
      She (weighed) only 54 kg.         (combine . . . ▲ part . . .)
      She wanted *something*.           (combine . . . that)
      Her desire was to give up.        (combine . . . inf/to)
      She persevered.                   (combine . . . but)

   e. Before her big swim, Marilyn was afraid of *something*.
      Marilyn did not like to (swim) in darkness.
                                        (combine . . . ger/-ing)

   f. Marilyn (won) a 42-km race in July, 1954.
      Marilyn felt she was ready for her big challenge.
                                        (combine . . . part/base #1)

      Her challenge was Lake Ontario.
                                        (combine . . . app)

   g. Marilyn's determination only increased.
      She felt eels attach to her body.
                                        (combine . . . when)

   h. She swam on.
      She (knocked) the eels away.      (combine . . . part)

   i. She survived by *something*.
      She (drank) corn syrup.           (combine . . . ger/-ing)
      The corn syrup was extended to her from the pilot boat.
                                        (combine . . . part)

   j. Marilyn (had) no sleep for over thirty hours.
      Marilyn was hardly aware of her finish.
                                        (combine . . . part/base #1)

k. She crawled up on the shore.
   S~~h~~e (heard) the voice of her friend.    (combine...inf/to)
   H~~er friend w~~a~~s~~ Joan Corke.          (combine...app)
   H~~er friend~~ (told) her *something*.      (combine...part)
   She had finished.                        (combine...that *or* ∅)

## Activity 19G    The Real Thing: Putting It All Together

1. Combine and rearrange the sentences in the following story about Wayne Gretzky so that you achieve sentence variety.
   a. Use some short sentences and some long ones.
   b. Move sentence parts around to help create variety.

2. Write a rough draft in your notebook and then edit it to produce a good copy.

3. Compare your version with that of someone else in your class so you can appreciate the sentence writing choices both you and your partner have made.

### Paragraph 1

The fans call him "The Great Gretzky." It's a nickname. He worked hard to win it. After all, people describe his skating as being like that of a scared chicken. The chicken is trying to escape a fox. He had to prove himself. Gretzky proved himself. He certainly did.

### Paragraph 2

Wayne is from an athletic family. His sister became a national track star. His brother is also an excellent hockey player. Wayne entered his family's athletic tradition at the age of six. He joined his first hockey team. That first year he scored one goal. He played with boys four years older than himself. The next year he got 27 goals. He got 104 goals the year after that. He scored 378 goals in 68 games when he was ten years old. He was on his way.

### Paragraph 3

He was sixteen. He was drafted by the Sault Ste. Marie Greyhounds. He ended his first season with 70 goals and 112 assists. He won

→

trophies. One trophy was for being the league's best rookie. Another trophy was for being the most gentlemanly player. He began to draw the attention of professional hockey scouts. At age seventeen he signed a $875 000 contract. It was with the Indianapolis Racers. The Racers were in the World Hockey Association. Wayne says that the most money he ever had of his own before that contract was $260.

**Paragraph 4**

The Racers folded. Peter Pocklington bought Wayne's contract. Peter Pocklington is the owner of the Edmonton Oilers. Wayne was earning $300 000 by twenty-one years of age. As a member of the Oilers, Wayne has won trophies. He has won the NHL's Lady Byng Memorial Trophy. This trophy is for gentlemanly play. He has won the league's most valuable player award.

**Paragraph 5**

Wayne has been good for the Oilers. He shattered almost every single season scoring record in the NHL books. He did this in the 1981-1982 season. He has set another NHL record. This record is for the most three-goal games. Nothing can compare with the thrill of winning the Stanley Cup. It was a great night for Gretzky. It was a great night for his teammates. They captured the Stanley Cup. They captured it for Edmonton. They captured it in the 1983-1984 season. Gretzky has an impressive hockey record. He still has a great career in front of him.

## This Is Your Hall of Fame

Maybe you didn't know Canada had so many outstanding sports heroes. Quiz your family and friends about some of the people you have discovered while building your writing skills.

You've worked with some of the choices available to you as you create sentences. These choices will allow you to write sentences that are different and varied.

Because all goals worth achieving come with practice—as all athletes will tell you—keep practising your sentence writing skills. You will never know when you need them.

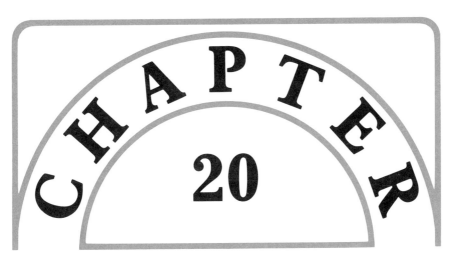

# RESOURCE CHAPTER
# GRAMMAR DEFINITIONS

Some people use specific terms when they are talking about language. They will use such words as noun, or verb, or proper adjective. This chapter gives you definitions of some of these terms. You can use the chapter almost as a dictionary to review grammar concepts that you learned in previous years.

However, always keep in mind the purpose for learning grammar. Grammar is a system that is used to describe the way sounds go together to make up words, and words go together to make up sentences. In other words, grammar is a system that describes the way people communicate.

Perhaps you can understand this definition of grammar better if you compare it to the universe. The universe is there—it exists, it has existed for eons, and it will continue to exist. The knowledge that humans have about the universe has nothing whatever to do with the way it works.

But humans have always been interested in the universe. We have looked at stars and planets, thought about them, written about them, and dreamed about them. We now know some things about the universe, and this knowledge has helped humans make technological advances such as sending people to the moon. But even though we know something about the universe, we don't know everything. And, as civilization continues to exist, we can expect to learn more about the universe, and this new knowledge will allow us to do new and different things.

Grammar is similar to this. It shows what we now know about language and the way humans communicate. But it is incomplete knowledge. As grammarians learn more about language, we will find different and better ways to help people use language to write better, to speak better, and to listen better.

Learning grammar is not the same as learning to write. Read the cartoon on page 310. Use it as a reminder that writing involves the process of composing—not the study of grammar. Now that you know what grammar is, let's get on with this glossary of traditional grammar terms.

# THE PARTS OF SPEECH

In traditional grammar there are eight parts of speech: **nouns, verbs, adjectives, adverbs, prepositions, conjunctions, interjections,** and **pronouns.** The following section defines each part of speech.

## About Nouns

Nouns are the words in English that name things. Here are some of the terms used to talk about nouns. An explanation of each term follows the chart.

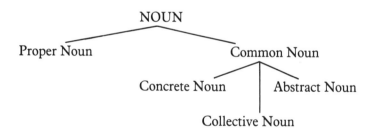

- **Proper Nouns**     nouns written with a capital letter: people and places or titles such as books, music, or television pro-grammes

- **Common Nouns**  nouns that are not capitalized when they are written. This category includes most nouns.

  **Concrete Nouns**     things you see, taste, or touch

  **Abstract Nouns**     things you think or feel, such as anger, hope, love, absence

| Collective Nouns | nouns that are singular in form but plural in meaning: |
|---|---|

- a herd of buffalo
- a crowd of shoppers
- a flock of chickens

*Examples*:

| sentence | description |
|---|---|
| • The *dog* ate the *bone*. | Both nouns are concrete/common nouns. |
| • The *deer* was chased by a *pack* of *wolves*. | concrete/common; collective/common; concrete/common |
| • *Cleanliness* is next to *godliness*. | abstract/common; abstract/common |
| • *Prime Minister Pearson* won a *Nobel Peace Prize*. | proper; proper |
| • *Love* came over *Hans* like a great *cloak*, and the *crowd* sensed the *change* in his *attitude*. | abstract/common; proper; concrete/common; collective/common; abstract/common; abstract/common |

# About Pronouns

Pronouns are words that take the place of nouns. For this reason they are closely linked with nouns. Many of the rules that apply to the place of nouns in sentences also apply to pronouns.

## Personal Pronouns

**Personal pronouns** distinguish the person speaking (the first person), the person spoken to (the second person), or the person or thing spoken about (the third person). The following chart shows the personal pronouns and how they are used.

Resource Chapter

| **Personal Pronouns** | | | |
|---|---|---|---|
| **Singular Forms** | | | |
| | *As subject* | *As object* | *Possession* |
| first person/person speaking | I | me | my, mine |
| second person/person spoken to | you (thou)★ | you | your, yours (thine)★ |
| third person/person or thing spoken about | | | |
|     masculine | he | him | his |
|     feminine | she | her | her, hers |
|     neuter | it | it | its |
| **Plural Forms** | | | |
| first person/person speaking | we | us | our, ours |
| second person/person spoken to | you (ye)★ | you | your, yours |
| third person/person or thing spoken about | | | |
|     masculine | they | them | their, theirs |
|     feminine | they | them | their, theirs |
|     neuter | they | them | their, theirs |

★an archaic or old form of the pronoun, no longer in common use

**Demonstrative Pronouns**
**Demonstrative pronouns** point out, or demonstrate something.

| **Demonstrative Pronouns** | |
|---|---|
| this | that |
| these | those |
| and occasionally *such* | |

*Examples*:
> *These* belong to Jacques. *Those* are Monique's.
> *Such* is the case.

*Note*: When demonstrative pronoun forms occur in a sentence as adjectives that modify nouns, they are called **determiners** (or sometimes **demonstrative adjectives**). See page 318 for an explanation of determiners.

*Examples of determiners*:
   *These* examples help clarify the point.
   We had never encountered *such* animosity before.

## Relative Pronouns

**Relative pronouns** perform two functions in sentences. They act as conjunctions, joining two basic sentences, and they relate or refer back to nouns that precede them. These nouns are called **antecedents**.
   The relative pronouns are **who, whom, that**, and **which**.

        antecedent     relative  pronoun

*That* is Georgette, *who* was once a flight attendant.

demonstrative  pronoun

This sentence means:
That is Georgette and Georgette was once a flight attendant.

        antecedent     relative  pronoun

*This* is the house *that* Jack built.

demonstrative  pronoun

This sentence means:
This is the house and Jack built the house.

        antecedent     relative  pronoun

*This* is the song in *which* the high note occurs.

demonstrative  pronoun

This sentence means:
This is the song and the high note occurs in the song.

## Interrogative Pronouns

You use **interrogative pronouns** when you ask questions. They appear to be the same as relative pronouns—*who, which,* and also *what*—but they do a different job in a sentence.

*Who* is centre forward?
*What* are you doing?
*Which* answer is right?

## Reflexive and Intensive Pronouns

| Reflexive and Intensive Pronouns | |
| --- | --- |
| I myself | we ourselves |
| you yourself | you yourselves |
| (thou thyself)* | |
| she herself | |
| he himself | they themselves |
| it itself | |

*an archaic or old form of the pronoun, no longer in common use

**Reflexive pronouns** are a special use of personal pronouns. They refer or relate back to the personal pronoun as a way of adding special emphasis in a sentence. Or more specifically, a reflexive pronoun is a personal pronoun ending with the affix *-self*, occurring as the object of a verb, and referring to itself as the subject of the verb.

*Examples of reflexive pronouns*:

I went *myself*.
They saw *themselves* in the movie.
I signed the document *myself*.
The bird hurt *itself* when it flew against the window.

**Intensive pronouns** are exactly the same ones as reflexive pronouns, but they occur in a slightly different place in sentences. They are placed right beside the word that they are helping to emphasize or intensify.

*Examples of intensive pronouns*:

I *myself* will go with you.
We gave the prize to the queen *herself*.
We gave the secret of peace to the generals *themselves*.

## Indefinite Pronouns

**Indefinite pronouns** received their name because they refer to no person or thing in particular. You cannot tell from the sentence exactly which noun an indefinite pronoun stands for. Here is a list of some of the more commonly used indefinite pronouns.

| Indefinite Pronouns | | |
|---|---|---|
| anyone | someone | everyone |
| something | no one | anything |
| anybody | everybody | nobody |
| somebody | everything | nothing |
| none | any | each |
| many | much | more |
| most | all | few |

*Note*: Some indefinite pronouns can take an *apostrophe* to show possession: everybody's mistake.

## About Adjectives and Determiners

Some adjectives in the following paragraph have been italicized. This paragraph is the introduction to the novel *Crossbar*. In this novel, a young athlete, who has lost a leg in a farm accident, fights his way back to self-respect and success.

> The sun had not risen high enough to warm the *prairie* day. By mid-afternoon it would be almost *unbearable*, but now it hung, *reddish* and *lifeless*, just over the top of the *still-dewy* wheat that stretched *unbroken* toward the *eastern* horizon. It was *cold*, cold enough for *woolen* sweaters and *flannel* shirts and for blowing *your* hands when they start to stiffen. Still, Aaron Kornylo was sweating. He was also breathing heavily—actually gasping sometimes—and moaning and thrashing around in *his* bed, the quilt and blanket and sheet long-since kicked aside. His eyelids flickered wildly, threatening to open, wanting to open, to deliver him from this *grotesque* dream one more time. But no, first the noise—the *machine's* noise—would have to come, closer and closer; and closer and...then the pain, so terrible that the brain, in its *mysterious* wisdom, shut down the system...just after the scream.
>
> John Gault, *Crossbar*

The italicized words show that adjectives are **describing words**. They tell you something about nouns—how many, how large, whose, what kind, and so on. Some grammar books say that adjectives **modify** nouns and pronouns. The word modify means the same thing as describe or qualify.

There are two basic categories of adjectives: **descriptive adjectives** and **determiners or limiting adjectives**.

## Descriptive Adjectives

Descriptive adjectives tell you more about nouns or pronouns. They add detail to writing.

*Examples*:

a *thick* book                         a *wild* horse

a *foggy* morning                    a *blue* mountain

Sometimes adjectives are so dominant in a sentence that they take on more importance than the nouns they modify. Consider the following examples.

- Jonathon has a tooth.
  Jonathon has a *sore* tooth.
- Germaine saw the wave.
  Germaine saw the *tidal* wave.

The first sentence in each example doesn't say very much. These sentences are uninteresting and give information that everyone knows. But add an adjective to each sentence and it becomes more meaningful. Adjectives give specific information about specific situations.

## Proper Adjectives

You will recall from your study of nouns that some nouns are classified as proper nouns. These nouns begin with a capital letter because they name a specific place or person: *Canada, Asia, Mars, Paris, England, Germany.* Adjectives that are formed from proper nouns—**proper adjectives**—also begin with a capital letter:

*Examples*:
  *Canadian* flag                    *Asian* philosophy
  *Martian* invader                *Parisian* style
  *English* class                     *German* language

## Determiners or Limiting Adjectives

The second category of adjectives is the **determiners**. They always precede the noun they describe or modify, so some grammar books call these words **noun-markers**.   Contrast the following two phrases:

*a* mistake                              *the* mistake

The determiner *a* tells you that the noun refers to mistakes in general. The determiner *the* pinpoints the meaning of the phrase to one specific mistake.

Here is a chart of the more common determiners.

| Determiners | |
|---|---|
| 1. Articles | a/an, the |
| 2. Possessives | my, your, his, her, its, our, their |
| 3. Demonstratives | this, that, these, those |
| 4. Relatives/Interrogatives | which, what, whose |
| 5. Numerals | one, two, first, second, ninety-ninth |
| 6. Indefinites | all, another, any, every, both, each, few, many, more, most, much, no, other, several, some, such |

You may notice that the classification of the determiners is similar to that of pronouns. Note in the following examples how a word can change its function in a sentence from a pronoun to a determiner/adjective.

*Examples*:

*Which* is the correct answer?   pronoun
*Which* answer is correct?    determiner/adjective

**Nouns As Adjectives**
Nouns can sometimes function as adjectives. Here are some examples:

*store* front                      *fence* post
*Easter* holiday                   *Christmas* present
*Air Canada reservation* desk      *Pacific Ocean* cruise
*Manitoba* maple                   *Alberta* crude oil

The **apostrophe** (') can also turn nouns into a special kind of noun/adjective:

the answer of Tom          Tom's answer
the whiskers of the cat    the cat's whiskers

The history of the apostrophe is rather interesting. English speakers several centuries ago used to say something like this:

Tom *his* answer            the cat *its* whiskers

But since speakers of English usually look for a shortcut to say words, they began to slur the two words together. To show that some letters are left out, the apostrophe was introduced:

Tom *h̸is* answer                    the cat *i̸ts* whiskers

### Degrees of Comparison

Notice that adjectives change their form when things or people are being compared:

Here are three cakes. This cake is *big*. That one is *bigger*. The third one is *biggest*.

When the affixes *-er* and *-est* are added to make a comparison, the form of the adjective is called the **degrees of comparison**. The word *degree* is used here in a special sense meaning stages. (*Degree* comes from the French word *degré*, meaning step or tread.)

| Degrees Of Comparison | | |
|---|---|---|
| **Positive Degree** | **Comparative Degree** | **Superlative Degree** |
| *1. Regular Comparison* | | |
| big | bigg*er* | bigg*est* |
| tall | tall*er* | tall*est* |
| lonely | lonel*ier* | lonli*est* |
| *2. Irregular Comparison* | | |
| good | better | best |
| bad | worse | worst |
| much/many | more | most |
| little | less | least |
| *3. Comparison with Long Adjectives* | | |
| beautiful | *more* beautiful | *most* beautiful |
| clumsy | *more* clumsy | *most* clumsy |

## About Adverbs and Intensifiers

Just as adjectives describe—or modify or qualify—nouns, so adverbs describe verbs.

Adverbs can be classified into different kinds. The chart on page 321 gives you examples of the main kinds of classification of adverbs.

| Classification of Adverbs | | |
|---|---|---|
| **Kind** | **Example** | **Question Answered** |
| *1. Manner* | He asked hastily. | How? |
| *2. Time* | I went yesterday.<br>She spoke briefly.<br>They jogged frequently. | When?<br>How long?<br>How often? |
| *3. Place* | You are here. | Where? |
| *4. Degree* | I nearly fell. | How much? |

**Formation of Adverbs**

Many adverbs have their own form. You can recognize them because they are words that are different from words in other parts of speech:

so, too, not, soon, here.

But most adverbs are formed from adjectives.

| Formation of Adverbs |
|---|
| **1. by adding -ly to the adjective form** |
| bad + ly            badly<br>great + ly          greatly |
| due + ly            duly<br>true + ly           truly |
| merry + ly          merrily<br>funny + ly          funnily<br>dry + ly            drily |
| shrill + ly         shrilly<br>full + ly           fully |
| drastic + ly        drastically<br>ironic + ly         ironically |
| **2. by adding -s to some adverbs of place** |
| upward + s          upwards<br>toward + s          towards |
| **3. no change from the adjective to the adverb form** |
| long                long<br>fast                fast<br>close               close |

## Comparison of Adverbs

The general rule to form the **degrees of comparison** among adverbs is to add *more* for the comparative form, and *most* for the superlative form. Some adverbs form their degrees of comparison in the same way as adjectives do.

## Position of Adverbs

Most words in English have only one slot where they fit into a sentence. Adverbs of manner, time and place have the remarkable ability to move about within a sentence.

---

- Suddenly the wind blew the roof off the barn.
- The wind suddenly blew the roof off the barn.
- The wind blew the roof off the barn suddenly.

---

The change in position of the adverb changes the emphasis of that adverb within the sentence.

## Intensifiers

Some grammar texts will tell you that adverbs perform functions in sentences in addition to modifying verbs. They also modify adverbs and adjectives.

A simpler way to look at this function is to call the words that modify adjectives and adverbs **intensifiers**. Intensifiers are words whose function is like *very* and *rather*. They always occur before the word they intensify.

- Matilda has *very* blue eyes.

- Henrietta ran *very* impressively in the last race.

- The child looked up with *rather* dull eyes.

- The dog finished off the bone *rather* slowly.

- She ate her *barely* warm soup.

- We sang *quite* frequently around the campfire.

- The torch has an *extremely* hot flame.

# About Verbs

For many years, grammarians have argued about whether the noun or the verb is the most important word in a sentence. Nouns name the actor; verbs tell what the action is. Probably both sides are correct. Yet it is the verb that must appear in (almost) every sentence or clause. It tells what the action is,

> • The prime minister signed the treaty.

or it mentions the state or condition that something is in,

> • The sheriff is ill.

It will be easier to understand the nature or characteristics of verbs if you look at some examples and illustrations.

### Transitive and Intransitive Verbs

Verbs are classified as transitive or intransitive. With **transitive verbs**, the action goes from the subject/noun to the verb, and then out to the object/noun.

*Examples*:

> what
> • The plane hit the ground.

> what
> • The horse cleared the jump.

> what
> • The snow blocked the driveway.

In other words, the object of the verb receives the action suggested by the verb.

With **intransitive verbs**, no action goes from the verb to the noun which may follow it:

*Examples*:

> • The rabbit hops, skips, and jumps.
> • The conductor leaned on the podium.

The meaning of the sentence comes from the subject/noun and the verb alone. There is no noun/object that receives the action suggested by the verb.

### Linking Verbs and the Verb *to be*

A special classification of verbs is the **linking verb**. Linking verbs act as a link or connector between two nouns or a noun and an adjective in a sentence. Some examples of linking verbs follow. Note that either the noun that follows the verb means the same thing as the noun/subject, or the adjective that follows the verb modifies or describes the noun in the subject part of the sentence.

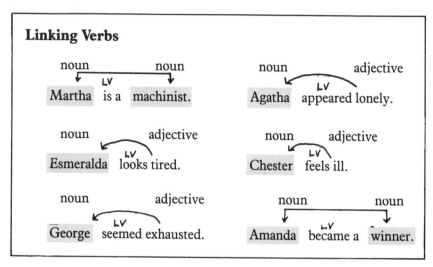

The most common linking verb is the verb **to be**. Below are some of the forms of this irregular verb.

| The Verb *to be* | | |
|---|---|---|
| **Present Tense (Time)** | **Singular** | **Plural** |
| first person | I am | we are |
| second person | you are | you are |
| third person | he/she/it is | they are |
| **Past Tense (Time)** | | |
| first person | I was | we were |
| second person | you were | you were |
| third person | he/she/it was | they were |

### Active and Passive Verbs

Transitive verbs occur in two **voices,** or forms: **active** and **passive**. Note how systematically a sentence written in the active voice is changed to the passive voice.

active voice:    The explorer found a new planet.

passive voice:    A new planet **was** found **by** the explorer.

Here are the rules that describe how a sentence is changed from the active voice to the passive voice.

> 1. The noun/object is placed at the front of the sentence.
> 2. The noun/subject is transferred to the end of the sentence.
> 3. The preposition *by* is placed in front of the noun/subject.
> 4. The appropriate form of the verb *to be* is added to the verb.

*Note*: All the sentences in this chart of rules are passive.

## The Verb Phrase

Verbs are frequently written with one or more helping words, or **modals**, connected with them. The helping words are sometimes called **auxiliary verbs** and the cluster of verbs is called a **verb phrase**. Here is a list of some of the more common auxiliary verbs, or modals.

| **Modals or Auxiliary Verbs** |
| --- |
| 1. All forms of the verb *to be*. |
| 2. will, shall |
| 3. has, have, had |
| 4. can, may, could, might |
| 5. must, ought |
| 6. should, would |
| 7. do, does, did |

*Examples*:
- The eagle *has* seen its prey.
- I *could have* won first prize if I *had* known the last answer.

## Simple Tense Forms: Present and Past

The word **tense** refers to the time dimension that is implied with a verb. The simple tenses are present time and past time. But there are ways in English to be much more specific than the simple tenses are to designate the time when an action happens. The verb forms can become quite complex.

| **Simple Tense Forms** | | |
| --- | --- | --- |
| **1. Regular Verbs**<br>Add *-ed* to the present form to make the past form. | | |
| *infinitive* | *present tense* | *past tense* |
| to like | like | liked |
| to walk | walk | walked |
| develop | develop | developed |
| **2. Irregular Verbs** | | |
| *infinitive* | *present tense* | *past tense* |
| to eat | eat | ate |
| to sing | sing | sang |
| to shoot | shoot | shot |

*Note*: To find the right form for the irregular verbs, you have to know the principal parts of the verb and choose the appropriate form from there. You probably know most of these irregular forms.

**Future Tense**

There is really no future tense in English. You will note in the chart of the principal parts of irregular verbs that there are separate forms for present and past tenses. There is no separate form in English to show future tense. Rather, future tense or time is shown in several ways. The most common and simplest to understand is the use of the auxiliary or modal *shall* or *will*.

> • School will end tomorrow.

But there are also other ways to show the future time. Each of the following sentences implies the future in its meaning:

> • School ends tomorrow.
> • School is going to end tomorrow.
> • School must end tomorrow.
> • School should end tomorrow.
> • School could end tomorrow.

So you see that you can form the future tense in several ways. When you are given questions in which you are asked to form the future tense, they are usually referring to the use of shall or will.

### The Progressive Tense

What is the difference between the sentences below?

> • I *walk* to school.
> • I *am walking* to school.

In the first example, the action of walking occurs once, and then is over for the day. In the second example, the action of walking is still in progress— "I" have not yet reached the school:

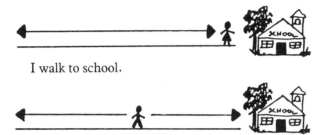

I walk to school.

I am walking to school.

The second example illustrates the **progressive tense**. It suggests action that is still happening or is still in progress.

The progressive tense is made from the appropriate form of the auxiliary *to be* and the present participle or *-ing* form of the verb.

Below are various examples of the progressive tense:

| Progressive Action of Verbs | |
| --- | --- |
| **1. Present progressive tense**<br>I *am* walking.<br>You *are* walking.<br>He/she/it *is* walking. | We *are* walking.<br>You *are* walking.<br>They *are* walking. |
| **2. Past progressive tense**<br>I *was* walking.<br>You *were* walking.<br>He/she/it *was* walking. | We *were* walking.<br>You *were* walking.<br>They *were* walking. |
| **3. Future progressive tense**<br>I *will/shall be* walking.<br>You *will be* walking.<br>He/she/it *will be* walking. | We *shall/will be* walking.<br>You *will be* walking.<br>They *will be* walking. |

### The Perfect Tenses

While the progressive tenses describe action that is going on, the **perfect tenses** tell you that action is finished. The following example will illustrate this idea:

- Jean *sang* a song when the lights went out.

- Jean *was singing* a song when the lights went out.

- Jean *had sung* a song when the lights went out.

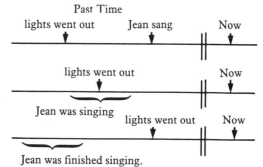

The perfect tense is formed from the appropriate auxiliary of *to have* and the past participle form of the verb.

| Perfect Tense |  |
|---|---|
| **1. Present perfect tense** |  |
| I have sung. | We have sung. |
| You have sung. | You have sung. |
| He/she/it has sung. | They have sung. |
| **2. Past perfect tense** |  |
| I had sung. | We had sung. |
| You had sung. | You had sung. |
| He/she/it had sung. | They had sung. |
| **3. Future perfect tense** |  |
| I shall/will have sung. | We shall/will have sung. |
| You will have sung. | You will have sung. |
| He she/it will have sung. | They will have sung. |

## About Conjunctions

Conjunctions are words that join various structures together. In this example, a conjunction joins two basic sentences or clauses:

The hurricane came *as* the people fled its force.

However, in this example, the conjunction links a series of prepositional phrases:

He walked to the end of the wall, turned the corner, *and* faced the crowd.

Conjunctions can be classified as coordinating conjunctions and subordinating conjunctions. **Coordinating conjunctions** link together structures that are of equal grammatical value, for example, two nouns, two phrases, or two clauses.

*Examples:*

> noun + noun
- John *and* Jeremiah sank their ship.

> noun + noun   verb + verb
- Zeke *and* Steve sang *and* danced at the end of their project.

> noun + noun          phrase + phrase
- Sarah *and* Sonjia went to the movies *and* to a party.

>                      sentence + sentence
- The grade nines went to the basketball game *but* they were not pleased with the result.

**Subordinating conjunctions** also join structures together. Usually these structures are complete sentences.

*Examples*:

>     sentence            sentence
- We saw the horizon when we went over the hill.

>        sentence        sentence
- Since I knew the answer, I didn't try very hard.

>     sentence               sentence
- I went to see what happened because I heard a weird noise.

## About Prepositions

**Prepositions** join nouns with nouns or nouns with verbs. Whereas subordinating conjunctions join complete sentences, prepositions join words. The unit of words that goes with a preposition is known as a **prepositional phrase**.

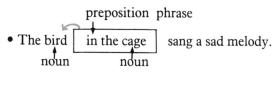

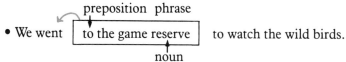

*Note*: "To watch" is an infinitive phrase, not a prepositional phrase.

## About Interjections

**Interjections** are also known as exclamations and are signalled by the use of the exclamation mark (!). Here are some examples:

- *Ah!* There you are.
- *Oh!* What should we do?
- *Poor Harvey!* He didn't know what to do.
- *Heavens!* I didn't know that.

Interjections, with exclamation marks, are not used very often in writing.

# INDEX